the
*d*ragon *k*eeper's
handbook

About the Author

Shawn MacKenzie had her first Dragon encounter at four years old and has kept them close ever since, warding the daemons of the dark with fire and whimsical tales, reminding her that there's so much more to the universe than most of us see. A graduate of Bennington College, Shawn is a writer of sci-fi/fantasy and an editor of crossword puzzles. Her stories have been published in *Southshire Pepper-Pot* and the *2010 Skyline Review*, and she is a winner of the 2010 Shires Press Award for Short Stories. A Vermont transplant, Shawn is an avid student of myth, religion, philosophy, and animals real, imaginary, large, and small. Visit her at http://mackenziesdragonsnest.com.

the *∂ragon keeper's* handbook

Including the Myth & Mystery,
Care & Feeding, Life & Lore of
these Fiercely Splendid Creatures

SHAWN MACKENZIE

Llewellyn Publications
Woodbury, Minnesota

First Edition
First Printing, 2011

Book design by Steffani Sawyer
Book edited by Nicole Edman
Cover art © 2011
            Background image: iStockphoto.com/Brandy Taylor
            Dragon: iStockphoto.com/Alexey Bakhtiozin
Cover design by Kevin R. Brown
Interior artwork © 2011 Don Higgins

Llewellyn Publications is a registered trademark of Llewellyn Worldwide Ltd.

Library of Congress Cataloging-in-Publication Data
MacKenzie, Shawn, 1954–
   The dragon keeper's handbook : including the myth & mystery, care & feeding, life & lore of these fiercely splendid creatures / by Shawn MacKenzie.
      p. cm.
   Includes bibliographical references.
   ISBN 978-0-7387-2785-1
1. Dragons. I. Title.
   GR830.D7M34 2011
   398.24'54—dc22
                                        2011006977

Llewellyn Worldwide Ltd. does not participate in, endorse, or have any authority or responsibility concerning private business transactions between our authors and the public.
   All mail addressed to the author is forwarded but the publisher cannot, unless specifically instructed by the author, give out an address or phone number.
   Any Internet references contained in this work are current at publication time, but the publisher cannot guarantee that a specific location will continue to be maintained. Please refer to the publisher's website for links to authors' websites and other sources.

Llewellyn Publications
A Division of Llewellyn Worldwide Ltd.
2143 Wooddale Drive
Woodbury, MN 55125-2989
www.llewellyn.com

Printed in the United States of America

contents

introduction Dragon Gestalt   ix

Part I: From Tooth to Tail: The Natural History of Dragons

one   True or False: Dragon Species
& Genetic Variations   3

two   Where the Wild Weyrs Are:
Habitats & Habits   55

three   A Year in the Life   81

**Part II: The Long & Winding Road:
Dragons' March Through Millennia**

four   Dragon Evolution: Which Came First,
the Ouroboros or the Egg?   107

five   First Encounters: Cosmic Dragons
& the Origin of Our Species   121

six   Taming the Chaotic, Suppressing the Wild   153

seven   Dragon Survival: Acts of God, Acts of Man   167

Part III: The Care & Feeding of Dragons

eight   Wild Dragons Near & Far   193

nine   Coddled Eggs and Orphans:
Welcoming a Dragon to Your Table   203

ten   The Early Years   219

eleven   Wellness in a Dragon's World   237

twelve   The Turns of Mortal Coil   247

epilogue Standing Alone Together   259

glossary   263

bibliography & suggested reading   283

It is as large as life and twice as natural.

—*Lewis Carroll,* Through the Looking-Glass

introduction

Dragon Gestalt

Thank the gods there are Dragons, or we'd surely have to invent them. And what a tall order that would be, to fashion out of whole cloth such fiercely splendid creatures! Such wild guardians and sage counselors, champions of sky, earth, and sea!

Granted, today some people are less familiar with Dragons than others, less "at one" with the reality of the Dragon, if you will. There are even people who see no relevance for Dragons in modern life and could-not/would-not see them if they were standing square in the warm umbra of a Dragon's breath.[1] To these most disbelieving amongst us, I ask: If there are no such things as Dragons, how is it that our disparate, barely erect ancestors, struggling across the still-drifting continents, imagined beings so universally similar in aspect and purpose? How did they manage to keep this myth alive through millennia? And how, even today, does *everyone*—skeptics included—know exactly what Dragons look like? Who among us would not recognize a Dragon crossing the boulevard or rabbiting at the country club?

---

1. In the immortal words of Mark Twain, "You cannot depend on your eyes when your imagination is out of focus."

Mere coincidence, some might insist. Stories spun around long-ago dinosaur discoveries. The genetic memory of all that awed our primordial kin—serpent, raptor, and ravening feline—wrapped into one so seemingly improbable being.

Improbable being the operative word.

When discussing Dragons, we are well served to remember the maxim of Sherlock Holmes: "When you have eliminated all which is impossible, then whatever remains, however improbable, must be the truth." In the case of Dragons, it is their very existence which, though improbable to some, remains a truth embraced by millions from pole to pole.

That the undeniable logic of this does not convince everyone is simply the way of the world. There will always be neat, modern people who want neat, modern explanations for the strange and unusual. People who honestly believe Homo sapiens are separate from and even superior to all other creatures. Who pride themselves on their cities and conquests, their strip malls and strip mines. People who put fear before wonder and, in the process, dissolve the ties that hold nature and spirit together. Such attitudes have pushed Dragons to the brink of extinction and necessitated radical conservation efforts around the world. We brought the black-footed ferret back from the abyss; surely we can do the same for Dragons.

To succeed in this endeavor, we must understand these wild and mystical beings from first breath to last, know their habits and habitats, their needs and dangers; what they once were, what they are today; what they want from us and what we need from them. The awe-inspiring and the ordinary, the harrowing and the gentle, the blithe and the heart-rending. We need to know it all.

In short, the sum of all Dragons.

We must remember their history so we can safeguard their future. We must know how to share this world with them to the benefit of all.

With each bit of information we arm ourselves against the non-believers—even win over a few converts—and bring Dragons more intimately into our lives.

It shouldn't be that difficult, right? Since prehistoric times we have lived with Dragons. We've summoned them from the mists with our longing and banished them twice as quickly with our fear. But what do we all actually know about Dragons?

Dragons are, according to established orthodoxy and a battery of lexicons, large—some might say mountainous—scaly creatures with leathern wings, cavernous maws, and incendiary breath. Western legends have them hoarding treasure and adopting a gourmand's appreciation for virgins in distress and the errant knights who might hazard their rescue.[2] Simply put, they are monstrous.

As with most appraisals of the mystical, this one is cursory at best, stereotypically prejudiced and erroneous at worst.

Dragons are so much more than this.

They are elemental, capable of commanding earth, wind, fire, and water. They fly across the face of the moon and dive deep beneath the seven seas.

They are loyal, loving, elegant, musical, fierce, and wise. They are weyr[3] builders and enchantment weavers.

They know more about this world we share than we humans can hope to glean in a thousand lifetimes.

They are wildness and mystery; bringers of death and symbols of eternal life.

This is the gestalt of the Dragon, as absolute and elegant as the Dragons themselves. Dragons are so much more than the simple collection of their parts. Such wonder deserves nothing less than appreciation and understanding in all its brilliantly monstrous complexity. It is a prodigious undertaking.

Let us begin.

---

2. What about Eastern Dragons, you ask? Though artistic representations present them in a more ophidian aspect, they are actually more similar to their Western cousins than different. We will examine the details of species variation in due course.

3. For those of you new to Dragons, a *weyr* is, essentially, a Dragon community; an *enchantment* is a Dragon clan. Be sure to consult the glossary at the back of this book for the definitions of any unfamiliar terms.

*p*art I

From Tooth to Tail: The Natural History of Dragons

You must not know too much or be too precise
or scientific about birds and trees and flowers
and watercraft; a certain free-margin, and
even vagueness—ignorance, credulity—helps
your enjoyment of these things.

—Walt Whitman

one

True or False: Dragon Species & Genetic Variations

When the sun rose over the primitive hominids of the ancient Rift Valley, there were Dragons. As late as eleven thousand years ago, our Mesolithic ancestors would have been well acquainted with Dragons both True and false. Indeed, with the exception of size,[1] True Dragons have not changed appreciably since the latter half of the Paleolithic Era.

The same cannot be said of false dragons, or pseudo-dragons, of course. Their bloodlines are far more fragile, more open to mutation, than their True Dragon kin. This has led to a host of lesser dragons of every shape, size, and temperament cropping up in every corner of the world. Though often hard to find, the vitality and mutation rates of these ersatz dragons provide priceless indicators of planetary health. They may not be as flashy as their True kin, but, as any cryptoherpetologist will tell you, we need them nonetheless.

---

1. There is some anecdotal evidence that our modern Dragons are roughly 20 percent smaller than those of the Golden Age (c. 5000 BCE). This is most likely the result of modern pollutants and habitat limitations. Like goldfish, Dragons will grow only as large as conditions allow.

For those new to the mysterious and rare, cryptoherpetology is, plainly put, the study of "hidden reptiles." More fanciful circles refer to it as Secret Serpent Science or even Remarkable Reptile Research, but it's Dragon Studies, plain if hardly simple.[2] Contrary to the assumptions of academe, cryptoherpetologists follow the same rigorous methodologies as do their more orthodox counterparts. Questions are raised; hypotheses formed; through observation, experiment, and empirical research, conclusions are reached; and results are shared. This may come as a shock to hard-core skeptics who view those working beyond the fringe of academia as hacks, eccentrics, or fools. Of course, if these skeptics bothered to look, they'd realize the sanctioned roster of natural sciences (and a few social sciences, too) has exploded in the last century, including a plethora of fields which would have been considered crypto studies as recently as a generation ago.

Granted, some central questions of Dragon Studies are hatched from eggs hard-shelled by myth, but that is hardly an unusual genesis when it comes to scientific inquiry. Before Thomas-François Dalibard and Benjamin Franklin played with kites and keys, lightning bolts were explained away as the temper tantrums of the gods: atmospheric javelins from the hands of Tlaloc and Zeus, sparks from Thor's hammer, etc. And, granted, the crypto sciences are frequently hampered by the inherent natures of their subjects. Draconic researchers contend not only with a meager fossil record and historical accounts more fiction than fact, but also with the very real risk of getting injured—even killed—trying to study Dragons in their natural habitat.[3] But ordinary scientific pursuits are also complicated by access and hazards—the boon of particle accelerators and the dangers of space travel immediately leap to mind.

---

2. The fact that Dragons, while reptilian, are not, strictly speaking, reptiles gives you some idea of the problems inherent in the discipline. It's a dicey starting point, to say the least, and one which has given skeptics plenty of ammunition over the years.

3. In addition, cryptoherpetologists must deal with the inability to do detailed examinations of subcutaneous draconic anatomy: vivisection is not a big hit in Dragon Studies for reasons both obvious and obscure.

George Santayana wrote that

> science is nothing but developed perception, interpreted
> intent, common-sense rounded out and minutely artic-
> ulated. It is therefore as much an instinctive product, as
> much a stepping forth of human courage in the dark, as
> is any inevitable dream or impulsive action.
>
> (*The Life of Reason*, Vol. V, p. 307)

There are now (and may always be) people who diminish—even dismiss—the scholarly bona fides of Dragon Studies. This is hardly surprising in a world that is still debating the truth of evolution. We suggest that such parochial thinking betrays a perception deficit on the side of traditional academia rather than any problem with the crypto sciences themselves. One has only to think of strange quarks and expanding universes, of gravity's binding force and the exquisite beauty of the double helix, to grasp the essential audacity at the heart of scientific curiosity, up to and including the exploration of the unknown and unexplained. If human erudition was limited strictly to that which was seen and appreciated by the powers that be, we'd still be diapered infants floundering in the intellectual sandbox.

That said, with open minds and courage enough for a stroll through the darkest dark, let's embark on a minutely articulated examination of Dragons, both True and pseudo.

True Dragons

True Dragons are among the universe's most perfect beings. This is a useful bit of information. Squirrel it away like a nugget of Fafnir's gold; take it out and burnish it now and then as we proceed.

There are three distinct species of True Dragons: Western or Occidental Dragons; Eastern or Oriental Dragons; and the Feathered Dragons of the Southern Hemisphere. While, from a distance, some of their larger poor relations can almost pass for True Dragons, there is one sure way to tell them apart: sacred geometry.

Were the early titans of sacred geometry—Phidias, Pythagoras, Euclid—staring in wonder at Hellenic Dragons when they had their Eureka! moments and codified the golden ratio? It is a reasonable conjecture. Being most-perfect creatures, True Dragons are proportionate to the sacred harmonies of the natural world. These proportions are easier to see in Western Dragons, their solid form standing four-square before us, crying out to be drawn and tape-measure quartered. Their physiques are in precise accord with the golden ratio used in sacred geometry: a+b/a = a/b = φ [$\varphi \approx 1.618$] (see Diagram 1).

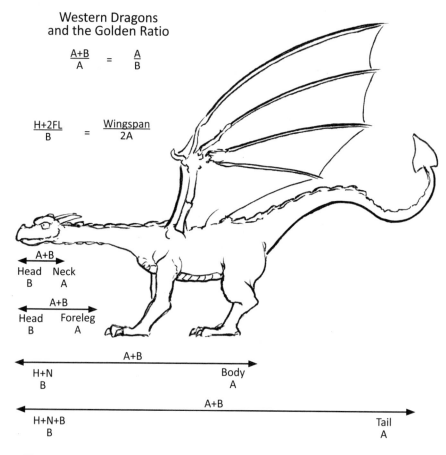

Diagram 1

The best way to understand the relationship of Dragons to the golden ratio is by looking at the parts first, then the whole. Plug the parts into the equation and—voilà!—all becomes clear.

Thus: Neck = A; Head = B

$$\frac{\text{Neck} + \text{Head}}{\text{Neck}} = \frac{\text{Neck}}{\text{Head}} = 1.618$$

These same proportions continue along the entire length and breadth of a Dragon's body:

Body = A; Head + Neck = B

$$\frac{\text{Body} + \text{Head} + \text{Neck}}{\text{Body}} = \frac{\text{Body}}{\text{Head} + \text{Neck}} = 1.618$$

Tail = A; Head + Neck + Body = B

$$\frac{\text{Tail} + \text{Head} + \text{Neck} + \text{Body}}{\text{Tail}} = \frac{\text{Tail}}{\text{Head} + \text{Neck} + \text{Body}} = 1.618$$

Wingspan = 2A [½ Wingspan = A]; Head + (Foreleg × 2) = B

$$\frac{\text{½ Wingspan} + \text{Head} + (\text{Foreleg} \times 2)}{\text{½ Wingspan}} = \frac{\text{½ Wingspan}}{\text{Head} + (\text{Foreleg} \times 2)} = 1.618$$

Consequently, if a Dragon's head was 2 metres long, his measurements would be (approximately): Head = 2 metres; Neck (and Forelegs) = 3.24 metres; Body = 8.5 metres; Tail = 22.25 metres. In all, he would be roughly 36 metres from the first scale on his nose to the last on his tail. His wingspan would reach almost 27.5 metres. A formidably perfect being!

The divine ratio is less evident in full grown Eastern and Feathered Dragons, getting easily lost in their sinuous physiology. However, when still in the shell, their True-Dragon proportions are very noticeable. There, snug and secure, they grow, coiled in a neat golden spiral. The Fibonacci sequence[4] provides the simplest approximation of this embryonic form and is a fitting approach for those of you who took a pass on post-graduate calculus (see Diagram 2).

---

4.   0, 1, 1, 2, 3, 5, 8, 13, 21, 34, 55, 89, 144, 233, 377, 610, 987, 1597, 2584, 4181, 6765…

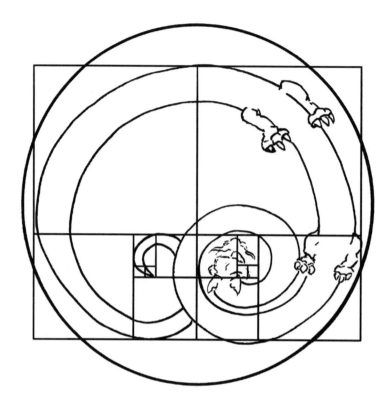

Diagram 2. Embryonic Eastern Dragon & the Fibonacci Spiral 0,1,1,2,3,5,8,13,21 ...

Once out of the egg, Eastern and Feathered Dragons mature in a manner corresponding to the golden ratio discussed above (see Diagrams 3a and 3b).

Also, if you get close enough to an Eastern Dragon—and are very polite—you will find that their scales, from tail to crown, multiply in a precise Fibonacci progression. There are reports that this is true of Western Dragons, too, though they are not exactly eager to have their scales counted. Consensus has it that Westerns are decidedly more titillative than their Oriental cousins, thus making for dicey fact checking even with the most affectionate Dragon. All else taken into consideration, it still makes perfect sense regardless of scale-by-scale documentation. As anyone steeped in Dragon Studies knows, a great many things must be taken on faith.

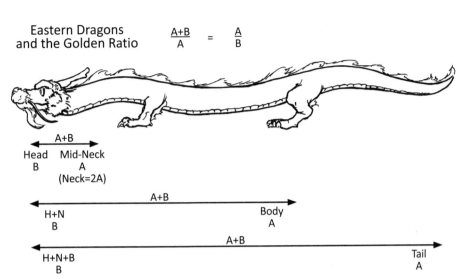

Eastern Dragons
and the Golden Ratio $\frac{A+B}{A} = \frac{A}{B}$

A+B

Head   Mid-Neck
B   A
(Neck=2A)

A+B

H+N   Body
B   A

A+B

H+N+B   Tail
B   A

Diagram 3a

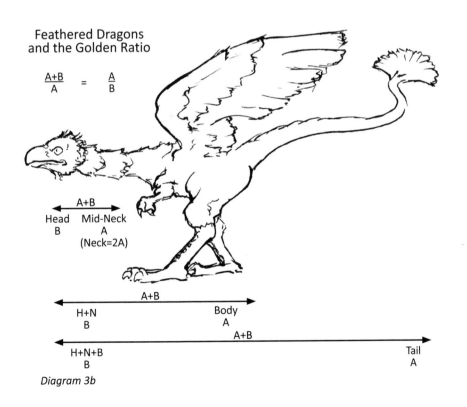

Feathered Dragons
and the Golden Ratio

$\frac{A+B}{A} = \frac{A}{B}$

A+B

Head   Mid-Neck
B   A
(Neck=2A)

A+B

H+N   Body
B   A

A+B

H+N+B   Tail
B   A

Diagram 3b

Western Dragons

What image comes most readily to mind when talk turns to Dragons (as it no doubt does frequently in your daily life)? Chances are it is that of the Occidental or Western Dragon.

From Siberia to Persia, through Europe and North America, these magnificent creatures have roamed the world, tipping their wings over mountains, steppes, river runs, and arid wastes. They are and always have been the most numerous of the True Dragons. They are also the most gregarious. That said, it is all the more puzzling that they have so long suffered the slings and arrows of atrocious public perception.

Through the centuries, Western Dragons have been depicted as fierce, bloodthirsty, winged fire-breathers who pilfer livestock, dine on ill-fated maidens, and guard their treasure-packed lairs from all comers. True, they do breathe fire—something to bear in mind when approaching them in the wild—and they are attracted to precious metals and stones, especially when brooding.[5] But the rest is mere fiction created by clerics in search of converts and/or knights who wanted something to brag about around the castle keep.

The temperament of the Western Dragon makes them adaptable to a splendid diversity of environments, including those in close proximity to quasi-urban centers. They are extremely bright beings who, contrary to popular belief, tend to be somewhat laid-back and retiring. And, like all True Dragons, they are loyal, often to a fault.

Vital Statistics

Mature Occidental Dragons measure between 8 and 12 metres in length, not counting their tails, with wingspans of proportionate size. Tails are close to two-thirds the total length of a Dragon but are flexible enough to curl neatly out of the way in intimate spaces. Well-conditioned Dragons are muscular with a pantherlike sleekness to their physique and can weigh in at two to three tons. True, this is massive; yet for their size, Dragons are actually featherweights—as they need to

---

5. See Chapter Three, Dragon Days of Autumn.

be—thanks to hollow bones and flight-sacs filled with lighter-than-air gases that help them soar aloft.[6] Like human fingerprints, tail spades, neck furls, and spinal ridges vary from individual to individual, though there can be hereditary similarities within families. Such shared characteristics, subtle though they may be to human eyes, serve as effective identifiers within large enchantments and during forced migrations.

Western Dragons come in both scaly and smooth varieties—though scaly types are the more prevalent.[7] Smooth-skinned Dragons sunburn with relative ease and thus are poorly suited to tropical/subtropical/desert habitats. For skin care, both varieties look to regular

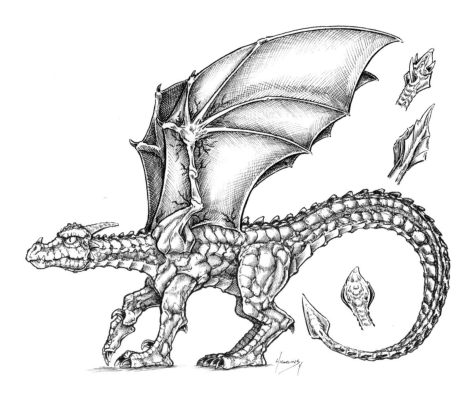

---

6. See Peter Dickinson's *The Flight of Dragons* for an extensive and fascinating dissertation on a Dragon's flight-related physiology.

7. It is possible that the smooth-skinned Dragons are simply more hermitic, rather than less numerous.

bathing in water and dust—the latter serving to combat any external parasites that might find their way into draconic locales.

Colour among Western Dragons is positively prismatic, so much so that a weyr on the wing is like an impressionist painting hanging in the clouds. That said, some hues are more common than others—if anything about Dragons is ever common. Most frequently seen are green, blue, red, and variations thereon; the metallics (silver, bronze, and gold) are less typical. White Dragons are the rarest of all. Diet plays a considerable role in subtler shade distinctions. Dragons who, for example, enjoy a consistent diet of crustaceans and mollusks— especially langouste, mitten crabs, and abalone—ingest significant amounts of copper. This can give a red Dragon a warm, auburn tinge or a green Dragon a slight verdigris underhue. All Western Dragons have an iridescent, chameleon quality, which enables them to adjust their colour at will or whim and blend into their surroundings, a defi- nite advantage when playing hide-and-seek—or fleeing for their lives.

Soft, leathery wings are one of the Western Dragon's most dis- tinctive characteristics. Flexible enough to fold neatly along a Dragon's back, these ribbed appendages are strong enough to carry a Dragon into the oxygen-thin stratosphere. Unfortunately, a Dragon's wings are among her most vulnerable features. Scholars insist that many of the ancient tales of Dragon slayings were only possible once the Dragons in question had been grounded by having their wings grievously lacer- ated. For this reason, Dragons must take precautions and preen their wings daily: a wing-damaged Dragon is a vulnerable Dragon.

Early imagination-challenged naturalists described Western Dragons as having equine heads, which is not only inaccurate but also unfair to Dragon and horse alike.[8] Though both sport long, rather spatulate crania, Dragons are much broader across the brow than horses. This is an evolutionary quirk that accommodates resonance

---

8. The confusion may well have arisen when early naturalists mistook water horses and kelpies for surf-frolicking Dragons. To this day, there are parts of the world in which water horses are still considered draconic kindred, proving once again that it is far easier to make a mistake than it is to correct one.

chambers for sonorous communication (speech and song) as well as their third eye, a species-specific enlarged pineal gland.

Teeth and horns distinguish Western Dragons from more mundane fauna as well as from their Eastern and pseudo kindred.

Male and female alike, Dragons are born with vestigial, temporal nubs. These harden by their fifth year and grow in a family-specific fashion, either straight, spiraled, or in a tight curl. Within these three general categories, Dragon horns can be as varied and spectacular as the vast treasury of antelope racks. They are used for defense and display and do require considerable care.[9]

Look a Western Dragon head-on and you cannot help but notice a formidable mouthful of teeth—fifty-six to seventy-two in number. That's enough to give the most intrepid naturalist pause! However, contrary to popular misconceptions, they are not all savage sabres like

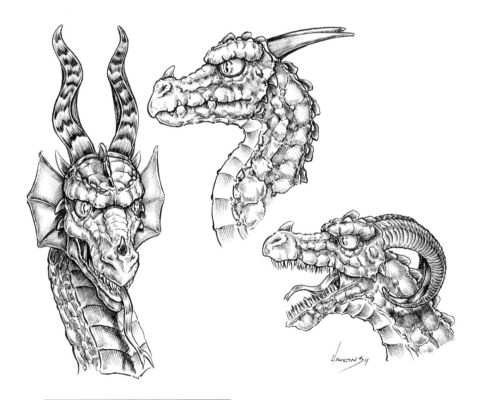

---

9. See Chapter Two.

those flashed by carnivorous sauropods or modern crocodilians. In testament to a Dragon's inclusive diet, thirty-six deep-rooted bicuspids and mandibular molars back up her impressive frontal array of fangs and incisors. With dental plates like these, Dragons can easily rend and masticate flesh, bone, and shell as well as grind up a variety of foliage, from delicate leaves to crisp, cellulose-laden branches.

As wide ranging as Western Dragons are, it is important to bear in mind that this makes them the most likely of the True species to cross human paths. When this happens, always remember: they were here first. The trespass is ours.

Eastern Dragons

Honored rather than reviled, Eastern Dragons have fared far better in the popular imagination than their Western relations. Though their range is limited to the more temperate parts of India, all of China, and the western Pacific Rim, they have wandered in spirit around the globe. They are represented in Dragon festivals across Europe and the Americas, including Dragon Boat Festivals in locales as diverse as Lethbridge, Alberta; Denver, Colorado; and Kiev in the Ukraine. That these beings are revered as one the wisest on Earth reminds us that the differences between Eastern and Western Dragons are as much cultural and philosophical as they are physiological.

An extreme loss of habitat has made Oriental Dragons not only rare but reclusive. Survival has taken precedence over their once benevolent, even extroverted, existence. As understandable as this is, it puts cryptoherpetologists at a distinct disadvantage, having to rely more on hearsay and legend than on empirical knowledge. This should in no way deter serious Dragon aficionados, particularly those who prefer to learn firsthand rather than from books. In short, the field is open for exploration.

That is not to say that we don't know some remarkable things about these sinuous beings. Oriental Dragons have a traditional and well-deserved reputation for being honorable, benevolent, lucky, and very ingenious. In dynastic China, the descendants of the First

Celestial Dragon, Golden Lung, symbolized power and good fortune and inspired near-divine awe. Though the people of China often referred to themselves as *Lung Tik Chuan Ren*—the Children of the Dragon—only the emperor was worthy enough to display the Celestial Dragon's likeness.[10] The emperor was China personified. Imperial robes and banners were embroidered with the auric five-toed Dragon so that his sovereign self—and, by extension, all China—might came under Golden Lung's personal protection. This is a far cry from the put-upon Occidental Dragons fending off questing knights at every turn!

Vital Statistics

Legend has it the Oriental Dragon is a being of nine aspects or anatomical resemblances: head of a lion (or camel); horns of a stag; eyes of a hare (or demon); ears of a cow; neck of a snake; belly of a tortoise;

---

10. The emperor also laid claim to the likeness of Shen Lung, the spiritual Dragon who ruled the rains, the Azure Dragon of the East, and so forth. To play it safe, no one outside of the Imperial family would even consider placing a five-toed Dragon on their banner or robe.

scales of a carp; paws of a tiger; and claws of an eagle. They are also described as being an amalgam of all the other zodiac animals—the quintessential astrological hybrid. Interesting theories, to be sure, though seeing any creature as a patchwork of others is not only bad science but demeaning to all concerned.[11] We advise against it.

The differences between Eastern and Western Dragons are evident at first sight. Where Western Dragons present a four-square lizardlike aspect, their Asian kin are more elongate and ophidian. They are, paradoxically, also the most mammalian of the True Dragons. They have a particularly leonine facial aspect, luxurious manes framing their regal heads, and wide, whiskered, well-toothed mouths which give the impression they are smiling with inscrutable mirth.

There are three separate families of True Oriental Dragons, each readily distinguished by the number of digits on their feet: the three- and four-toed of the Pacific Islands (including Japan, Indonesia, and the smaller nations of Micronesia) and the five-toed of the Asian mainland. The most prevalent is the Chinese five-toed. These charming pentadactyls were so common in the past that they were believed to be the root stock for all Oriental Dragons, travelling and mutating as their new environments demanded.

Within the three families, there are two other distinctions: horned and hornless, flying and flightless. Our human need to create hierarchies and order in the world reveres the five-toed, horned, flying Dragon as the epitome of the species. Since a medley of traits can be found within a single enchantment—sometimes even within a single clutch of eggs—this says more about our human discriminatory nature than it does about the Dragons.

Oriental Dragons move through their habitats with low-to-the-ground serpentine grace. Their soft ankle and tail tufts catch pollen with ease and contribute to the health of flora in their environments. Unlike their Western cousins, they do not breathe fire. They also

---

11. Cast your mind back to the platypus and the zoological brouhaha kicked up by the discovery of this "duck+beaver" creature and you'll get the idea.

don't have wings. How Eastern Dragons fly without them remains a mystery considered more philosophical than physiological.

Flying Eastern Dragons, regardless of toe count, are larger than their landlocked kin. There are credible reports of such Dragons reaching up to 30 metres in length. Substantially shorter and stockier than these ethereal beauties, flightless Dragons measure, on average, only half that when full grown.

The colours of Oriental Dragons are habitat specific: earth Dragons lean toward muted mineral tones: umbers, ochres, and rusts often flecked with glistening gold or copper; forest Dragons come in a wide variety of greens; water Dragons are aqueous in blues and greens; and sky Dragons shimmer with silvers, greys, and pale azures. In contrast to the showy chameleon excesses of their Western kin, Asian Dragons seem to prefer stillness and natural *feng shui* for camouflage. Of course, the respect afforded them in their native lands gives them greater freedom of movement. They require far less stealth in their daily lives than their Western relatives. This also explains why Eastern Dragons rarely venture west of the Urals: they would be fools to go where they're not appreciated.

And Dragons are seldom fools.

Feathered Dragons

Feathered or Southern Dragons are the smallest and the most scarce of the True Dragons. They flit in and out of the rain-forest canopies, wrapping their lithesome tails around boughs of kapok and purple heart trees. In environments full of the unknown and unusual, Feathered Dragons are the epitome of both—so much so that some doubt they even exist. But long before the Maya and Moche civilizations in the New World and the Dahomey and Khoisan in the Old World, Feathered Dragons were catching the sun on their quills and dancing like living rainbows across the sky.

Vital Statistics

Compared to other True Dragons, our feathered friends, while not minute, are definitely on the miniature side. This is a strict function of habitat. Living in and on the edges of the planet's dense rainforests, these exquisite beings cannot sustain the great size and bulk of their cousins. Theirs is a realm in which lightness and flexibility mean survival.

Mature Feathered Dragons rarely grow to more than 6 metres in length or weigh much over 300 pounds—about 10 percent of that being their colourful, plumed integument. They have lean, reptilian musculature stretched over a hollow-bone frame. Scales protect the belly and lower legs; feathers are everywhere else. Dense bristle feathers run from head to nape, forming wide facial discs and ornate crests radiating around barely visible hornlets which never develop beyond the nub stage. Lustrous contour feathers blanket the rest of the body. Despite the Dragons' enormity, the outer plumes are comparable to those of the large avians in their environs—macaws, harpy eagles, horn bills, and eagle owls. On the rare occasions that such feathers make their way to the forest floor, they are generally assumed to come from more mundane species. This misconception affords the Dragons welcome protection from hunters' sanguine ways. A fine undercoat of semiplumes and careful preening make Feathered Dragons naturally waterproof—just the thing to shed the weight of incessant forest showers or when cooling off in crystal *cenotes*. Where their range bleeds into semi-arid plains (lands deforested by climate change and human greed), this same plumage provides them with insulation against the daytime heat and nightly cold.

Their shimmering wings span a good 3 to 3.5 metres, far and away the most impressive feathered array in the forests.[12] Using their broad, plumed tail spades as rudders, they undulate through the skies, looking not unlike a sleek cetacean traversing an airy sea.

---

12. In all of the avian world, only the wandering albatross has a wingspan to even approach the Feathered Dragon's reach.

Feathered Dragons are the most diurnal of the True Dragons, using stark daylight shadows to camouflage their hunting and foraging through the treetops. With encyclopedic palates and more stealth than any creature their size has a right to, they pluck from the bounty around them not only a wide variety of foliage but also cacao nuts, jagua fruit, fish, monkeys, and the occasional peccary, kinkajou, or boa constrictor. While all Dragons have superb eyesight, Feathered Dragons have the most excellent of all. In a realm so densely undergrown, visual acuity is absolutely essential if they hope to hunt with success.

Though they spend much of their time—both awake and drowsing—in the canopy and above, Feathered Dragons nest exclusively in secure cliffsides and inaccessible plateaus.[13] An enchantment will honeycomb an entire escarpment, digging out dens and tunnels, up and down, front to back. There the females lay their eggs in nests of branches and kapok fibers. Throughout the nesting period, the males come and go, bringing their mates select morsels and relieving them for requisite baths and wing stretches. Fledgling Dragons will stay in the nest until their flight feathers come in and they can maneuver through the environment with safety. While we tend to think of Dragons as virtually invulnerable, top-of-the-food-chain predators, land-bound Dragonlets can themselves fall prey to voracious reptiles, big cats, or anacondas.

These feathered beauties are the rarest jewels of the True Dragon triad. With rainforests vanishing at an alarming rate, we must take particular care not to drive them forever from our world.

Defense Mechanisms

We humans have proved ourselves monstrous when it comes to designing bigger and better ways to hunt and kill. And, as the canon of draconic mythology attests, no being—not even the amplest, most

---

13. Reports of Feathered Dragons nesting in the floating islands above Venezuela's Gran Sabana likely proved inspirational to Sir Arthur Conan Doyle when he was penning *The Lost World*.

ferocious Dragon—is immune to attack and murderous dispatch. In such a harsh landscape, Dragons have developed an arsenal of species-specific defense mechanisms which, while not exactly leveling the playing field, do give them a fighting chance when needed.

All True Dragons (and many pseudo-dragons) face the hostile world armed with intimidating size, fierce aspects, and thick hides. Even the seemingly fragile Feathered Dragons, when mature, have plumage so dense and hard that it repels nigh-on-all fangs and talons, as well as simple human weaponry—spears, blades, and small-to-medium caliber bullets.

Though generally preferring flight over fight, if pressed or cornered, Dragons will not hesitate to use tooth and claw to good effect. They have razor-sharp front talons which can grasp or rend as needs be. Their powerful back feet can throw up mounds of dirt, blinding foes with sod and soil, and, in extremes, eviscerate an adversary with one swift kick. Draconic jaws exert a crunching force of between 20 kNs[14] for Feathered Dragons and a staggering 90 kNs for Western Dragons—roughly four times stronger than the bite of the saltwater crocodile. While these are serious bites by any stretch of the

---

14.   kN = kiloNewton. 1 Newton = 1 kg m(etre) s(econd)^2

imagination, the vulnerability of an open maw at close range with gun or blade makes this a Dragon's less-than-ideal first choice of defense. Better to take wing or turn tail and get a little distance, a little perspective. Or, as Shakespeare's Falstaff said in *Henry IV*, "The better part of valor is discretion, in the which better part I have saved my life."

Speaking of turning tail, this is not a sign of draconic weakness. Far from it! Among Western and Eastern Dragons, it is a bold and four-square defensive ploy. With whiplike speed and devastating accuracy, a Dragon's heavy, armored, spade-tipped tail can knock rider from horse, break the thickest of bones, and in short, inflict serious damage while courting little jeopardy.[15]

Unfortunately, for a Dragon's dogged enemies, no amount of defensive posturing or sage withdrawal will dissuade them from the hunt. Under such circumstances, a Dragon must take more affirmative action. This is when they reach into their species-specific bags of tricks and, if needs be, take no prisoners.

Fire

For Dragons, breathing fire is as iconic as—well, as breathing fire. This is actually a defense mechanism employed almost exclusively by Occidental Dragons and erroneously celebrated in myth and legend and too many Hollywood CGI-laden extravaganzas to count. The truth is, Western Dragons use fire for a variety of reasons, only one of which is protection—or, as anti-Dragon folks insist, "aggression." Brooding Dragons, for example, warm their nesting dens with the occasional blast during dark winter nights. This helps keep their maturing clutches at the optimum temperature and ensures the perpetuation of the species. Flaming an errant knight is the last thing on a maternal Dragon's mind. Dragons also use fire for mating-ritual panache, warning signals, and just plain fun. After all, if you have it, why not flaunt it?

---

15. Those of you unfamiliar with this behaviour in Dragons have only to look at the Perentie of Australia's Red Centre. Though lacking in the stature of their oh-so-remote kin, these savvy desert monitors use their tails to similar effect.

There are several theories swirling around the production of Dragonfire, all of which, one way or another, involve digestion, gas bladders, and timely sparks.

When it comes to fire, the main bone of contention for crypto-herpetologists involves the chemical makeup of the fire gas. Some insist it is a methane (CH_4) byproduct of digestive or intestinal fermentation, similar to that emanating from cows and other ruminants. But Dragons, to the best of our knowledge, are *not* ruminants. Though Dragons certainly ingest enough plant matter to produce masses of methane, there is no evidence that Dragons are anything other than monogastric, or single-stomached. It is, of course, possible that the digestive bacteria in their one stomach are potent enough to break down dietary cellulose and create voluminous reserves of CH_4. Unlike flatulent livestock who have been getting a lot of bad press in global warming circles, Dragons would store their excess methane in fire bladders for use when and as needed.

The other credible theory, put forth by such noted Dragon experts as Peter Dickinson, is that Dragonfire is the expulsion of excess lighter-than-air gases—mostly hydrogen—from their flight reserves.[16] This would explain why many portraits of Dragon/knight encounters depict lumbering, grounded Dragons. It is hard to maintain altitude if you have to use all your liftoff gas on self-defense.

Being methane or hydrogen-based, Dragonfire ignites by way of an esophageal tinderbox in which finely masticated chert (flint) powder is forced over a hard plate at the back of the throat, setting the flammable gases ablaze. A uniquely modified epiglottis allows Dragons to breathe and flame at the same time.[17] This fleshy tube protruding under the tongue is equipped with heat-sensitive valves which regulate respiration while protecting the lungs from super-heated air.

---

16. See Dickinson, *The Flight of Dragons.*

17. Cryptoherpetologists who, despite evidence to the contrary, insist that Dragons are reptiles, point to the epiglottal similarity between Dragons and serpents. A careful examination of a Dragon's mouth will show that this is an oversimplification at best.

These valves are also believed to act like carburetors, adjusting the oxygen content of a Dragon's flame for maximum effect. Fascinating as this concept is, even those in the vanguard of Dragon Studies have yet to verify it to a scientific certainty.

Despite questions lingering around anatomical anomalies and systemic technicalities, cryptoherpetologists can all agree on one thing: fire-breathing Dragons are basically dealing with volatile cases of indigestion. That they have learned to control their bodily functions so ingeniously speaks to the evolutionary complexity of the species.

Venom

Oriental Dragons, Feathered Dragons, and numerous pseudo-dragons produce venom with various qualities, strengths, and delivery systems. While small, lesser dragons traditionally use their poison as a hunting aid, it is strictly a weapon of last resort for True Dragons. If you get up close to an angry Dragon, you had better watch out: there is no antivenin strong enough to counteract a full-on wet bite. Of course, to paraphrase Butch Cassidy, "Antivenin! Are you crazy? The bite will probably kill you."

True Dragons have true venom, a complex, glandular cocktail of proteins not to be confused with the nasty bacteria-laced slobber of Komodo dragons and other monitors.[18] Indeed, our quilled rain-forest friends are the only feathered creatures on Earth with a poisonous bite.

Feathered Dragons have venom glands situated between the upper jaw and the cheek bone with a duct leading to a fierce pair of retractable front fangs, 15–20 centimetres (6–8 inches) in length. Compared to, say, your average pit viper, these glands are proportionately quite small; however, strength and lethal delivery system more than compensate for the discrepancy. Feathered Dragon venom is a hemorrhagic hemotoxin so potent that one drop can cause a bull elephant to bleed out in a matter of minutes. While a Feathered Dragon

---

18. This is not to say that some of the more reptilian pseudo-dragons don't have toxic saliva.

at odds with an elephant is a highly unlikely scenario, you can imagine how the sight of such massive blood loss might have affected the primitive peoples in their environs.[19]

The venom sported by Oriental Dragons is of a very different nature. Living in an essentially Dragon-friendly environment, theirs is a poison designed to stun rather than slay: a neurotoxin, diluted, atomized, and absorbed through the victim's skin. Chinese Dragons are a prime example of this. Through the years, what has often been interpreted as frost mist or ice breath billowing from the maws of some Eastern giants is, in fact, a fine spray of relatively mild paralytic venom. Forced through outward facing holes in their front fangs, the venom vaporizes on the back of warm Dragon breath and settles over foes like a low-lying cloud.[20] In moments, the mist "freezes" its target and the Dragon can depart at her leisure. In time, the freezee will come around, stiff, headachy, and suffering some short-term memory

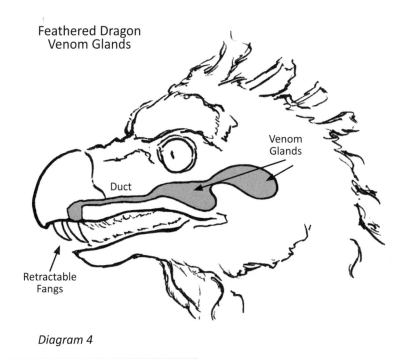

Feathered Dragon
Venom Glands

Venom
Glands

Duct

Retractable
Fangs

Diagram 4

19. The blood-letting rituals of the Maya and Aztec people come readily to mind.

20. Think highly modified spitting cobra and you'll begin to get the idea.

loss but with few lasting effects. The amnesiac qualities of the toxin are particularly beneficial, making "I ran into an angry Dragon" rantings sound like little more than a hallucination. Some Pacific Rim Dragons use soporific toxins to similar effect, producing a sleep cloud over their adversaries. If all goes well, little blood is shed and Dragon haunts remain secure.

With an Eastern Dragon, volume trumps concentration when it comes to venom. To this end, her toxin starts out as an extremely potent fluid produced in small vesicles tucked back in her jowls, just below her lower mandibles. When needed, a minute quantity of venom flows forth, watered down in a pair of much larger salivary glands, and then stored in reservoirs pouching along the Dragon's upper lip. From there it streams out on torrid breath and the job is done.

The pseudo-dragons who pack a venomous punch come in both front- and rear-fanged species. The latter, like their ophidian counterparts, are the safer of the two, employing hemotoxins and cytotoxins as hunting and digestive aids rather than weaponry. A bite from such a lesser dragon, while certainly painful—and, depending on the species, potentially deadly—is not likely to be toxin-laced. On the other hand, front-fanged pseudo-dragons can be very dangerous. Not only is their venom generally more lethal than their rear-fanged kin, they tend to be more aggressive too.[21] Lacking the intelligence and discretion of True Dragons, they will not hesitate to use all the defenses at their disposal. This includes injecting copious amounts of poison into their enemies, be they real or merely perceived. Only master Dragon handlers using the greatest of care should even attempt to approach these creatures.

Sound

The stentorian thunder of a Dragon is a sound not soon forgotten. Quintessential defense mechanisms, the voices of True Dragons are used to shock and stun, to rock foes right back on their heels and

---

21. The Hydra is a perfect case in point. See page 33.

send them heading for the hills. Ranging from 95 to 160 decibels, well above the safe level for human ears, a draconic roar can, in close proximity, cause nausea, disorientation, permanent hearing loss, and even death. The accompanying subsonic shock wave will rattle the earth and, in mountainous terrains, easily produce landslides or avalanches.

A Dragon will start his roar deep in his chest, with a huge breath cascading up and out by way of larynx and cavernous resonance chambers in his skull. Then he has only to open his mouth and say "GRRRRAAAHHHHRRRRRHHHHHH!!!!"

Understandably, this is an excellent long-distance defense. Dragons can bellow from hiding, and even work in consort, bouncing their voices back and forth, further disorienting their foes and protecting their enchantments with minimal risk. This ploy is particularly useful in open environments where a solo Dragon yawping in front of his den becomes a dead-set target for Dragon hunters.

Shape Shifting

Some may argue that shape shifting is an odd sort of defense for a Dragon. After all, who is stronger, fiercer, or more high flying than a Dragon? Still, there are times a little transformation comes in handy.

In the canon of draconic legends, there are numerous tales of shape-shifting Dragons. In the West, reports of shape shifting generally involve sorcerers and magi turning hapless princes and unwitting individuals into Dragons for punishment or much-needed life lessons.[22] It's vile treatment totally in keeping with the anti-Dragon sentiments of the region. Such conjured Dragons were usually wyrms or drakes rather than True Dragons, and the spells often served to put them in danger rather than protect them. There were far too many warriors and would-be heroes about just waiting for a chance to dispatch a Dragon, or, as the case might be, a confused human in a magical Dragon suit.

---

22. C. S. Lewis used this to fine effect on young Eustace in *The Voyage of the Dawn Treader*. Of course, the curse Eustace falls under apes the one that afflicts Fafnir of Rheingeld fame.

Things were very different in the East. Not countenancing human interference, Oriental Dragons are in control of their own lives. And they can be particularly transformational beings.

In Japan, for example, Dragons are one of the four *henge*, deities who can metamorphose between animal and human forms. Three of the four, the Kitzune (Fox), Tanuki (Raccoon Dog), and Tengu (Bird Man), are real pros at mischievous alterations, needing only the slightest impetus to change.

Dragon *henge* activities are of a very different nature, reflective more of the mortal storytellers than of the Dragons themselves, for humans are always more envious of draconic qualities than vice versa. To this end, we find stories like the Tale of Hoori. Hoori, a young hunter, falls in love with and marries Otohime, the daughter of Ryujin the Dragon King. As these things go, the princess eventually became pregnant, which was cause for great celebration by all concerned. But it had been years since Hoori had seen his family and homesickness weighed heavily on him. So the Dragon King sent Hoori and his bride out of the Sea Kingdom that their baby might be born on land, in the bosom of his son-in-law's kin. In the way of her Dragon kind, Otohime had to shift back into her true form for the actual birth. She made her husband swear not to look at her in her real shape, but, of course, Hoori could not keep his word.[23] Caught clothed in her Dragon scales, Otohimi felt such shame she fled back to the sea, leaving her son behind her. Hoori was aghast to discover he had married a Dragon and sired a half-Dragon son—though this was a decidedly anti-Dragon position for such a pro-Dragon part of the world. What father wouldn't want his offspring to have the strength, wisdom, and good humor of a Dragon? Hoori, for one, walked out the door without a second thought, leaving the child behind.

Raised by Otohime's sister—the one person who had not abandoned him—the young prince grew wise and vigorous with all those draconic qualities intact. In time he loved and married the woman who stuck by him, and they had four children, each with a full

---

23. Cupid and Psyche had nothing on these two promise-breakers.

measure of Dragon blood flowing through their veins. The youngest, Jimmu, powerful and judicious, became the first emperor of Japan and served the people long and well. While a direct self-defense link might be a stretch, you can make the case that sharing draconic DNA disposed the emperors of Japan kindly toward their ancestors, which made the world safer for one and all.

At the end of the day, such stories, as delightful as they may be, are more fancy than fact.

Pseudo-Dragons

Pseudo-dragons—small *d* dragons for our purposes—are as numerous and varied as the environments they inhabit and the peoples they inspire. Some cross cultural and international boundaries; some prefer to remain within more parochial realms. All of them are fascinating, even if they're not True Dragons. Though it would require volumes to explore each and every species in depth, we will look briefly at a few of the more colourful pseudo varieties, both familiar and rare.

Wyverns

One of the most recognizable of the pseudo-dragons, wyverns have, in art and literature, frequently been mistaken for True Dragons. In fact, through the ages, artists no less than Paolo Uccello, Gustave Moreau, Rogier van der Weyden, and Domenichino[24] have erroneously placed wyverns at the mercy of their St. Georges. Of course, a quick limb count should disabuse anyone of this notion.

Bipedal and winged, wyverns are indigenous to Northern Europe and parts of Siberia. They are considerably smaller than True Dragons, averaging around 6 metres long from their toothy heads to the tip of their spiked tails. Not tiny, true, but definitely not Dragons. Like bats, they have clawed, leathery wings, useful for holding onto perches

---

24. Uccello, *Saint George and the Dragon*, 1470. National Gallery of Art, London; Moreau, *Saint George and the Dragon*, 1890. National Gallery; van der Weyden, *Saint George and the Dragon*, 1435. National Gallery; Domenichino, *Saint George Killing the Dragon*, 1610. National Gallery.

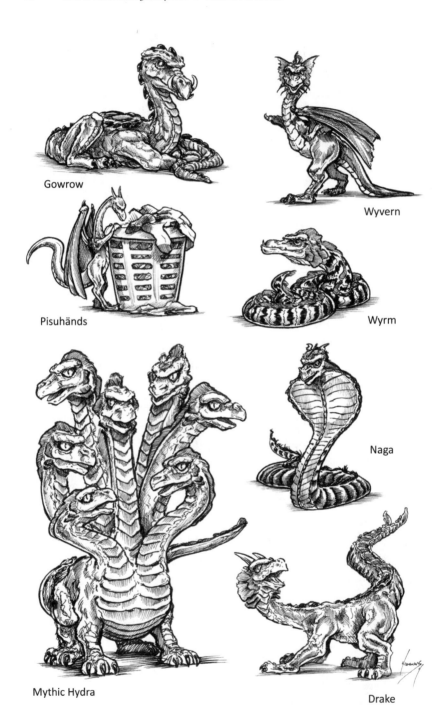

Gowrow

Wyvern

Pisuhänds

Wyrm

Naga

Mythic Hydra

Drake

or prey, but otherwise not terribly dexterous. In contrast, their powerful back feet dig and tear and grasp with great expertise. They have angular features and, when aloft or at a (great) distance, have been mistaken for very large raptors.

Wyverns are solitary creatures, coming together briefly to mate, then parting. The female lays a clutch of three to five eggs, buries them, then departs. From the start, the hatchling wyverns are on their own, trying to make their way in a hostile world. This birthing arrangement, while familiar among more mundane reptiles, makes their survival precarious at best. This not only accounts for their limited numbers but also for their aggressive, territorial dispositions. When scrapping for every morsel since day one, good manners tend to get left by the wayside.

Historically, we have seen wyverns as symbols of war, envy, pestilence, and spite. In our typically contrarian fashion we've also taken them as heraldic emblems of strength and bravery. Houses with wyverns in their crest stand, to good effect, under wyvern protection.

Wyrms

There is considerable confusion in some European quarters about what a wyrm—or würm or worm—actually is. Some people insist it is simply the Old Norse word for Dragon. While that connotation still lingers in parts of Scandinavia, it is no longer accepted in modern scientific and academic circles.

Today, wyrms are classified as long legless creatures with impressive horns and venomous fangs; in aspect, they are one of the most ophidian of the pseudo-dragons.[25] Their scales are tight and hard, affording them protection and streamlined movement through both land and water. Massive though they are, wyrms do not come close to the near 100-metre lengths reported in legend. (A large old wyrm

---

25. There are numerous sub-species of wyrm including the guivre of France and, some even insist, the two-legged, wingless lindworm of the East encountered by travellers along the Silk Road. Given the geophysical qualities of the Asian steppes, it is more likely that the lindworm is a cousin of the land-loving aspises or basilisks.

might grow to 100 feet with a solid 12-foot girth.) Spending much of their time in the dark and semi-dark, their eyes are extremely large and light sensitive. This makes them vulnerable in the bright light of day but perfectly designed for nocturnal forays. Thus, the best time for wyrm sightings is shortly after sunset or in the dark before the dawn.

Most wyrms are found on the British Isles and in the lowland countries of Western Europe. A few of their cousins have even been recorded in the watery wilds of North America and masquerading as sea monsters near the Grand Banks off Canada.[26] Shunning the places of man, wyrms prefer to live in deep caves with ready access to flowing water. This choice of habitat has led some to speculate that the Loch Ness Monster is, in fact, a wyrm with underwater cave access to the loch for feeding or a leisurely swim. This would explain why sonar sweeps have failed to catch sight of Nessie: she makes a speedy and discreet exit through a wave-covered channel and there's nothing but lake to see!

In story and song—such as "The Ballad of the Lambton Worm"— wyrms are notorious for their ravenous appetites and total disregard for boundaries and personal property. They eat when and what they choose, up to and including people. The truth, however, is far less dramatic. Wyrms are certainly dangerous but seldom cross human paths unless there are serious food shortages or territorial disputes.[27] When human villages were morphing into towns, then swelling into cities, both of these conditions were present and bloody clashes, while not commonplace, were frequent enough to become a fixture in the local ethos. Today, with numbers greatly reduced, they pose the greatest danger to unwary spelunkers and greedy geologists drilling where they ought not.

---

26. The scientific consensus holds that Ogopogo (aka Naitaka) out in Okanagan Lake, BC; Tatosok (aka Champ) in Lake Champlain, QC; and Memphre of Lake Memphremagog, QC, are wyrms of considerable age and size.

27. You can't blame them. We've hardly treated them well in the past. Some interactions are just not worth the potential hassles.

Draks/Drakes

Like wyverns, draks—or drakes—have often been mistaken for True Dragons. And, as with wyverns, a cursory limb count works wonders. Draks are land-bound, propped up on four sturdy legs but with nary even a vestigial wing nub in sight. In fact, the absence of alar limbs leads some cryptoherpetologists to hypothesize that draks are the fruit from an eccentric branch on the Thecodont family tree. Familiarly, draks are known as the grizzly bears of the draconic world.

Native to Europe, Asia, North America, and even the lusher parts of Africa, draks reside in well ventilated caves—abandoned mines are a particular favorite—and range through foothills, forests, and plains. This last proves problematic in the modern world: unable to fly, lumbering afoot, and slow to fight, their best means of escape is to hide from view. Open grasslands, while good for hunting, leave them far too exposed for comfort.

In the dimensional continuum, draks are medium sized at best, but what they lack in magnitude they more than make up for in attitude—most of which is pure fanfaronade. With thick hides, variegated neck furls, and horny protuberances, they readily adopt a fierce demeanor, preferring to bluff their way out of tight spots rather than go at it with tooth and talon.

This is not to say that draks can't be formidable opponents. One of the more family oriented of the pseudo-dragons, drak parents will do whatever they must to protect their own. If pushed, they will not hesitate to roast a foe to a fine turn or rend them, stem-to-stern, with razor claws. This reluctant ferocity made a serious impact on Europeans who honored draks with the eponymous drake, a small yet powerful cannon used in the seventeenth and eighteenth centuries.

Like their ursine counterparts, treat draks with respect and caution; better yet, simply leave them alone.

Hydras

Steeped in myths as deep as their native wetlands, hydras are longtime residents of that amorphous realm between fact and fiction. Thanks to the narrative abilities of ancient Mediterranean peoples, one particular dragon, the Lernaean Hydra, stands in the fore. From Hesiod to Seneca, the hydra of Lake Lerna has been celebrated and reviled as the bane of Hellenic life and victim of Hercules's second labor. This much-maligned creature is considered by many to be the template for all hydras, regardless of the scientific facts of the matter.

So let us begin with the myth, for, despite the heavy doses of fantasy, it does contain illuminating tidbits about the species.

According to the ancient Greeks, the Hydra (and there was only one) was a draconic being with nine heads—the center one being immortal—and a fearsome territorial instinct. Hera raised the offspring of Typhon and Echidna with tender loving care, letting her roam large and strong through the marshes round Lake Lerna. When people moved into her neighborhood, the Hydra would, naturally, venture out and raid their flocks or ravage their fields.[28] Hercules was tasked to slay the creature and free the local people from her tyranny. With flaming arrows, he goaded her off her nest and into the swamp. There he hacked at her nine heads, only to face two new-grown heads for every one he lopped off. In the end, with the help of his friend Iolaus and cauterizing fire, Hercules brought the Hydra down. He then dipped his arrows in her poisonous blood, guaranteeing that any wound they inflicted would be incurable.[29] Needless to say, Hera was not pleased; the enmity between her and Hercules, her husband's *nullius filius,* continued with ever-mounting intensity.

Sifting through hyperbole and rank invention, we do find some salient truths hidden in this tale. As their name implies, hydras are water creatures, residing in marshlands and near sheltered pools from the Balkans, Greece, around the Black Sea to Asia Minor and the

---

28. Some might say this was malice, though it seems more a matter of the Hydra demanding her home back from the human interlopers.

29. It is karmically apt that, according to some, a robe coated with the Hydra's blood was the cause of Hercules's own agonizing death. Other stories insist it was the blood of the centaur Nessus, whom Hercules killed with one of his Hydra-blood-tipped arrows. Either way, what goes around comes around.

Levant.[30] Thus, it is certainly possible that a hydra inhabited the verges of Lake Lerna. Unfortunately, this also puts them at odds with humans who not only need water but, in the past, considered such pools sacred sites. Clashes are inevitable.

Like wyverns, hydras prefer a solitary post-mating lifestyle. The lone female lays her eggs in nests of wattle and mud and guards them against all dangers. If, as some stories insist, the Lernaean Hydra was brooding when accosted by Hercules, her hostility would have been understandably defensive rather than aggressive. A mother must protect her clutch.

Physically, hydras are quite different from their classical portraits. To begin, they stand about 2 metres at the shoulder—not exactly gargantuan—and they have only two heads (not nine), neither of which is immortal. They do sport a long tail with a fleshy end which, like the shingleback skink's, passes for a faux head in times of fight or flight. If lost, the tail will grow back, but a severed head remains severed—there is no magical two-for-one regeneration. Confusion on this point likely stems from poetic license coupled with the extraordinary speed with which an attacking hydra moves. In the heat of battle, they are a furious blur of long necks, long tails, and teeth … lots of teeth. With due respect to mythologists, specifics tend to get lost under such circumstances.

The reported dangers of hydra blood are real. Like that of True Dragons, hydra blood is a corrosive toxin which burns through flesh and steel. So potent is it that ancient poisoners, alchemists, and medieval toxicologists used onyx jars to contain their hydroid supplies.[31] Today, heavy glass, while not as elegant, serves in place of stone. For easier storage, the blood can be desiccated and pulverized. In this state it is less volatile, inconspicuously applied, and quickly regains full strength

---

30. A hydra sighting on the Greek island of Patmos may well have inspired the seven-headed dragon St. John mentioned in Revelation 12:3. Who inspired the young woman in the story is anyone's guess.

31. Any stone softer than a 7 on the Mohs scale, such as marble, simply dissolves at the touch of hydra blood. No doubt Hercules's arrows were flint-tipped and his sword flint-bladed.

when rehydrated. This was likely the substance used on the tunic which brought Hercules down. A blood-soaked garment would have raised some serious red flags even for a man known more for brawn than brains.

Though a hydra census has not been taken in a generation, there were a handful of verifiable sightings fifteen years ago in the remote marshlands of Greece and Turkey and round the hidden inlets of the Sea of Marmara. Clearly they are an endangered species in an often troubled part of the world. If you come across a hydra in your travels, first, give her a wide berth. Then report your find to the World Wildlife Fund (WWF) or your local chapter of the World Association for Dragons Everywhere (WAFDE).

Nagas

Slithering from the forests of the Indian sub-continent to the lush fringes of Indochina is the naga. This ancient species of pseudo-dragon wound his way into many a Vedic and Buddhist tale. Some say they are the divine form of the king cobra, and though the king may be a distant relation, the naga is genetically closer to the European wyrm than to any mundane serpent. Their size and ability to spit fireballs put them squarely in the pseudo-dragon phylum.

Aside from broad hoods and ophidian bodies, the mythic naga's physical and metaphysical traits vary from culture to culture across his range. In Malaysia and Cambodia, for example, the naga is a large multi-headed creature. In keeping with the balance of yin and yang, the males are odd-headed and represent timelessness, infinity, immortality; the females are even-headed and symbolize mortality, physicality, and the Earth. The Vedic nagas are single-headed and regarded by turns with reverence and disdain. In the *Mahabharata*, for example, they are the instrument of a deadly curse against King Pariksit.[32] On the flip side, the Great Naga Vasuki (aka Basuki) helped the gods recover *amrita,* the elixir of eternal life. The Eternal Naga, Ananta, served as a throne for Ganesha, guarded the sacred lingam, symbol

---

32. *The Mahabharata*, Adi Parva 20–36.

of Shiva. In the *Bhagavad Gita*, Krishna invoked him as an analogy of his own universal divinity.[33] For nobility and commoners alike, nagas are nature deities, guardians of rivers and bringers of fertility to field and flock. They dwell in a watery subterranean region and are charged with keeping the dragons of chaos from running amok with the seasonal rains and flooding the world.

One of the most iconic nagas is Mucalinda of Buddhist lore. When Siddhārtha Gautama was meditating his way to enlightenment, a great tempest churned in the firmament and torrential rains poured down upon him. Naga King Mucalinda, a giant of a creature, emerged from his underground realm and rose up, tall and strong as a Bo tree, and spread his massive hood over the Buddha, protecting him from the inclement elements for seven days. Some scholars insist this is a variation on a much older Vedic tale of the multi-headed Naga who sheltered Vishnu. Either way, the legends speak volumes to the high regard in which nagas are held.

Scientific truths about the naga are nearly as fascinating as these spiritual fancies. Measuring 10 to 20 metres in length with luminous scales and elegant hoods, full-grown nagas are rare sights even in the densely populated regions they call home. Spending most of their daylight hours underground, these crepuscular-verging-on-nocturnal creatures emerge only in the cool of the late day. They meander through the tropical undergrowth, slaking thirst and hunger and surveying their realms. Once every fifty years, male and female come together, court, and mate. This is a stylized ritual in which they dance around the banyan trees, rising up on coils and mating spurs—short faux limbs at their pelvic girdle. Unlike some primitive snakes—boas, pythons, and anacondas—who have short, free-floating anal spines used to facilitate the mating process, naga spurs are fully articulated, temporal growths

---

33. "Of the many-hooded Nagas I am Ananta, and among those born in the waters I am Varuna, their lord. Of spirits of the fathers I am Aryama, and among the dispensers of law I am Yama, the lord of death." *The Bhagavad Gita*, 10.29.

approximately 1 metre long.[34] They emerge first in the female when she enters estrous; the male's spurs sprout shortly thereafter in response to the female's potent pheromones. After mating, these appendages disappear: the male casts them off with his next slough; the female absorbs them back into her body, using the extra calcium and proteins to fortify her eggs. Six months later, a clutch of baby nagas will hatch. They grow quickly and can easily be mistaken for large king cobras when they are just a year old, slithering through the wilds, swimming in lakes and rivers, and throwing up fireballs for fun and defense.[35]

Nagas are very curious, especially about people and the baggage we call civilization. They are fond of milk and rice, welcoming them as a tasty supplement to their basic diet of frogs, lizards, small mammals, and serpents. Generous offerings of milk do help compensate for deforestation and loss of habitat. Because of their connection with rivers and springs, nagas are particularly vulnerable to pollutants flowing through the world's waters. Proverbial canaries in the ecological coal mines, a healthy naga population serves as a sign of a healthy environment.

Pisuhänds, Aitvaras, and Other Household Dragons

Household dragons are familiar sights in the rural regions of Europe to this day. Originating in ancient Britain, they migrated to the Continent shortly after Boudicca and the Iceni fell into Roman hands around 60 CE. It was an understandable move: the Romans had a different view of Dragons in general, being less-than-kindly disposed towards even the most innocuous of the species. Once plentiful from central Europe to Scandinavia, urbanization and the bustle of industrial life drove these small, benevolent creatures to the rural parts of the Baltic nations, Finland, and eastern Russia. In the late-nineteenth and early-twentieth centuries, political and financial forces upended

---

34. At first blush, this seems huge, but you must bear in mind the overall size of the naga and put things in proper perspective.

35. The Dragon-illiterate often confuse naga fire with *ignis fatuus*, or will-o'-the-wisp, a mistake no first-year cryptoherpetologist should ever make.

Eastern Europe, compelling millions to immigrate to the New World, many with their household dragons in tow. Thanks to this Atlantic traversal, these creatures are now endemic to the temperate regions of North America, from New England to British Columbia.[36] Give them a few more generations and they might even be called natives.

In modern Europe, the most common household dragons are the Estonian pisuhänds. Political borders being a human construct no Dragon heeds, these delightful creatures range where they will,[37] picking up local appellations, such as puuk or puky, along the way. Four-footed, just over ½ meter long, pisuhänds seek out a family when their egg smell still lingers on their scales. A warm hearth, fresh milk, and friendly scratches under the chin are all the enticement they need to feel right at home. Raiding dressers for bits of fabric, gnawing on brooms for straws, they will find snug niches up in the rafters, at the back of closets, or under stairwells and build themselves a comfortable nest. Socks or scarves gone missing? Check with your house dragon.

Once ensconced in their new digs, pisuhänds set about earning their keep. Known as the lucky magpies of the pseudo-dragon set, they make moonlit flights to pilfer trinkets, jewels, and precious metals for their masters/mistresses.[38] All draconic grace and speed in the air, on the ground these stealthy dragons slink about like large house cats and are able to come and go quite inconspicuously. Back home, they will guard their treasure troves—and any other valuables within their home[39] against all comers. *Loyalty* is their watchword, so much

---

36. Curiously, there are no records of Dragons of any stripe passing through Ellis Island, which leads cryptoherpetologists to assume pisuhänds are capable of extreme camouflage or rudimentary shape shifting.

37. Recent sightings in western Poland and Germany signal a European comeback in the making.

38. During the Middle Ages, feudal lords would keep whole flocks of pisuhänds to help supplement their already-disproportionate wealth. This was a grievous misuse of the creature's wiles. By the Renaissance, as sweet as their sinecures were, many voluntarily left their cushy existences for simpler, more rewarding lives among people who really needed their help.

39. Such as their family's children. Pisuhänds make excellent watchdragons.

so that, once you've welcomed a pisuhänd into your life, you're stuck with each other. This devoted nature wound up being their ticket to far off places and benefitting us all.

Kin to the pisuhänds are the Lithuanian aitvaras. Small dragons with fiery tails and temperaments to match, they find their way into a homestead and bless it with good fortune, asking for little more than a roof over their heads and a daily omelette in return. Though fond of simple dishes of eggs folded around fresh herbs, no self-respecting aitvaras would turn up his nose to wild mushrooms or a little caraway cheese thrown into the mix. Profoundly nocturnal, they fly through the starlit sky, their flaming tails dancing in the dark. Like their puukish cousins, they have the antisocial habit of stealing wealth and goods from neighboring homes to please their masters. This can create enmity in otherwise peaceful communities. Remember: aitvaras are only following their natures, being loyal to their house, and giving back to their keepers. They also spread their nutrient-rich excreta over the fields and gardens, making them fertile beyond belief.[40]

When Grand Duke Jogaila Christianized the region in 1387, the legends swirling about the aitvaras took on a decidedly malignant tone. In the past (and the present), sudden good fortune in a small town had a way of garnering attention, usually of the negative variety. Religious forces, eager to establish their power and collect their tithes, would pounce on the newly affluent with zealous scrutiny. Add to that the anti-dragon stance of most Western religions, and aitvaras quickly transformed from household benefactors into shape-shifting instruments of the devil. To church eyes, only witches or those who'd made pacts with Lucifer and his minions knew the companionship of the aitvaras. Of course, these "Satan's servants" were clever and discreet: during the day they might be a black cat or cockerel, passing without notice among mundane pets and farm animals. But at night, they'd resume their dragon forms and let their devilish natures emerge. And the true cost of an aitvaras's aid was no mere plate of eggs by the hearth. No. According to church elders, it was the souls

---

40. And putting modern agrichemical businesses to shame.

of everyone in the aitvaras' houses. Even if you drove him away—with holy water, consecrated candles, even bits of Eucharistic bread mixed in with his breakfast—he would simply return. And the minute your guard was down, he'd snatch your soul and haul it kicking and screaming down to hell. Or so the clerics said.

Such vile, diabolical interpretations of purely natural beings served to persecute these pseudo-dragons and their people and enrich the already rich who confiscated the "evil" wealth.[41] That any aitvaras survived such superstitious times is a testament to their resilience and the few brave souls who gave them refuge.

Happily, the enlightenment of science now eclipses much of the fear and greed of the old ways. Today, for pisuhänds and aitvaras alike, a little training and an unequivocal return policy on stolen items goes a long way to keeping peace in one's community.

Guardian Dragons: Daimones, Iaculi, and Žaltys

While the majority of pseudo-dragons keep their distance from humans as a matter of survival, a few thrive on close, one-on-one mystical relationships with people. These beings watch over their charges, guiding them through their years, keeping them on a just path. In short, they leave their mark on the world as guardian dragons.

The people of the Aegean and Adriatic Seas were very familiar with such dragons. Known as *agathos daimones* ("good spirits"), these creatures looked like large winged serpents and were believed to be the physical manifestation of caring and, some might say, meddlesome ancestors. In shape and purpose, they're comparable to the legless amphipteres, watchers of the world who serve as aegises for warriors as fierce as they. Physiology aside, daimones are more akin to the Roman lares, penates, and genius loci—or, in Judeo-Christian parlance, guardian angels.

In exchange for offerings of the finest wine, daimones hover round the individual entrusted to their care, whispering sage advice

---

41. Of course, no stigma was attached to those who thus added the "devil's" gold to their coffers. Such are the privileges of the powerful.

into their ear, blessing them with fortune and fine harvest, especially in the vineyards. Those who shun their obligations to the daimones must fend for themselves against woes both divine and profane. Against the weight of all that, respect and a glass of wine is truly a small price to pay.

Travel south into Africa and you enter the world of the iaculus. These winged pseudo-dragons have been interacting with humans since the time of the pharaohs. Denizens of tombs and cemeteries iaculi watch over the departed and mediate between the living and the dead. This gives them the ability to pass wisdom from generation to generation, to instruct the young and oversee their moral maturation.

Gentle with those under their protection, iaculi can be deadly when it comes to strangers intruding upon their territory. According to the "Aberdeen Bestiary":

> The iaculus is a snake which flies. Lucan says of it: "The iaculus that can fly" (*Pharsalia*, 9, 720). For they spring into trees and when anything comes their way, throw themselves on it and kill it. As a result, they are called *iaculi*, "javelin-snakes". [42]
>
> (Aberdeen University Library, Folio 69v)

To keep them happy, heed their sibilant whisperings, treat them to a daily bowl of warm beer, and introduce all newcomers with deference and care.

Where the iaculus is dangerous, the Baltic žaltys is mild. Sacred to Saulė, goddess of the sun, this relatively small, short-legged dragon is a messenger and intermediary between gods and men. In their natural habitat, these diurnal creatures spend much of their time basking in the sun or blessing pools and streams with their scaly touch. There, to the ignorant or uninitiated, their serpentine physique and gentle

---

42. The obvious error here is in not recognizing a pseudo-dragon when it's right under one's nose.

manner give the žaltys the guise of a harmless grass snake. Only the Dragon-savvy will recognize them for what they truly are.

When found in the wild, žaltys are treated with the greatest respect[43]—any slight or injury to them being a slight or injury to the goddess. A dish of milk and a cooing invitation might persuade them to latch onto an individual or family and move into their house. Once there, they curl up in a down-lined dragon basket by the stove and watch. If their people are righteous and kind to humans and creatures alike, the žaltys will bestow fortune and fertility upon them. If, however, the ways of the house turn stingy and mean, the žaltys will depart and take all her blessings with her. No other of her kind will ever cross that threshold as long as it remains with the same family. Some say this is harsh punishment; others, a simple lesson in good manners and draconic ethics.

Though not all cultures honor žaltys with the same esteem, they remain one of the world's more abundant pseudo-dragons, found from Europe to Central Asia and across the Mediterranean to North Africa. The well-travelled cryptoherpetologist is likely to see dozens of them in her lifetime. In the United Kingdom, despite their numbers, they are on the protected species list: you can keep your own žaltys—if one will have you—but a license is required to trade them with others. Not that žaltys take kindly to the idea of being an object of barter; this falls squarely into the category of immoral actions. Should you follow this path to acquisition, much repentant care and affection must follow. In the absence of such attentions, the žaltys will leave you faster than Gou Mang on a mission for the gods.[44]

Lake Dragons

The most ubiquitous of the pseudo-dragons is the lake dragon. Found on every continent except Antarctica, they have as many names as there are peoples who have met them. There are knuckers in Europe;

---

43. Even by those who take them for mere serpents. You can't be too careful.

44. Gou Mang is one of the Chinese Cosmic Dragons, who, along with his darker counterpart, Rou Shou, were messengers to the celestial deities.

gaasyendiethas, stvkwvnayas, mashernomaks, and wakandagis in North America; dards and dhakhans in Australia; and glyryvillus in South America, to mention but a few. In short, any body of freshwater that supports a diverse ecosystem is capable of supporting a lake dragon or two.

Though there are localized variations within the species, your basic lake dragon appears, at first blush, like a cross between the Eastern and Western Dragons. They are long, proportionately short-legged, with webbed feet, paddle tail spades, and scales and heads almost classically draconic, including impressive frills and horns. Despite reports of massive creatures reaching up to 20 metres in length, your average lake dragon, constrained by the size of her habitat, seldom exceeds half that size. The exceptions to this rule are the great horned serpents of the American Great Lakes and the less well known dragons of the world's large lakes such as Baikal, Tanganyika, Ladoga, and Titicaca.[45] European oral tradition holds that the lake dragons simply move to the sea when they have outgrown their freshwater homes.

Through the centuries, people have spun great yarns about the rapacious lake "monsters" who would kill you with venom, fire, or a lethal bite as soon as look at you. As is the case with most draconic legends, these stories tell more about the human response to the unusual and the unknown than about the creatures themselves.[46] The facts are quite different. Most lake dragons are retiring, even shy. As people have moved into their environs—particularly around small lakes—the dragons adopt a cautiously defensive posture, much preferring to hide than to seek. This makes daylight sightings particularly rare, at best involving little more than the glimpse of a tail-tip vanishing

---

45. Much as we like to think we have left our human footprint all over the globe, there are still vast regions—especially aquatic regions—crying out for the exploration and study of dedicated cryptozoologists.

46. Some shamans see through their own fear and are able to appreciate the lake dragons in all their magnificence. One particular example of this affects the kitzinachas who were revered by the Lenape and Algonquin peoples, their blessings invoked by the shaman with dance.

under the waves. Of course, our past treatment of their kind was so atrocious that many, no doubt, wish we'd ignore them altogether. They'd be much safer that way. That said, the observant cryptoherpetologist is apt to find more dragon signs ashore than on the water: scale-scraped tree trunks, tail swathes swept through leaf litter, and, in oozy mud at the water's edge, paw prints too large to be anything but draconic.

Left to their own devices, lake dragons spend their days playing among the reed forests, disguising themselves as moss-caped boulders along lake shores. Farther out in the depths, between banquets of muskellunge and bass, arawanas (dragon fish), catfish, the occasional wigeon or smew, and mouthfuls of milfoil and salvinia, they doze on soft lake-weed and churn the lake beds with tail dancing.[47] And with their hot breath, they raise the morning mists then lounge ashore, hidden in the haze, until the sun burns the water clear.

In the winter, lake dragons in less temperate climes slow heart and breath and retreat to caves far beneath the winter ice, in virtual stasis. There they hibernate until, with spring abandon, they crack the surface and return. It is during this vernal renaissance that, circumstances permitting, lake dragons will mate. However, pairing off does not always mean reproduction: in small lakes with limited resources, they may go decades without laying a single egg.

The greatest threat to these diverse creatures now is human encroachment in all its manifestations: loss of habitat, pollution, and overfishing of the waters. The last can drive lake dragons up on shore to hunt the forests or dine on livestock; this is not their diet of choice, it is something we have pushed them to, only to then vilify and slay them for doing what they must to survive.

Today, with our fresh water reserves in rapid decline, we would do well to learn from our wiser ancestors and rethink our relationship

---

47. In large waters which can support whole pods of lake dragons, scientists witness them using their flat tails to corral fish with team mud-ringing behaviour similar to that used by certain Gulf dolphins.

with the world's lake dragons.[48] Not only are they wonders to behold, they are also one of our last, best defenses against pollutants and invasive species. It is in their nature to keep the waters clean, balanced, and bountiful. The more we poison our lakes, the more keenly we need lake dragons.

Snallygasters

In the northern Blue Ridge Mountains, from southern Pennsylvania to Maryland and on into Ohio, lives one of the most unsavory of the pseudo-dragons, a creature who strikes fear into the heart and gives children nightmares: the snallygaster.

In the early eighteenth century, a community of German immigrants reported being besieged by a winged creature they called a *Schnellegeist*, or "quick spirit." Over time, the name underwent linguistic modulations, settling into the modern vernacular as snallygaster.

The dragon transformed over time, too. Original accounts described a hybrid of bird and ghoul with a killer beak, wicked talons, and a serious thirst for blood. It would swoop down upon the settlers' farms and drain a chicken or two, then depart. This was an evil nuisance, to be sure, but nothing a few well-painted septigrams on barn and house couldn't deter. By the nineteenth century, this predator had morphed into a more traditional draconic being, all of 20 feet long with green scales and massive wings. The avian beak remained, now lined with rows of razor-sharp teeth. Some accounts even mention kraken-like tentacles emerging from the mouth to grasp prey. The snallygaster's blood-lust was replaced by a more inclusive diet: whole animals, children, even small adults, were carried off with owlish stealth. Nary hide nor hair nor splintered bone of the victims was ever found.

---

48. A shining example of this in the West is the respect the Algonquin of Quebec bestowed upon the misiganabic. This lake dragon was alarming in size and considered by some to be a harbinger of death if looked upon, but the Algonquins knew it also maintained the waters and made their lives possible.

In February 1909, the *Middletown Valley Register* printed a story about an Ohio man who claimed to have seen one of these pseudo-dragons winging its way towards Maryland. This account sparked a series of sightings throughout the Blue Ridge Mountains, including several by hikers who swore they saw lone nesting creatures up in the hills, brooding single eggs large enough to hatch a horse.[49] If spotted, the beast would let out a thunderous boom followed by deafening screeches which sent casual observers into full-fledged panic mode. The adventurer's response was quite different. These reports inspired curiosity, and, in due course, snallygaster safaris were organized across the region. The Smithsonian Institute and Teddy Roosevelt even expressed interest, and the National Geographic Society was preparing an expedition to memorialize the creature on film. However, before the president donned his hunting gear, the *Register* published an article detailing the snallygaster's demise. Needless to say, this prompted speculation that the whole thing was a hoax designed to drum up readership for a flagging paper. There may have been truth in this theory, but it presupposes that there was only one snallygaster in the entire region. Hardly likely.

As recently as 1976, Gordon Chaplin, under the auspices of the *Washington Post,* mounted an expedition to track down the snallygaster. The results were dismal: he found not so much as a paw print. (This was likely due to a foolish lack of cryptoherpetologists in his party.) Fortunately, the state of Maryland was not swayed by a lack of evidence and put the snallygaster on their endangered species list in 1982.

Snallygaster sightings have diminished in the last thirty years though the rich oral tradition of the Blue Ridges keeps them alive and well, especially for children. Nothing stops a recalcitrant child in their tracks faster than the admonition: "Keep that up and the snallygaster will get you."

---

49. Some accounts say the egg could hold an elephant, a claim which stretches credulity.

Gowrows

Tusked dragons are a rarity in the modern world, gowrows being among the last in the Western Hemisphere.

Native to the Ozark and Ouachita Mountains of Arkansas and Missouri, the gowrow—aka golligog and bingbuffer—is an American original. Travel to the region and you will find souvenir stands hawking draconic figurines on every corner. There's nothing wrong with that, in theory—just another sign of robust capitalism at work—but from a scientific viewpoint, these scaly tchotchkes look far more like Godzilla cast-offs than actual gowrows. This is but another reminder of all the misinformation out there demanding to be set straight.

So, what is the truth about this unusual creature? Briefly, the gowrow is a 5-metre-long, wingless pseudo-dragon with a thick, plated hide, spiny ridges, fiery eyes, and formidable curled tusks.[50] In fact, standard descriptions conjure up a beast not unlike a terrestrial variation of Cetus in Piero di Cosimo's painting, *Perseus Rescuing Andromeda* (c. 1515; Uffizi Gallery, Florence), suggesting the dragon-watchers may have been as much students of late-Renaissance masters as of mid-American monsters. Illuminating reports from the 1880s mention gowrows also have marsupial-like pouches in which they carry their young, an incongruous indication of conscientious parenting. They spend their days in caves and under rock ledges, emerging at night to hunt and forage and let loose their distinctive "ggoowwwwrroooooow-www" from one end of the Interior Highlands to the other. Thirteen thousand years ago, this haunting yowl would have struck fear into the hearts of the Clovis people who settled the region and its sound would have kept them far away from the dragon's gaming and nesting grounds.

Where the gowrows came from and how they got to their particularly isolated environment are questions to which the modern scientific community can offer only sketchy answers. Some cryptoherpetologists postulate that they are Ice Age revenants from the late Cretaceous who

---

50. Tales of modern gowrows reaching 20 to 30 feet are, charitably speaking, exaggerations. They may well have been larger in the distant past, but such giants cannot be sustained by today's over-hunted, over-populated Ozarks.

crossed the Bering land bridge and turned right. Others suggest they're not dragons at all but modern cousins of the *Arkansaurus fridayi*, a bipedal theropod native to the area.[51] At present, both theories fail to encompass species-specific anomalies—tusks and pouch[52]—and so are regarded as educated hunches in dire need of substantive proof.

We have better luck with diet and habitat. In the Boston and St. Francois Mountains, spelunkers have stumbled upon lairs thick with whitened bones from possums and rabbits (for hatchling gowrows) all the way up to deer, bear, and even hapless humans. Fortunately for the explorers, these cryptozoological caches were long-abandoned; they walked away with information *and* their lives.

Up until the early twentieth century, gowrows were frequently heard, if only occasionally seen. This made their study problematic at best. In 1897, one William Miller reportedly killed a gowrow who was pestering livestock in Searcy Country, Arkansas, and shipped the corpse to the Smithsonian. It never arrived. That was one of the last detailed accounts of a hands-on gowrow encounter, and with good reason. In 1911, the Army Corps of Engineers began a fifty-year construction plan geared towards transforming the White River with a series of six dams. The reservoirs and lakes created by this massive waterways project were a boon to the tourist industry but totally disrupted the gowrow's natural habitat. Fishermen, boaters, and a steady influx of people have driven these tusked dragons deep into the remotest parts of the Ozarks, which remain human-free. Though their singular voice still sparingly cuts across the Arkansas night, no living gowrow has been sighted since 1951.[53]

---

51. This flies in the face of the region's oral tradition, which paints the gowrow as a rather drakish quadruped.

52. The pouch is of particular interest, as gowrows are the only pseudo-dragon outside of Australia known to have this feature.

53. See Vance Randolph, "Fabulous Monsters of the Ozarks." *The Arkansas Historical Quarterly*, Vol. 9, No. 2 (Summer, 1950): 65–75.

Ropen

In the dense, little-explored jungles of Papua New Guinea and sur-rounding isles, among fairy cuscus and tree kangaroos, explosive cassowaries and sartorial birds of paradise, resides the mysterious ropen.

Due largely to topography and sociological isolation, we knew virtually nothing about the ropen until as recently as the mid-twentieth century. In the 1950s, Christian missionaries set their sights on converting the indigenous peoples of the region and, in the process, created one of the first cultural/scientific links between the islands and the outside world—a rare instance of Western theologians actually aiding Dragon Studies.[54] The subsequent accounts leaking into the cryptozoological community described the ropen as a small, bipedal pseudo-dragon with leathery wings spanning 1 to 2 metres[55] and a long, luminescent tail. Large eyes—the better to see you with, my dear—highlight their angular heads, while serious incisors and scalpel-sharp claws give them a threatening mien.

Originally believed to be a breed of giant bat, or megachiroptera, ropen are actually one of the closest living relatives of Triassic pterosaur/proto-Dragon hybrids.[56] And, like their ancestors, they travel in familial flocks, inspiring fear more by their numbers than any display of innate aggression. For, though as well equipped as any predator in the rainforest, ropen are carrion-eaters by nature. As custodians of their realm, they keep the jungle free of decay and attendant disease. Patrolling the evening skies, they taste the air with their tongues, sorting through the jungle bouquet. They pinpoint fallen fauna littering the forest floor from as far as a league off, then descend *en masse* to

---

54. In recent years, creationists have latched onto the ropen's dinosaur-like aspects to promote the idea that dinosaurs and humans walked the planet contemporaneously. In their single-minded efforts, these folks fail to appreciate the obvious evolutionary changes millions of years of cross-breeding and mutation have wrought.

55. Females are larger than males by almost a third.

56. The greatest threat to the ropen is being mistaken for a flying fox and hunted in error. Minimizing such blunders is important both as a matter of conservation and preservation: no tribe wants a blood feud with a congregation of dragons.

feed. In hard times, they will disrupt human funerals, but this is a rare occurrence, more unsettling to the mourners than actually dangerous.

To some of the islanders, the ropen are the mystical eaters of the dead. They may not quite be gods, but they're not simply animals either. It is perhaps in recognition of this quality that the tribesmen of Ceram Island in the Maluku Archipelago elevate ropen from creature status and refer to them as the *Orang-bati*— "men with wings."

Whether ropens were revered or feared, the humans who share their habitat usually appreciate the niche they fill in the ecosystem and leave them alone.

Aspises

Pound for pound, the aspis is the most dangerous pseudo-dragon in existence. They also give truth to William Congreve's words, "Music hath charms to soothe the savage breast."

Once common throughout central Europe, aspises hatch out of their eggs, wingless and two-legged. A mature apis will grow up to 1 metre long, and those rare souls fortunate enough to reach the half-century mark will sprout wings astride their mid-dorsal vertebrae.[57] They are fast through the grass and lightning quick on the attack if disturbed.

Tales of deadly human/aspis encounters clutter the annals of medieval lore. For their size, they have huge venom glands and fangs as sharp as brand-new hypodermic needles; in combination, they deliver bites which, even in the age of antivenin, prove 100 percent fatal. As ominous as that sounds, this is not their most dangerous trait. Aspises have fine, downy setae between their spiky scales, each fiber coated with microscopic nematocysts. At the slightest touch, the scales flare up, slicing flesh—or gloves—and the nematocysts release a flood of venom into the attacker's system, resulting in crippling pain and almost-certain death. Scale lacerations are not essential to the poisoning. If the skin's integrity remains intact, the venom can still

---

57. For years there were conflicting reports about the aspis, some insisting they were winged, some wingless. Only recently have we been able to age aspises and sort out the confusion in the scientific record.

seep in through the pores. The process is slower than direct contact with the blood but no less virulent. So be careful: even dead, with scales inert, this little pseudo-dragon can inflict a mortal wound.

In the face of such an onslaught, what is a person to do? What is the aspis's Achilles heel? Thanks to the wisdom of the medieval alchemists and venomologists, we have an answer to that question: music. Mellifluous harmonies[58] are soporific to the species, causing them to let down their defenses and, quite literally, unwind. As a countermeasure to this tonal assault, some aspises would put the tip of their tail in one ear and push the other flat to the ground. While keeping them free from the music's effects, this ridiculously contorted position makes it impossible for them to attack. Think smart, step lively, and you will have plenty of time to retreat to safety.

Kiaus

No examination of pseudo-dragons would be complete without a visit to China. In the immense shadows of the great Lung and his True kin live a variety of lesser species, both righteous and sinister. One of the more interesting is the kiau, or marsh dragon.

A word up front: this charming creature is not to be confused with the fierce water behemoth of the same name. That singular Kiau was a menace to the fisherfolk along Chien Tang River for hundreds of years, dispatched at last in the twelfth century by a local hero.[59] There is speculation of a much-diluted blood connection between the two species—that the lesser dragons were the bastard offspring of the

---

58. Pipes and/or simple strings are the most efficacious deterrents; in a pinch, a well-pitched song will do, too. This probably explains why there are so few accounts of troubadours or minstrels, even melodious shepherds, falling prey to aspises in the field.

59. It is possible that Kiau was actually a sea serpent, washed up river by one of the great tidal bores for which the Chien Tang is famous. As with whales who get stranded in freshwater channels, he likely became turned around and confused. Unable to return home, he simply made the best of a bad situation, much to the dismay of all others who relied on the river for their livelihood.

greater—but the harsh light of scientific inquiry considers the notion guesswork at best.

The small *k* kiaus are free of foul tempers and predacious appetites. Barely 2.5 metres of mostly neck and tail, these green and gold marsh dragons populate wetlands from central China down through Laos, Thailand, and the Malay Peninsula. One of very few true vegetarian dragons, they dine almost exclusively on duckweed, water chestnuts, and the invasive water hyacinth. Not only do they clear out smothering vegetation, but, with their heavily whiskered mouths, they filter the wetlands of impurities. Indispensible when it comes to keeping waterways clean and healthy, these guardians of fish, frog, and waterfowl have earned the respect of all who cross their path.

That said, because of their size, kiaus can fall prey to large crocodilians, tigers, and even some of the larger, less discriminating Oriental Dragon and pseudo-dragon species. Unfortunately, as with so many creatures today, their greatest threat is loss of habitat and unscrupulous poachers.[60] China's Three Gorges project, for example, while a boon to the nation's power supply, flooded one of the most productive breeding grounds in Hubei Province. The loss decimated the kiau population of central China. Without diligent conservation efforts, it will be generations before their numbers recover.

---

60. Dragon parts, even from small pseudo-dragons, are a poacher's ticket to Easy Street. Believed to have mystical and medicinal properties, they're worth their weight in diamonds on the black market.

Even the most winged spirit cannot escape physical necessity.

—Kahlil Gibran, "Sand and Foam"

two

Where the Wild Weyrs Are: Habitats & Habits

Imagine a midsummer's afternoon in New England, the sky shimmering like a Kashmir sapphire, a light breeze keeping the mosquitoes at bay. Just right for a trek through the Green Mountains to enjoy a little birding or caving along the way.

And a little Dragoning, perhaps?

Despite their limited numbers and cautious ways, to the sharp-eyed and open-minded, Dragons are there to be found.

What is the best way to start on such an adventure? Simple. Know the signs—the needs and ways of Dragons in the wild. Their habitats and habits.

Weyrs: What, Why, and Where

As any self-respecting dracophile knows, the fundamental unit of Dragon life is the weyr. This is a community for Dragons, similar to a human village or a stronghold like the fortress Alhambra. Within each weyr reside an amicable collection of clans, or enchantments. Despite a lack of empirical evidence, some experts insist ancient weyrs were more like cities than simple villages, capable of supporting up to fifty enchantments at a time. The wondrous scope of it boggles the imagination. Regrettably, modern weyrs can sustain a scant two to five enchantments, at best. This is having a deleterious effect on the draconic gene pool, a subject we'll take up in Chapter Three.

While the particulars of these communities are species- and location-specific, there are a few constants shared by all.

There must be shelter against inclement weather. This usually takes the form of caves—either natural or Dragon-made—or deep scrapings. In rare cases, smaller Dragons will avail themselves of abandoned human mines, though they have to be *long* abandoned.[1] Remember, Dragons are what one might call easy keepers; except during climatic extremes, they need little more than a ledge over their heads. There is, of course, a marked difference between creature comforts and comforts of choice, even for Dragons.

All weyrs have hatching grounds. These are not to be confused with nesting areas, which are within an individual Dragon family's living quarters. Hatching grounds are the public spaces to which a brooding Dragon moves her eggs in the last weeks of incubation. These spaces can be sub- or superterranean, depending on climate and species, but must be large enough to accommodate mother, clutch, and whatever relatives may drop by.[2] They are the emotional heart of the community, resonating with joys and sorrows, with the fragility of life and the certainty of death. Recent studies of an abandoned weyr on Lake Baikal, Siberia, for example, found the walls of the hatching ground studded with stone circles around bits of broken eggshell. It's believed that the circles were placed there in silent memorial to Dragonlets lost. As breeding cycles would leave the grounds empty for much of the year, there is growing speculation

---

1. Recent studies have shown that Dragons find the taste of human excavations most unpleasant. Something about the mix of industry and too-frequent death plays badly across their Jacobson's organs (a sensory organ used to detect pheromones and other chemical messages).

2. For further details on the whole nesting process, see Chapter Three.

about what the space would have been used for when not full of eggs or nascent hatchlings. Voices from the intellectual camps have suggested it's used as a retreat of sorts, a quiet spot for contemplative Dragons—very Zen and the Art of Dragonry. The more common notion is that enchantments would use it as an infirmary: an isolated place for the injured or (rarely) ill Dragon to heal and get her strength back. Either way, it's one of the many curious and as-yet-unresolved questions of cryptoanthropology.

Adjacent to the hatching ground, one usually finds a bathing/dusting area. This provides a means for the nesting Dragons to stay refreshed and parasite-free without having to go far from their charges. And, once the Dragonlets are born, they can have a quick

splash-about—or, if water is not available, a vigorous roll in fine sand—and clean off any residual egg clinging to their shiny new scales. Relatively small and distinct and very separate from the communal laving stead, this is usually the one bathing area which affords Dragons a modicum of privacy.

Finally, every weyr has a communal area. The exact purpose of this is unclear. Some in academia believe it serves as a meeting place where the weyr gathers to socialize and strategize, tell stories and sing songs, celebrate births and mourn deaths. The height of romantic anthropomorphism? Perhaps. But even the most hardcore cynic has to admit there is something enticing about the prospect of Dragons basking in the waning sun while sharing their day's adventures and night's dreams. If we can see a bit of ourselves in Dragons, we might be less inclined to treat them so badly.

One thing is for certain: weyrs give Dragons a sense of place and security in the world. Dracophile or dracophobe, we should all be able to appreciate that.

So, where do we find these enchanted communities?

While Dragons can live most anywhere, some habitats are more to their liking than others. Aside from considerations of diet and clime, a detailed map of electromagnetic energy or ley lines—both major and minor—remains one of the most reliable means of narrowing down possible weyr locations. This dynamic network crisscrosses the world from Rapa Nui (Easter Island) in the Pacific to Glastonbury, UK, from Uluru in Australia to Mount Kailash in the Himalayas of Tibet, and a plenitude of points in between. Dragons have always established their weyrs in those places most alive with earthly energy, where the elemental forces speak most clearly.[3] The lesser lines are particularly helpful today as the areas around the primary leys have been densely settled over the years.

Familiarity with local lore can also be useful if you are confident in the veracity of your sources; if not, you might as well be chasing

---

3. In Dragon-friendly China, such lines are even known as *Lung-mei,* or "Dragon currents."

rainbows for Unicorns. Beyond that, the best tools for weyr finding are a solid understanding of earth sciences, common sense, and open eyes. *Bonne chance!*

Water

Life on Earth needs water. It is one of those immutable facts no one can escape, not even Dragons. From the beginning, observant weyr watchers have celebrated what they believed was a rare, even super-natural connection between Dragon and wave, both sweet and salty. They took the natural draconic affinity for water and turned it into tales of gods and kings of rains, rivers, lakes, and churning high seas.

In the natural world, Dragons do not need honorifics, just clear, fertile depths that they can fish and graze and enjoy. Unfortunately this elemental need of theirs has, over the millennia, placed Dragons in direct conflict with human beings time and time again. For inland enchantments, spring- and glacier-fed lakes and headwaters fit the bill perfectly. By and large, such waters remain clean and are capable of supporting a wide variety of flora and fauna. Though lacking the Unicorn's ability to purify lake or stream, Dragons work assiduously to maintain the balance of the aquatic ecosystems upon which they rely. They have an uncanny way of discerning which species in their environment are endangered and will go to great lengths to protect them, particularly nesting waterfowl. Some pseudo-dragons can be decidedly troublesome in this respect, but they have a tendency to be ecologically short-sighted and eat indiscriminately from the fare at hand.[4] Where large waters are not available, small springs and tarns will suffice, though the lack of aquatic life necessitates Dragons going farther afield to fill their bellies.

Dragons also relish mucking about in the mud and are known to push up dams and other earthworks in the process. Modern his-torians believe they may have contributed to the lore surrounding

---

4. Lake District marsh draks, for example, are particularly fond of garganey eggs, and have contributed to tipping these lovely dabbing ducks to the brink of extinction in the British Isles.

certain unexplained structures in the remote parts of Canada, Russia, and China. The massive dam, for example, in Wood Buffalo National Park, Alberta, while ascribed to a bevy of beavers, might well have felt the slap of draconic tail spades in its making. On the flip-side, when the spring thaw hits the far north, Dragons will break ice- and log-jams as needs be to keep the waters flowing clear.

The major rivers of the world have become far too urbanized to serve modern Dragons well, and vice versa. Feathered Dragons in the South American rainforest, for example, have been particularly tasked by the silt from runoff of clear-cut areas being claimed for agriculture. Hindered by their size, they could easily use the heft of an Oriental enchantment or two in their efforts to keep the Amazon and Orinoco Rivers flowing as they should. That said, Dragons are aware, as was Leonardo da Vinci, that, "Very great rivers flow underground."[5] Mountain and desert Dragons are particularly adept at finding such waterways and making the most of them.

Coastal Dragons mirror their inland cousins' aquaphilia, amplifying it to equal the splendid scale of the seas around them. From cliffside perches they soar over the waves, fishing and frolicking at their leisure.[6] Like Galapagos iguanas—though on an appropriately gargantuan scale—they are able to filter and expel excess salt from their systems in amounts which would easily kill lesser beings. This gives them the freedom to live without being tied to supplies of fresh water, a life-or-death limitation to virtually all other land species. The minerals in seawater are not only a boon to fire breathing, but, as a dietary constant, produce some of the most colourful Dragons around.[7] The raising of "natural" ayres and dredging of fjords and estuaries are frequently attributed to ancient enchantments, though how much of that is truth and how much wishful imagining is conjecture at best.

---

5. *The Notebooks of Leonardo da Vinci.*

6. Though there are "sea monsters" in the oceanic depths, nine times out of ten what are called sea monsters are actually Dragons larking about between surf and turf.

7. The elements also create flame variations the likes of which rival the spectral phenomena of the most festive fireworks displays.

Today, our ever-escalating demand for seafood, oil, and gas, not to mention the ineffable way we use the oceans as a dumping ground, have placed humans increasingly at odds with marine Dragons. The North Sea shores, Pacific Rim, and coastal Yucatan, once teeming with Dragons, now see their magnificent kind only once in a blue moon.[8] They have, almost to a wing, relocated inland or, in some cases, to more remote shores which have yet to be plundered and fouled.

Terrain

Among criteria for Dragon habitats, space follows fast upon water. As their global presence attests, room to spread draconic wings can be found—even today—across a range of topographies and climates. Weyr watchers everywhere have simplified the canvas, placing Dragons in four basic ecological regions: mountains, upland forests, lowlands, and deserts.[9]

Mountains

The majority of post–Industrial Revolution weyrs are located in alpine and semi-alpine expanses. These are environments ill-suited to human habitation, which pleases Dragons very well indeed. Above the timberline, Dragons can make the world their own, taking full advantage of all the land has to offer. There are caves to shelter even the hardiest enchantment from the elements, adroit sheep and goats to nosh upon, and, best of all, a dearth of meddlesome humanity. True, the water does not flow as freely as down below, but in modern times, security takes precedence over the pleasures of swimming holes.[10]

---

8. One wonders, were wholesale habitat devastation not a certain result, if Dragons might not consider bringing the oil rigs down and reclaiming the waters once and for all. Of course, being part of the Big Picture, they might just be waiting us out, along with our attendant folly.

9. Some cryptoherpetologists add maritime regions to the list, though it is generally held that upland and lowland ecospheres sufficiently overlap and cover all coastal bases.

10. Besides, a breath of fire across the snow can warm up even the most glacial of waters.

In what is known as the Himalayan Quad, there are, to this day, no fewer than eight known weyrs. One of the oldest is nestled in the inaccessible heights of Mount Kailash. The local Dragons thrive on the ley-line energy which thrums through the mountain and, in return, protect the sacred peak from humans who would climb her without understanding her. Ironically, in the process, they also save droves of high-altitude daredevils—more bombast than brains— from themselves. A mountain may not scare them, but Dragons are another story! The merest whoosh of a wing can turn snowfields into avalanches, not to mention how Dragon dancing can open chasms, dislodge climbers' pitons, and generally ruin a mountain adventurer's day. It's enough to make even the densest climber think twice.

A note to the ecologically misinformed: Dragons will melt snow for their own use, but Dragonfire is not responsible for the diminishment of the world's glaciers. Using the presence of enchantments *anywhere* to debunk climate change is pure junk science. Dragons are being impacted by global warming like every other species, not causing it. The scientific community would be better served setting the blame game aside and looking at how Dragons, for all their size and flame, move through the world with a virtually negligible carbon paw print. Understanding *that* could revolutionize our human relationship with energy and save all the glaciers.

As is true of all habitats, the mountains offer a mix of blessings and inconveniences. The paucity of vegetation, for example, forces high-altitude Dragons to be situationally carnivorous. This can be tricky: extreme dietary deficiencies can potentially result in scale softening and/or cracking. To combat this, they get their daily allotments of vitamins from the rich internal organs—especially the liver—of their prey, and while this meets their needs, it does not satisfy winter-weary palates. Come the first blush of spring, when the sap begins to rise, enchantments will descend from their high homes and gorge themselves on new shoots and leaves below the timberline. The sight, while spectacular, can give unprepared humans the shivers imagining raids on herd and home—raids which occur only following winters of baleful longevity and bitter cold. Think serious Ice Age distress.

An alpine Dragon's annual greens binge does wonders for his disposition and scale strength and gets him ready for the hectic spring and summer months to come.[11] While a lack of flora has its dietary drawbacks, nothing is better for fire practice than a treeless expanse. Young mountain Dragons can huff and puff to their hearts' content without fear of setting their surroundings ablaze.

For those living on the verge of the tree line, the story is slightly different. The altitude makes the air very dry and the resinous conifers of the region can go up in a flash should an errant spark fly in from the wrong direction. Thus, care with fire is the requisite exchange for a more omnivorous menu. It is a testament to enchantment vigilance that more forest fires—at any elevation—are the result of lightning strikes and felonious human intent than reckless Dragons-in-training. It makes elementary Dragon sense: you don't set your home on fire— at least not on purpose.

Mountain winds also play both fair and foul with Dragons. Gentler updrafts and thermals are perfect for first flights, giving that extra bit of lift to a neophyte aviator still unsteady in her wings. It's the storm winds that can be dangerous. When you are looking at habitats above 3,000 metres, winds whipping about at between 10 and 12 on the Beaufort Scale—60 to 100+ mph—are not uncommon, particularly during the winter. Even the most experienced Dragon can get battered silly trying to fly in such conditions. At times like those, enchantments will go deep underground, warm their weyr chambers, and wait the inclemency out.

Upland Forests

Come down from the mountain tops, through the sparsely treed transitional zone, and you enter the province of the upland forest weyrs. Here the waters flow sweet and clear, and the vegetation is plentiful. There are also natural caverns or, where they are lacking, ground fit to be tunneled. The climate being reasonably temperate, some Dragons are even inspired to rough it out of doors for a good eight to ten months of the year.

---

11. See Chapter Three.

The Scottish Highlands, the Scandinavian lake country, much of Canada, the northeastern and northwestern United States, Siberia, and Manchuria—all these regions and more have topography which suits upland weyrs nicely. The trees are largely coniferous and the undergrowth hardy and rich with nutrients. The expanses also support a variety of game, from hare to goral to wild bison, with waters fit to be fished of salmon, trout, and pike. Though sharing the environs with other large predators—bear and wolf immediately leap to mind—the reptile-slow metabolism of full-grown Dragons helps assure there is enough food for all, man and nature willing. Their main problem is that humans have likewise found these regions to their liking, though more often for hunting, lumbering, and mining than for residential use. Still, it is anyone's guess which of these activities causes Dragons more distress.

To personalize their digs, forest enchantments will clear shelves for basking and fire practice, often leaving stands of strategically placed trees to mask their presence from all save the most discerning observer. Though there are no guarantees when it comes to Dragons, knowing precisely what you're looking for takes you a long way towards finding it. Look for unusual scrapings on bark, spade-swept paths, and undergrowth almost too perfectly "natural" in its configuration, as these are all helpful signs when highland Dragoning.

Travel south to the tropics and you will find comparable environments, especially in the foothills of the Andes and Southern Alps and in the upper jungles of Asia, Africa, and northern Central/South America. The dense, torrid uplands provide quantity and quality of vegetation upon which Dragons and their prey freely dine. In a more open space, such abundance might produce giants; not so in the near impenetrable rainforests. The native Dragons—almost exclusively of the feathered or sinuous Oriental variety—are dwarfed by their surroundings, needing smaller, suppler physiques to navigate among close brakes of ceiba, bamboo, and monkey puzzles, not to mention the even more restrictive jungle undergrowth.

Until the late 1800s, upland rainforest weyrs were considered safe havens for Dragons. Despite the milder climate, their isolation was on a par with that of the mountain communities. Age upon age, enchantments lived without seeing more than a handful of humans, and the few who happened to wander through their neighborhood did so with appropriately awed respect. The recent clearing of the forests for land and rare woods has had a devastating effect on all who call them home, from largest Dragon to smallest beetle.[12] Though upland weyrs are still more secure than their lowland cousins, there is a growing concern among cryptoherpetologists that it is only a matter of time before they are reduced from thriving communities to bastions beleaguered by an intrusive world. Worries aside, South American places like the Iguazu River basin and Canaima National Park have just the abundance of water and dramatic landscapes to thrill the wildest of Dragons.

Lowlands

Once upon a time, back when our ancestors were first rising up off all fours, weyrs positively littered the lowlands of the world. These are the regions of lake, river, and coastal plains, of old-growth forest and rolling grasslands. Here there was water, plant and animal life, and space enough for even the largest Dragon to spread her wings. These were the lands of deciduous trees, of orchard and grove, of sacred oak, ash, sakaki, and banyan trees—Dragons curled round them, dining on their fruits and lounging in their shade.

Though natural shelters were not as prevalent as in the hills, there were cliffsides, perfect for excavating rooms with aquatic views. On steppe and open plain, the soil was soft and easy to mound and tramp into enchantment-cozy abodes. (For beings capable of carving through mountainous rock, kicking up dirt and fieldstone is like slipping talons through butter.) From Clovis mounds to modern, eco-friendly Hobbity homes, lowland Dragon earthworks proved positively inspirational.

Such idyllic environments held a natural appeal for humans, too. Look at any map and it will be clear: humans settled and multiplied in these same accessible spots. They used the waters to travel and trade,

---

12. That includes the indigenous peoples of the regions.

and the fertile plains to graze and sow. The lowlands made it possible for humans to move beyond the provincial to the cosmopolitan. In the process they could not help but come into conflict with the local Dragons. It took centuries, but in the end, people won out, especially along navigable waterways.

For the sake of history, entire weyrs were often distilled into the persona of one notable Dragon—fiercer, more sanguine than the others—who stood between man and a prime patch of real estate. Smok Wawelski was just such an exemplary Dragon. Wild and (according to legend) murderous, he dwelt on a hill overlooking the banks of Poland's Vistula River.[13] When people moved into the valley, they looked upon the location of his weyr and coveted it in their hearts. The king thought it was a perfect spot for his castle; the bishop, for his cathedral.[14] Of course, they did not bother to ask the resident Dragon if the construction was okay with him. Why should they? They were humans, and he was but a monster! Naturally, Smok took a stand. He defended his home the only way he knew how: with fire and fang, terror and talon. At this point, the lore of the region veers off into faërie-tale territory. Smok becomes an evil Dragon, extorting the people to the amount of one girl a month lest he slaughter flocks and scorch crops with abandon. King Krak was more than willing to pay the fee as long as it involved peasant children. As happens in these tales, in time there was only one girl left in the tribe: his daughter. Suddenly, the Dragon's sinister demands were no longer acceptable. A call went out for a dragon slayer but none of the usual suspects answered, neither knight nor wizard nor seventh son of a seventh son. When the king was about to give up all hope, a wily cobbler stepped forward. He left a sulfur-dressed lamb outside of the Dragon's den and waited. As any proper Dragon would, Smok scarfed the lamb, stuffing and all. The sulfur gave him a voracious thirst which he tried to slake by practically inhaling the waters of the Vistula. He drank

---

13. Advances in Dragon Studies suggest he was not a solitary Dragon as reported, but the alpha Dragon of the local weyr.

14. A reminder of the connection between ley lines, Dragons, and human religious sites.

and drank until there was nothing for it: he simply exploded. Nasty, but his bursting came just in time for happily-ever-afters. The cobbler was given the princess's hand, keep and church were erected just as king and priest wished, and the city of Krakow grew and flourished around them. In the end, it was not courage or skill at arms or faith that slew this Dragon. In the end, Smok Wawelski was dispatched by his own hunger and the inglorious trick of a tradesman.

Of course, the *prima facie* absurdity of this story hardly bears noting. It is yet another fiction to justify Dragon displacement. That said, it serves to illustrate the inevitable clash which occurs when acreage-hungry humans run into established enchantments.

Today you have to trek long and hard to find a lowland weyr fit for anything other than an archaeologist's dig. Across the Northern Hemisphere, between 55 degrees N and the Tropic of Cancer, there's nary a lowland tract not cultivated with concrete or corn. London, Vilnius, Dublin, Quebec…cities large and small sprouted up where once only Dragons ruled. If you head into the back of beyond, towards the desolate Arctic—Southampton Island in Nunavut or the northern Siberian Plain, for example—you can find taiga lowlands so remote and forbidding that humans have kept their distance. There, amongst brooding snow geese and migratory lemmings, Dragons live in relative peace, though one can't help thinking they'd prefer the verdant expanses and warmer climes they once called home. While we have yet to supplant these indigenous enchantments, oil exploration and boreal mining will soon threaten even these isolated weyrs.

On the flip side, there are places we call home which True Dragons consider uninhabitable: coastal deltas and floodplains too unstable to bear the weight of one gravid female, let alone an entire weyr. No self-respecting enchantment, for example, would put down roots in the Mississippi Delta, with or without barrier islands, seawalls, and Army Corps of Engineers–approved levees. Whether it is their abundance of common sense or an ability to extrapolate an area's long-term topographical changes,[15] Dragons leave such trembling prairies to the mundane fauna: cottonmouths, barking frogs, migratory waterfowl, and the occasional swamp rabbit, nutria, or marsh panther—and humans convinced they can hold back the tides. Though certain small solitary pseudo-dragons—swale tangies, fen flappers, and the like— have been spotted in these fragile environments, it is unclear if they're permanent residents or just passing through. More study is required.

Such boggy tracts aside, one can say without fear of contradiction that no draconic biome has been afflicted by the presence of humans as much as that of the lowland weyrs.

Deserts

It is hard to imagine any environment able to beat back beings as resilient as Dragons. Mountain cold, hill and valley deforesting, mining, and widespread urbanization—every habitat presents obstacles, and yet nothing compares to the inherently inhospitable nature of a desert. Bare, wind-blown anvils of sand and rock upon which the sun beats relentlessly, deserts comprise one-third of our planet yet claim barely 10 percent of the world's Dragons.

Still, for our scaled friends, it is not the heat they mind, it is the aridity.[16]

As the stories of Aido Hwedo and other primordial desert beings teach us,[17] Dragons quite enjoy spending hours soaking up the rays and dusting in the warm sands as long as they can cool off with a luxurious swim at day's end. Mawu, the Creator, understood this and gave Aido Hwedo the oceans. And, in the distant past, when deserts themselves were so much smaller, most desert-dwelling Dragons lived

---

15. Long-lived and elemental, Dragons are acutely aware that, in the ebb and flow of ecospheres, ultimately, water will out.

16. Not to mention the fact that deserts can get downright cold depending on altitude, season, and time of day. The Gobi has been known to reach -45 degrees F in the winter and even the Sahara goes sub-zero on January nights.

17. See Chapter Five.

close enough to sea or river that they were able to maintain a balance of water and sand, sun and shade. The enchantments were content.

But that was long ago.

The climate has since changed: the sun turned ruthless, the winds roared, and mountains fell into sand. In this way the deserts multiplied. As did people. That which could sustain small nomadic tribes was insufficient to the needs of the growing population. We humans needed land, lots of land, on which to farm and build. Inching our way along the anthropological timeline, we walked out of the hostile wastes, settling along coasts and waterways. In the process, we forced the Dragons inland to dunes and hard-baked wilds as dry as the mountains of the moon.

As this poverty of water defines the environment, so it defines everything about a desert weyr: location, size, even certain evolutionary adaptations of the Dragons themselves. Protection from the desiccating properties of the sun makes caved sites—north-facing where available—essential. Think *The English Patient*, sans petroglyphs. Sand replaces water when it comes to bathing, with a good roll in the dust scouring off most parasites and grime. The uncompromising habitat means there is little wildlife and what is there tends to be stunted by a nutrient-poor diet.[18] This is true of the Dragons, too: it's hard to reach draconic proportions on a diet of spinifex and jerboas. The enchantments of the Aïr Mountains of the Sahara Desert, for example, have become dwarfed over the years until now they are a full 40 percent smaller than their nearest lowland relatives.[19] Spare resources also place strict limitations on weyr size. Deep-desert weyrs can support no more

---

18. Xeric shrubs, cacti, and tough, spiny grasses are the standard flora of the ecosphere and, hardy though they may be, they prove more filler than nourishment for Dragons. Still, in a lean season, they can keep the most draconic stomach from rumbling. If things get really rough, desert Dragons have been known to estivate (a summer hibernation) until the rains come.

19. Marvels of adaptive morphology, the Aïr Dragons also have heavy brow ridges over their eyes which serve as sun shades, and exude protective oil when molting, which helps prevent sunburn.

than a score of individuals,[20] and those few inhabitants will, of necessity, forage across 10,000–20,000 square miles.

As is true of all desert dwellers, the enchantments live—quite literally—for the rejuvenation that comes with the seasonal flash of lightning and the brief rains that follow. They drink their fill and stuff their bellies with tender budding greens and short-lived blooms. Like baleen whales inhaling krill, they swoop, mouths open, through locust swarms, scooping up great, crunchy mouthfuls of protein. And when the oryx antelopes emerge to slake their thirst at the swollen wadis, there is a feast to be had!

---

20. Despite the low numbers, the weyrs will still have two or three enchantments to maintain a strong gene pool. In such adverse conditions, every little bit helps.

Such bounty does not last, of course, and desert Dragons are well adapted to times of privation. Though they prefer not to have to test their endurance, they can go up to three months without food or water. To hedge against this extreme scenario, they are on intimate terms with every patch of shade and salt flat, every guelta, watering hole, and oasis to be found within their range. They can also find aquifers far beneath the sands and track the flows with precision to where they can be tapped with ease.[21] Should you ever be caught without water in the desert and happen to see a Dragon overhead, by all means follow them. Their extraordinary water-sense might just save your life.

Today, with the loss of more auspicious environs, a few enchantments discomforted by the very idea of human neighbors have been turning to the duned wastelands as refuges of last resort. It is a tall order off the adaptation menu, for sure. But it is their choice and if any beings can do it, Dragons can. More disturbing from a cryptoherpetologist's perspective is how short-sighted overfarming and deforestation are devouring once fertile lands. Without grass and trees to hold moisture and topsoil, the deserts will continue to grow. In time, habitat choice may no longer be in Dragon paws. Or in ours.

Habits

To the best of our knowledge, Dragons do not bite their talons, gamble, or do drugs, and they only smoke in a natural, internal-combustion sort of way. Yet, like most living things, they are creatures of very specific habits. We are, of course, speaking in zoological terms, of habits as day-to-day instinctive behaviours or characteristics. These are not the broad-brush seasonal activities which highlight a Dragon's yearly agenda.[22] Rather, habits are the daily routines and rituals which

---

21. There was speculation that Dragons could actually manipulate underground waters, calling them to the surface in times of distress. As with many things draconic, this is more magical/wishful thinking on our part than actual cryptozoological fact.

22. We'll be discussing their broader biological calendar in Chapter Three.

keep enchantments functioning as productive, tight-knit social units. These are the activities every Dragon needs to get through his day.

From Dawn to Dawn

To understand Dragon habits, you must understand two things: First, that they live under the tyranny of powerful chronobiological cycles starting with—but not exclusive to—well-established circadian rhythms. And second, that their lives revolve around the basic trio of concerns which occupy us all: food, family, and fun. Everything else— sleep, grooming, etc.—serves one of those three *F*s.

Light, temperature, social synergy, eating patterns—these are some of the exogenous (external) cues—the *zeitgeben*[23]—which inform a Dragon's internal clock, synchronizing it with their existential needs and environment. In this respect, they are not too different from the rest of us, save for the fact they are Dragons, which makes everything that much more...draconic. Their photo- and thermal-sensitivity can best our own by quite a lot. For Dragons in temperate and torrid zones, where day and night and the attendant temperature variations have certain daily consistency, this means they are able to keep active deep into the crepuscular hours. Such temporal latitude confused cryptoherpetologists for years, leading them to believe that Dragons were essentially nocturnal. While it is true that some love the nightlife more than others, it is more a function of self-preservation than biology, reflecting the eminent adaptability of the species. Dragons who live beyond 65 degrees N·or 65 degrees S, in the realms of Long Night and Midnight Sun, have a much more free-wheeling internal clock thanks to the extreme light/dark cycles. In those regions, other zeitgeben kick in, literally giving them time enough to balance out their daily routines. Polar Dragon vision, for example, is so acute that the pitch black of hibernal mornings seems no less impenetrable than a light mist rolling across the San Francisco Bay. More

---

23. "Time givers," a term popularized by chronobiology pioneer Jürgen Aschoff in the 1960s.

importantly, during the ostensibly endless Arctic summers, the artificial night of weyr dens provides them with much-needed dream havens.[24]

How then does a Dragon's day unfold?

Your average enchantment—to the extent that there is such a thing—starts its day in that darkest hour just before dawn. Sluggish from sleep, the Dragons emerge from their caves and head immediately to basking ledges to await the warmth of the sun. For years it was believed this was the Dragon being her primordial, ectothermic self, shaking off the night's torpor, priming her biothermal pump, and preparing for the first hunt of the day. Logical as that seems, it's no longer a truth of enchantment living—hasn't been for millennia. Dragons are far more complex than simple snakes or lizards, being a mixture of warm- and cold-blooded with a dash of the heat thief thrown into the mix; formally put, Dragons are endo-, ecto-, and kleptothermic. Even without such a metabolic mosaic, their size places them squarely among the gigantotherms—creatures so large that they can maintain a consistent, active body temperature for long periods of time. Recent studies indicate that the early morning bask is actually more behavioural than biological and serves as a sort of draconic kaffeeklatsch. The perfect way to start the day.

Unfortunately, not even a Dragon can loll about 24/7. Hunger calls—the need to hunt—especially if there are little maws to feed. As the morning progresses, social mores give way to biological necessity. Stomachs rumble like summer thunder. The Dragons break off into parties of four to six and head out to feed. Working in small groups, they alternate between hunting and patrolling the skies. One does not consider Dragons particularly vulnerable creatures; certainly while aloft, with wings furled and flame at the ready, they are as safe as a predator can be. However, caution is warranted when, during the light of day, Dragons spend long stretches on the ground foraging among the vegetation. Breakfast choices vary with species and

---

24. Imagine a dorm full of college students up for a week, cramming for finals, then multiply it by a hundred. That is a sleep-deprived Dragon. Remember, we all need to dream.

environment. In the far north or at high altitudes, high-caloric needs have our friends looking for meat from the get-go. Small catches will be noshed on the wing; large prey will be taken home to be divvied up among kith and kin.[25] Dragons in temperate or tropical climates frequently opt for a light repast of fruits and greens as their first meal, caching any game they happen upon for later use. Their systems digest plant matter with ease, allowing them to stay alert and fast on their wings. However, flying after a heavy meal of flesh and bone is a little like going cliff diving after Thanksgiving dinner. Cramps are certainly possible, not to mention bloat and a general lethargy. It is understandable that Dragons would prefer to follow such a gastronomic ordeal with a nap in the sun rather than aerial acrobatics.

Which takes us back to the weyr for elevenses and nap time. With talons full of the morning's catch, the valiant hunters return. Their bounty is taken to the communal dining area, usually a large above-ground space with good drainage for washing away blood and other refuse so as not to attract pests and scavengers. Not that your everyday carrion eater is apt to hang out with Dragons. Still, it is elementary Dragon hygiene: you don't want to foul your weyr. Any breakfast leftovers are deposited in the larder. This is a separate den, out of the sun and away from enchantment hustle and bustle. Though Dragons don't mind their game a little gamey, they prefer it as fresh as possible and certainly not rancid. Taking draconic appetite and judicious hunting into account, spoilage is a blue-moon concern.

A word or two about Dragon table manners would not go amiss here. If you are the least squeamish or fainthearted, the sight of feeding Dragons is not for you. Simply put, a weyr mess is a mess, bloody and visceral and positively stentorian. When Dragonlets and/or juveniles are in attendance, any meal will quickly elevate to a feeding frenzy. Part of this is an obvious function of size. Small Dragons need fuel to grow, lots of it. They are almost always hungry and eat with Rabelaisian relish. Like Tasmanian devils on steroids, they rip apart

---

25. This is essential when there are weyr-bound nesting females and/or hatchlings. See Chapter Three.

carcasses their elders might swallow whole and plunge into a bath of flesh and gore only to come up for air coated from muzzle to elbow in blood and fur. Time and again, they go back to the source until there is nothing left save a tell-tale stain on the dining rock and a splinter or two of rib stuck between their teeth. Emily Post would blanch at the sight. Oddly, as loud and furious as young Dragons get, they almost never hurt one another, even when tussling over the same shank or kidney. Messy they may be, but they know how to share. While no less vocal about their gastronomic pleasures, grown Dragons eat with large, clean, deliberate bites befitting their size and maturity. Compared to their offspring, they are positively decorous. *Caveat spector*: If you're out Dragoning and hear an unholy ruckus echoing through the hills, keep your distance. If compelled to approach, do so with extreme caution and a telephoto lens. Chances are you will go unnoticed, but accidents can happen in the heat of the moment, especially around rambunctious juveniles. You are far better safe than eaten.

Being atop the food chain, Dragons, like the big cats, can afford to sleep long and sound when they wish. By late morning, they will have scanned their environs for danger, eaten heartily, and settled in for a long siesta. Oh, to live the life of a Dragon! Again, these are routines tied directly to the social ebb and flow of the weyr.

Dragons spend their afternoons in what we might interpret as effective play. Flying, climbing, swimming, dodging fireballs … all are activities both fun and essential to survival. Proficiency builds agility, speed, stamina, and strong Dragon bodies.[26]

Play also works up an appetite. It is followed by a twilight hunt or, if enough food has been lardered, some Dragons may opt to spend a leisurely evening at home and dine in. As the day winds down, enchantments delight in postprandial family time. First, they will bathe and/or dust, ridding themselves of the worst of the day's muck and mire. This is followed by more intensive bonding as one Dragon grooms another,

---

26. In the Peruvean Plateau, Dragons have been known to fly speed trials along the Nazca Lines, an excellent place for a workout.

preening all those spots between scales and feathers which individuals can't reach on their own.

Grooming time also includes sharpening talons and charming horns. Charming is more common to Unicorn care than Dragon, but it means much the same thing regardless of species. A uniquely cryptozoological term, *charming* refers to periodic horn maintenance. Conveniently located pieces of basalt, granite, or hornfels are used to spruce up brow and blaze cornicles. These rocks are rough enough to remove a burr or reshape and hone a chipped tip, yet fine enough to minimize the risk of rubbing off excessive horn in the process. Not that they're foolproof; young Dragons, caught up in their adolescent zeal to have the sharpest horns in the weyr, have been known to go charming wild. The resultant nubs can require months—even years— to grow back. It is a lesson hard learned and seldom repeated. While Dragons can handle coarser filing than Unicorns, when it comes down to a really smooth finish, hornfels is the burnishing stone of choice for both. Horn-notched outcroppings of this small-grained rock send chills through savvy weyr watchers: Dragons are near!

Ablutions concluded, enchantments ease into the day's end. Dragons after dark are as idiosyncratic as people and even more mysterious. Some verge on the actively nocturnal, lighting up the night sky with Dragonfire and sparkling aerobatics.[27] Still others lounge about the weyr, engaging in what can only be called community song time, their sonorous voices filling the air with eldritch melodies. And then there are those who retire early, underground, perhaps to tell tales into the wee hours or to simply curl up and drift into dream time.[28]

Thus, teeth to tail, another circadian cycle comes round. Minor variations aside, a Dragon's daily habits will remain largely unchanged.

---

27. These individuals tend to be late risers or afternoon power nappers.

28. The nighttime rituals of Dragon dens are one of the last unexplored realms of cryptoherpetology, and with good reason. As benign as one's intention might be, startling a sleeping Dragon can have disastrous consequences. Better to leave such matters to one's imagination.

Mythic Misunderstandings

That the natural habits of Dragons have been distorted and maligned through the ages is unfortunate but to be expected. It falls on modern Dragon specialists to set the record straight. To this end, heed the following:

Damsels, In Distress and Out

Given their druthers, Dragons will not eat people. This is one of those fictions left over from the persecution of the Dark Times, c. 2000 BCE to 1450 CE. True, mathematical probability insists that, through the years, some humans—particularly those aggressively inclined—have wound up as draconic crudités. But the numbers do not jive with the accounts of maidens lost. One is left to wonder, though, what became of all those virgin sacrifices and damsels in distress. Were they spirited off to some distant shire or province? Perhaps left on the stoop of a local convent, babbling incoherently about great flying monsters? Either way, they disappeared, leaving Dragons to bear the brunt of horrendous press. Of course, it would have been so much easier for all involved had our ancestors simply let the occasional cow or sheep go and chalked it up to the cost of doing business in Dragon country. That they didn't do so says something rather unpleasant about the value placed on their daughters vs. their livestock.

Once you cut through the layers of archaic spin, the fact remains that humans don't particularly pique Dragon appetites. If they want something that tastes like chicken, they go for the real thing.[29] That is not to say that you can be reckless when in their territory. You wouldn't walk up to a polar bear or a tiger and just rub them behind the ears without a proper introduction. That's bad manners and a good way to lose a hand—or worse. Sensible precautions must be taken, particularly in times of drought or famine.

---

29. They are also inclined towards leaner flesh than humans are heir to. Too much fat will clog even Dragon arteries.

Hoarding

Dragons and hoarding is a good story to tell, spread around, or spin to your heart's content—but it's just not true. At least not in the way people mean it. It is said, "For where your treasure is, there will your heart be also."[30] When it comes to Dragons, some people have taken this literally, insisting it explains the great hoards of precious metals and stones with which they fill their lairs. This presupposes 1) that Dragons actually have vast stores of wealth, and 2) that Dragons place the same value on these things we do. Neither of which is true.

Well, not exactly.

Dragons do gather and guard rare and shiny objects, though seldom on a grand scale. This is a habit recognized in lore since the Greek legend of Ladon and the apples of the Hesperides. However, what we call hoarding, Dragons would consider simply gilding their nests. By placing precious minerals and stones among simpler, organic material—branches, moss, and the like—a Dragon creates a bed both soft and durable. And, more to the point for a brooding female, one which will hold sufficient heat to incubate her clutch.

Are these metals their "treasure"? Hardly—certainly not in terms we would relate to. Dragons have absolutely no worldly use for gelt, gold, or gems. They attach not a whit of intrinsic value to such objects. In fact, though they deeply resent treasure seekers intruding into their personal space, they rarely notice—or mind, per se—one or two individual pieces going missing from their collections. And contrary to popular myth, they seldom pilfer from human stores save when very young and enticed by the prospect of readily available sparklies. This is a game for Dragonlets, not a felony. After all, if we will go leaving our valuables about, someone is apt to take them. It might as well be a Dragon. Ultimately, it has always been easier for them to find their own gold and silver ores, raw diamonds and beryl, than to risk major run-ins with humans literally up in arms about property rights. Of

---

30. New Testament. Matthew 6:21.

course, this does suggest that Dragons can locate lodes with uncanny dispatch, which creates a whole new array of problems.[31]

Unfortunately, solid facts seldom trump extravagant lies. To this day, avaricious treasure hunters continue to seek Dragons' legendary troves, conservation regulations be damned. On rare occasions, they stumble across hatching grounds where eggs lay atop nests of soft, warm gold—a great thermal conductor which keeps a clutch at just the right temperature. Like infant Dragons, these people are blinded by shiny trinkets, going for the gold and missing the true treasure right in front of their eyes. Gold may be $1,200 an ounce, but a Dragon egg is priceless. (A heads-up to treasure hunters: Willfully breaking or poaching Dragon eggs is ILLEGAL. Not to mention that a Dragon will defend her nest to her dying breath. You have been warned.)

That said, the well-equipped cryptoherpetologist always packs a bauble or two in her field-kit. You never know when they will come in handy as an offering of friendship or distraction for a much-needed getaway. If swift-footed Atalanta of myth could falter at the sight of a golden apple, a shiny trinket might just have the same effect on an inflamed Dragon. It would certainly be a ploy worth trying should all else fail.

---

31. The Chinese, however, chose to honor Dragons for their treasure-finding ability, rather than exploit them. The noble Dragon Fu-Ts'ang, for example, was called the Dragon of Hidden Treasures and was guardian of all the rare minerals on Earth. The ultimate hoard.

*Spring blossom, Autumn moon, when will they
cease their come and go?*

—*Li Yü*

three

A Year in the Life

There is a saying bandied about Dragon circles: Only the wild and
the worm know the rhythms of nature, and nothing is as wild as a
Dragon.

A tad hyperbolic, perhaps, but true.

Much as their lives are micromanaged by circadian rhythms, so
Dragons are macromanaged by the ebb and flood of the seasons.[1]
We're talking cryptotheriogenesis, or Dragon Reproduction 101: mating, nesting, hatching, and growing. Each phase of an enchantment's
social and psychosexual existence is in synch with Earth and sun, the
planetary trimesters.[2] Their relationships are organic, hormonal, and,
at heart, sidereal. Proper appreciation of draconic nature is impossible
without a clear grasp of this concept.

Yes, to everything there really is a season.

---

1. And by the wash of decades and generations—even centuries—that follow.
   One of the perks of being exceptionally long-lived.

2. This is true even among equatorial enchantments, though not always easy for the
   lay observer to catch given the subtle nature of the seasonal changes in that region.

Sex and Reproduction

Sexuality is one of the most fascinating and least understood aspects of a Dragon's life. So first, here are some basics that are applicable—with minor variations—to all True Dragons.

Until recently, our knowledge of draconic procreative behaviour has been, at best, a crude, fanciful cobbling-together of legend and theories extrapolated from mundane species like dinosaurs, Komodo monitors, and the great raptors of the world. Well into the seventeenth century, for example, it was commonly believed that Dragons did not mate at all, but reproduced by way of spontaneous generation from the bowels of decaying human corpses. This is obviously a hangover from superstitious times dominated by fears of plague, death, and mortal decay. The absurdity of it is an insult to modern Dragon studies, let alone common sense. It does, however, speak to the embarrassing want of empirical evidence which has hampered the crypto sciences up to the mid-twentieth century.

Fortunately, we have made great strides in the last sixty years.[3] Current theriogenetic research has found Dragon relationships to be as intricate as any in the animal kingdom, humans included. Within a weyr, the members display the gamut of bonding behaviour: a few staunch individualists choose the solitary life, while others enjoy being attached to the weyr as a whole; most opt to pair off with that one special Dragon who sparks their heart.

Not all couplings lead to procreation, which is both intentional and imperative. Acutely aware of Earth's less-than-boundless capacity, not to mention their own limited resources of food and space, Dragons instinctively monitor—and, when necessary, control—their populations. This means that while Dragons bond for life and affection, sometimes two female Dragons will come together, sometimes

---

3. Because of their numbers and accessibility, our knowledge of Western Dragons is the most extensive and has a tendency to colour our thinking about all Dragons. While some traits may be shared amongst Eastern, Western, and Feathered Dragons, there are others at which, for lack of observation and study, we can only guess. This is another reminder of the need to constantly expand our draconic horizons.

two males, sometimes a female and male who choose not to breed. To certain human factions this seems just too politically correct for words, but, as mundane zoologists are discovering, political correctness be damned. Sexual diversity is as natural as breathing among virtually every species on the planet, be it Dragons, people, or hairy-eared lemurs.[4]

The majority of non-breeding partnerships evolve naturally out of youthful associations, with proximity and shared experience weighing almost as heavily on the romantic scales as animal attraction and draconic chemistry. Such alliances are often made and sanctioned years before the parties reach sexual maturity, which proves of great benefit to a weyr's general harmony. The Dragons tend to be more settled and less prone to explosive hormonal outbursts, and ugly courtship battles are, if not eliminated, at least radically curtailed.

Among Dragons inclined to procreate, the path to mated bliss wends along a more volatile route. First, in order to keep the genetic lines strong, breeder Dragons—Queens and Sires—never mate within their own enchantment.[5] This was a simple matter in the old days when weyrs were large and multi-enchanted. As any first-year biology student knows, the more clans a weyr could support, the greater their genetic diversity and long-term strength. Today, the threat of weakened gene pools is a real concern to Dragons and conservationists alike. Some individuals of mating age will fly off and try their chances with distant, unrelated weyrs. This is not a choice made lightly, for it entails true jeopardy to life and limb. Not only are they travelling hundreds of miles across unknown territory, but once they reach another weyr, they run the risk of being shunned or even attacked as

---

4. Anyone who objects to nature being natural is basically stuck in the Dark Times and not a proper Dragon person in the first place.

5. Romantics hell-bent on anthropomorphizing all things Dragon speculate on the number of star-crossed enchantment mates who choose egglessness rather than be separated from their "true love." While there may be a whit of something to this, for now it's considered faërie-tale thinking at best.

an invader. Still, for those driven to reproduce—and, ultimately, for all Dragonkind—the potential rewards outweigh the hazards.

Field researchers are noting another quite encouraging trend: groups of three to five Dragons striking out on their own, establishing separate weyrs. From their new homes, they send out calls to other Dragons until they have a diverse nucleus from which to reinvigorate their blood and expand their genetic pool. While not an easy undertaking, the movement itself indicates there are Dragon populations healthy enough to try, a fact that thrills even the most pessimistic ecologist.

Which leads us to a few draconic facts of life:

As with people, females mature in a holistic sense long before males, becoming fit to breed between 35 and 50 years of age. Males require another decade (sometimes two) to come into their own. Those extra years give them much-needed time for their mental and physical development to synchronize so they don't completely bungle their paternal responsibilities.[6] Mature Queens are capable of laying eggs once every quarter century. This not only prevents a population explosion but also allows one brood to grow up and leave the nest before the next clutch is hatched, a necessity for centuries when the anti-Dragon legions were out in force. During those dark times, it took all the vigilance and cunning a weyr could muster to keep their enemies at bay. Too many little ones under paw would have meant untenable risks and losses greater than the Dragons could bear. Generational procreation puts far less physical and emotional strain on both individual and group. While this may seem an interminable time between matings, one must remember to look at it through the lens of draconic longevity. Twenty-five years is a drop in their temporal bucket. The latest research also indicates that recreational sex is not an alien concept to consenting adults.

---

6. This is unlike humans, who are capable of reproduction without regard to our mental/emotional ability to cope. Dragons have enough problems in the world without worrying about adolescent parenting.

Dragon Days of Autumn

Here in the north,[7] we start our year when the days are short and the world is in stasis. Hardly an auspicious time to start anything. Dragons prefer to kick their year off in high style among the golden grains and fatted calves of late summer. This is the season for making little Dragons. The Harvest Moon of August and September's Singing Moon[8] shine upon enchantments frisky from months of warmth and plenty—on Dragons primed for romance, ripe as the grains, fecund and virile. This is when Dragon fancies turn to thoughts of love, when bonds are celebrated, and life begins. There could be no more perfect launch for a draconic year.

In preparation for the ritual and splendor of the time, all Dragons go through their late-summer molt, exchanging dulled, outgrown skin for new. This in itself is an intimate affair, as mutual grooming allows partners to share in the anticipation of what's to come. Since actions speak to intentions, couples not yet bonded have been known to break up over insufficient attention paid to this early—yet crucial—stage of courting. A cavalier attitude about the summer cast usually denotes immaturity; it's best, in the long run, that such a couple goes their separate ways.

Being little prone to waste, Dragons use the slough, an excellent insulator, to line their nests and fill unwanted cracks in their dens. A Queen will take the cast skin from her spade, mix it with horn filings, parsley, amber chips, and blood (or honey, if available), and roll it into a passion ball. She sets aside this aphrodisiac until, at the most propitious time, she shares it with her Sire.[9]

---

7. No slight intended to our Southern Hemisphere readers, but for simplicity's sake we will be referencing the Northern Hemisphere's moons and calendar. Add six months and you have the sub-equatorial equivalent.

8. Known in China as the Chrysanthemum Moon which, rightly, bathes the land with joy.

9. Unfortunately, tales of Dragon balls—or "ardor orbs" as they are familiarly called—got out and gave humans another excuse to harass and hunt enchantments just when they most desired to be left alone. It didn't seem to matter that these items are extremely toxic to anyone but Dragons.

With scales spectrum-hued and shiny as freshly minted coins—a lure no hot-blooded Dragon could ignore—Dragons enter estrus between the end of August and the Autumnal Equinox. In the old days, this was a time of battle and bravado, with males—and occasionally females—pulling out all the stops to vie for affections and breeding rights. Deadly bloodbaths were very real possibilities as enchantment parvenus and alien rogues offered challenge to established pairs. Dragons were forced to modulate their behaviour during the Dark Ages, when weyrs were beset on all sides and populations dwindled precipitously. After all, they'd be mad to help in the human campaign of Dragon eradication, and mad Dragons are rarities even in the worst of times.

Not that there aren't very real dangers inherent to the season. We are talking about Dragons, after all—beings of great size and strength, and passions equal to both. But modern Dragons have exchanged mortal practices for gentler suit, and for three fervent weeks, weyrs are awash with courtship, foreplay, and sex; with spade and frill displays, polyphonic Dragonsong—which sounds very like an Igor Stravinsky duet for calliope and vuvuzela; with Dragonfire, and dancing on the clouds. New bonds are forged and old bonds reawakened. In a nod to bygone days, some Dragons will engage in extreme, high-speed acrobatics to get their blood up and adrenaline flowing—a little risk can be a powerful turn-on. And then there are the pheromones. They are positively heady during this libidinous time. Field reports from the Ukraine, for example, speak of weyr auras redolently layered with rosemary, myrrh, bitter orange, and frosty spruce—a bit like Yuletide in September. Of course, how it smells to the Dragons is another matter entirely. [10]

As the weeks go on, food and treasures are gifted—the former, a time-tested show of a Sire's ability to provide, the latter a measure of admiration and affection. When at last both Dragons are ready, the

---

10. Naturally, there are variations from weyr to weyr, north to south, and species to species. Asian Dragon pheromones tend to be more spicy, tickling the nose with the likes of vetiver, clove, and the scent of green papaya.

Queen will collect her passion ball from its hiding place and the two of them will fly off for some much needed privacy. It is believed that each pair has their own secret mating space where, away from prying eyes, they will remain until they are out of season.

Actual Dragon sex is a personal affair. There is no draconic Kama Sutra, and no humans have ever witnessed the act—at least none who lived to tell the tale. In the absence of firsthand accounts, we must look to what we know not to be true, combine that with lessons from mundane fauna, and hypothesize. For a long time it was believed with great certainty that Dragons went in for free-fall, in-flight mating. It's dramatic, yes, but no more their way than that of eagles. This erroneous conjecture was likely made by some well-intentioned individual who spied a pair in close contention over territory or the catch of the day. The truth is, for creatures their size, the logistics of aerial coitus would make the act far more dangerous than blissful and would risk killing both parties, thus utterly defeating the purpose.

Water mating, while possible, perhaps even enjoyable—and certainly orthodox among kelpies and lake dragons—is too public for True Dragons. The lake or river being a shared resource, anyone from the weyr might just drop by for a swim or drink and destroy the couple's alone time.

This leaves terra firma to bear the passions of our concupiscent friends. For this model we look to others in the animal kingdom, particularly birds and primates. Researchers have come across secluded tracts adjacent to weyrs which show signs of abandoned bowers, tail-swept dancing grounds, and deep grooves clawed passionately into the hardpan. Specifics aside, one can assume that, for amorous Dragons, the earth does indeed move.

When the Autumnal Equinox arrives, Dragon behaviour turns from lusty to domestic. With a mere six weeks between conception and laying, an expectant pair returns to their weyr with a to-do list a mile long. First and foremost, the mother-to-be must tend to her nutritional needs. Her body is creating life, an endeavor which, powerful as she is, puts an obvious elemental strain on her system. Dragon eggshells are mostly calcium carbonate and amino acids, especially significant amounts of proline, which is essential for flexible shells. Nothing unusual here, as illustrated by a quick examination of your average bird and/or reptile ova. Unique to Dragon eggs, however, are high concentrations of silver, magnesium, cadmium, gold, beryllium, and/or copper. These minerals not only help modulate incubation temperatures but also reinforce the shell's structural stability. An insufficient diet leads a Queen to leach what she needs from her own bones and muscle, or, in times of extreme privation, reabsorb her eggs, forcing motherhood to wait for more propitious times. Against this possibility, increased quantities of fresh flesh and bone become part of a gravid Dragon's otherwise balanced fare. Her mate and others in her enchantment will help supply her provender. She is, after all, eating for the survival of the line. Those living on the coast turn to shells and coral to get exigent calcium; inland Dragons use dolomite, calcite, and limestone deposits for the same purpose. In fact, an observant cryptoherpetologist can often tell a pregnant Dragon by the rich auburn shimmer to her scales which comes from this extra calcium. For the trace minerals, a Queen will swallow metal-rich stones whole and simply let her digestive system do the rest.[11]

While his mate is eating for two—or as many as seven—the proud papa sets about preparing the nest for the clutch to come. From far and wide, he will collect bough and moss, stone and soil, thatch and frond. These he presents to his mate; if he's lucky, she approves of his offering. If not, he must try again. This is not always easy. There is no draconic Home Depot just over the next mountain. Studies of abandoned weyrs have discovered, for example, remnants of nests constructed of materials foreign to their environs: desert nests with cedar linings, palm fronds woven into taiga roosts. "Far and wide" is no hyperbole, and no length is too great to go for a Dragon eager to please his expectant lady. Again, this is where the social structure of a weyr comes in very handy; a Sire can take off on a long-distance quest assured that there is family at home to look after his Queen.

---

11. The extra stones in her stomach help break down her other food, increasing the efficiency of her digestion easily tenfold.

Once the materials are gathered, the pair will build the nest together. Atop the layer of summer slough, they place a mix of loam, precious metals, and rare ores. This is followed by a soft mix of vegetation, then more stones, dirt, and hoard bits. These strata are repeated, varied, and tweaked—this nugget moved here, that shock of rye there—until Mother Dragon is satisfied.

When all is right and ready, on the cusp of November's full moon, she lays her eggs.

Winter of Content

The cool nights and shortened days of early November find weyrs abustle with activity. For the majority of Dragons, it's time to prepare for the coming winter. Dens are secured and sleeping areas made snug. And there is lots of eating to be done: muscle and fat reserves must be built up against the possibility of lean months ahead.[12] In gelid climes, stores will be set by underground or frozen for later use.

The weyr's breeding Dragons enter the cool of the year at various stages of the gestational process. With eggs almost fully grown, couples who mated the previous year will be rounding into the home stretch of the year-and-a-half-long journey. Twelve months down, six to go, this is their second cold season, one spent in proud anticipation of the hatching to come. Theirs is an easy time, relatively speaking.

For the current year's parents, it is nesting time. Six weeks after conception, the pair retreats to their chamber and the Queen deposits her clutch. Typically, there will be between three and eight eggs. Newly laid Dragon ova are variegated ellipsoids with soft, corrugated

---

12. A sure sign of a healthy autumn Dragon is a tail plump with fat for the coming winter.

shells that look not unlike large, semi-inflated, origami beach balls [13] and, depending on the species, can be up to 1 metre from tip to tip.[14] The leathery folds allow for embryo growth—not even a Dragon could vent full-sized eggs without serious discomfort—and disappearing completely by the twelfth month. Thousands of tiny pores let the shell breathe, giving incipient Dragons a richly oxygenated environment in which to develop. Only during the last few weeks of incubation does the shell harden, a sign that hatching is imminent. But more on that in good time.

The laying itself can take hours, even days in the case of a large brood, and demands a Mother Dragon's complete mental and physical

---

13. For a time it was believed that the colour of an egg determined the colour and, consequently, the sex of the Dragon inside. This is an offshoot from the notion of colour-coded draconic dimorphism, which, among Eastern and Western Dragons has been disproved in recent years. Colour is slightly more helpful when sexing Feathered Dragons—conversely to birds, the females seem to be slightly more brilliant than the males—though more studies are advised. Size can be a distinguishing sexual characteristic among True Dragons, though this will not become apparent until a Dragon enters late adolescence.

14. In Asia, round Dragon eggs are considered the uniters of yin and yang. The embryonic Dragon is yang, the rest of the egg, yin. When the egg has been absorbed, yang and yin combined in the Dragon, she is ready to hatch.

attention.[15] While her mate is of little practical help, he remains by her side for the duration, singing to her and providing what moral support he can. As each egg arrives, it is carefully arranged in the nest and covered with layers of loam and organic material which, with a lick of Dragon breath, will keep it just the right temperature for hours. Once the nest is full, the Queen positions herself around her clutch, making sure each egg touches her scales to receive her warmth. Finally, content with her efforts and spent beyond believing, she sleeps.

While his mate rests, the Sire takes the opportunity to get out, stretch his wings, and hunt. He will return with food enough to share: his lady will be ravenous when she wakes. For a year and a half, this is essentially the way things go: she incubates their brood while he hunts and sees to her needs. Some members of the gender-equality police might see this as a sexist arrangement—males hunt and gather, females stay home with the kids—but there are very practical rationales for this division of labor. Female Dragons generate slightly more body heat than their male counterparts, which makes them far more suited to keeping the eggs at the proper temperature. They're also considerably more lithe and limber than their mates, thus more adept at ministering to the eggs without harming them.

From laying until early January, a Queen and her new clutch are inseparable. This is an anxious time—if anything can go wrong, it most likely will during these first weeks.[16] She monitors the eggs' growth, their respiration, their temperature. Every day she turns them so that her children might know her touch. Every night she sings to them, the pitch and timbre of her voice etching into their embryonic memories. By the rising of the full Quiet Moon of January, any damaged or sterile eggs will be culled and those remaining are repositioned in the nest. Now, with the days beginning to

---

15. Feathered Dragons are believed to lay faster than other Dragons. No one knows exactly why this is, though there is speculation it has to do with their slighter and more avian physique.

16. In the days of rampant DDT use, Decembers were mournful times for Dragons, particularly in the West.

lengthen, Mother Dragon can breathe easier, perhaps relax a little. And she will start to take time away from her brood. Not much, at first, but a little. After all, eighteen months on a nest can drive even the most devoted Dragon stir-crazy. Though maternal instincts naturally repress any long-distance wanderlust, it is essential for a Queen's mental and physical health to be periodically spelled from her duties. An afternoon out now and then gives her time to feed, bathe, regain her draconic mojo, and, in general, remain an active member of the community. To this end, other enchantment females offer to egg-sit as needed, knowing that when and if the circumstances are reversed, the aid will be reciprocated.[17]

Despite their mien of invincibility, Dragons are not exempt from the vagaries of life and death, and occasionally a Queen is deprived of support, without even a mate to help with her responsibilities to the next generation. This is when proper nest building and the careful application of Dragonfire work wonders. A Dragon under such duress will bank her nest with a mixture of twigs, soil, and seasoned dung, and set it asmolder. The eggs stay warm while she takes time to eat, drink, patrol her habitat, and so on. Thus, she keeps herself alive, her nest chamber safe, and improves her children's chances against long odds.

In regions of seasonal extremes, deep-winter weyrs are frequently blanketed with both snow and languor. This was originally believed to be a function of the frigid temperatures slowing Dragon metabolisms and inducing a hibernal torpor. Foolish though this seems today, it was a logical conclusion given the limited scope of pre-modern cryptozoology. Scientists naively assumed Dragons would react to the cold like other reptiles, an overly simplistic approach to our very complicated friends which totally ignores the existence of Polar Dragons. We are discovering that, save in instances of truly bone-numbing cold, Dragon activity during winter months is only restricted by the availability of food and their own desire to take a break from the elements. Less activity requires less energy; less energy, less food. When

---

17. Another reason that staggered breeding and extended families are a boon to all.

much of their usual prey has either migrated or gone to ground, Dragons conserve as best they can.

Expectant Dragons can find life with their winter-bound kindred a welcome distraction. Den fever creeps in under the weight of blizzard and frost, especially for those tied to the nest. One can imagine gatherings, warmed by body and breath, where games are played and stories told—certainly a cadre of season-weary nest-sitters standing by, ready to do their bit for the family. In this way, a weyr pulls together. Come sleet or snow or biting gale, they tend the old, the young, and the yet to be born, content to move through the dark of the year into the brilliant light of spring.

The Hatching Fire of Spring

There is a saying in Guinea, "No matter how long the winter, spring is sure to follow." And as resilient and hardy as they may be, Dragons—even Arctic Dragons—look forward to spring with the exuberance of starshine dancing across the night sky. In the first enchanted wash of vernal sun, they feel the sap beginning to rise. Shaking off winter lethargy, they eat, drink, frolic, and welcome the newest generation of Dragonlets into their fold. In warmer climes, the seasonal signals might go unnoticed by all save the most sensitive beings. Dragons certainly top that list, picking up the slightest taste of spring rising up from the deep-rooted soil. Of course, proud parents-to-be are blessed with a calendar that would make the Aztecs green with envy: they need only listen to their eggs and they'll know the year's passage down to the hour.

In the seventy-third week of nesting, the eggs, though still soft, have filled out round and smooth, the Dragonlets inside heading into the final stage of development. It is time for the Queen to move her clutch from nesting chamber to hatching ground.[18] The area has

---

18. If more than one clutch is due, the hatching ground can get quite crowded. True, there will be temporal overlap, but Dragons usually avoid the need for traffic controllers by giving each Queen her own moving day. Down the line, this means each clutch has their own hatching day, thus every Dragon family gets their moment in the sun.

been meticulously prepared, the Sire neatly composing new-growth boughs and the softest gold to pillow the precious orbs. While the rest of the weyr looks on approvingly, Mother Dragon transports her eggs, one by one. When all are relocated, she settles around them again, her warm, familiar touch soothing after their ordeal.

Over the next fortnight, the eggs will lose their leathery integument, maternal heat baking the shells as hard and chip-proof as bone china. This transformation signals that the Queen's nesting duties are coming to a close: three more weeks and the fruits of her patience, care, and sacrifice will hatch out.

Days and hours count down and the feeling around the weyr gets positively festive. Everyone stays close to home, not wanting to miss a moment of the blessed event. As squill and bloodroot begin to dot the hillsides, enchantments take the opportunity to do a little spring cleaning, removing winter detritus from their dens and making any necessary repairs. In anticipation of infant arrivals, the weyr larder is stocked, sand pits warmed, and the last ice cleared from pool and stream.

Back at the hatching grounds, Mother Dragon has been turning and adjusting her newly hardened eggs with care. She attends to the slightest changes both within and without, answering her Dragonlets' agitated thrumming with a soothing hum all her own. After a year and a half, they are understandably anxious to get out into the world, but timing is everything. And no one knows the rhythms and rituals of hatching like a Dragon Queen.

Among Occidental Dragons, one of the most spectacular birthing rituals is the use of hatching fire. This is the penultimate gift parents have to offer their clutch and marks the start of the last seventy-two hours in the shell. When the time is right, the Queen summons her mate to her side and together they blast the eggs with flames so intense they burn away all organic nesting, leaving the eggs buoyed on amorphous globules of gold and silver. More importantly, the fire gives the egg-bound neonates a quintessentially draconic nudge into the outside world. The searing heat puts a finishing shine on their development. Then, as the eggs cool, the otherwise impenetrable shells are weakened ever so slightly with fine crackle lines, spiralling like fractals out from the poles.

As a historical aside, one of the arcane myths of Dragon reproduction suggested that an embryo which is not annealed in hatching fire might emerge a wyrm, at best a wyvern, but *never* a proper Dragon. This is simply not true. A Dragon egg hatches a Dragon and only a Dragon. Scientists are finding evidence the fire bestows certain immunities on Dragonlets, though studies of the long-term effects are as yet inconclusive and ongoing.

Now we come to the May full moon. With incubation days enumerated in full, word goes out and, beneath what the Chinese so wisely call the Dragon Moon, the hatching ground quickly fills with family and friends. This is one of those situations where more room is better and an outdoor arena—if possible—makes a lot of sense. Once assembled, they have only to wait.

At a moment only she can feel, the Mother Dragon starts to channel her inner diva. Her scales luminesce as she dons the mantle of the Great Dragon—the Creator—and commands, from deep within, the most ancient of Dragon songs. No hymn, paean, or Wagnerian aria can equal the solemn joy that weaves across every note of her *antienne eclorsion* (birthing anthem). Trills and chills rime the hatching ground as she reaches out to her children encased in shell. Solo becomes duet when her Sire joins in, his rich timbre floating amongst her treble tones. Then the rest of the weyr chimes in, duet building to consonant canon until the air thunders with symphonic voices. This sumptuous clarion rouses the baby Dragons and they, in turn, set their eggs to rocking back and forth, knocking against each other, and opening wide the crackles formed by flame.

In the next heartbeat, the singing stops. The elders can do no more save hold their collective breaths, watch, and wait. One by one, throughout the night, the infants use their adamantine egg-teeth to chip their way free. As the last to emerge takes his first gulp of air, a rousing chorus of draconic cheering erupts, no doubt frightening the wee ones half to death and making them wonder just what sort of world they've stumbled into! Fortunately, fear loses out to neonate needs for first meal, first bath, and, most importantly, first moments with mother, father, and nestmates.

Newborn Dragonlets are scruffy little creatures. To start, their scales are sticky with residual shell membrane, which Mother Dragon removes as best she can before showing her brood how to bathe themselves in dust and/or pool. Once clean, their physical qualities come more neatly into focus. Your average Occidental hatchling is about the size of a full-grown Great Dane. They are unsteady on their feet—real klutzes—and initially clueless about their tails, often getting tangled in their whippy length and tumbling, all snort and chuff, spade over teakettle. Eventually the concept of tail-as-balancing-aid sinks in and they're able to get around with ever-increasing grace. Their wings are disproportionately undersized at birth, sheathed in plush velvet, and totally useless. Baby scales covered with a fine coat of fur afford them an extra layer of protection in their youth. For most Dragons, this fur is shed completely during the summer of their third year, yet Dragons near the poles have been known to hold on to a rich mane of neck and chest fur well into adulthood.

Western Dragons are the most well understood of Dragons, though there is evidence that infants of other species are similar in some ways (and different in others, of course). Feathered Dragonlets are smaller and covered with fine down which will fledge into flight feathers within a year. Oriental Dragons are longer and, naturally, more ophidian. Of the True Dragons, Orientals are the most like miniature versions of themselves right out of the egg—including the presence of fully functioning venom glands. Aside from size, Dragonlets are distinguished by skimpy manes and ankle tufts which fluff out nicely by first molt.

Once cleaned up, hatchlings want to eat. Since Mom has had her hands full, it falls to Dad to provide them with their first meal. Immediately following the hatching ceremony, he slips off to the larder, which has been well stocked for just this moment. He returns with a gullet full of masticated meat and greens, which he regurgitates for his offspring's gastronomical delight. For the first few weeks of their lives, this will be primarily his job, giving his mate time to recuperate from her long nesting duties. Not that she doesn't take her share of feedings and spend a great deal of time with her children; she was bound to them from the moment she first wrapped herself round their eggs and nothing will alter that connection. Indeed, long life and relatively slow maturation make the bonds between Dragon parents and hatchlings as strong as those reserved, in scientific circles, for humans and primates.

In the spirit of the extended family, other enchantment members are eager to chip in too. Modern studies show that they gladly tend and teach the little ones, especially in years of multiple broods, turning hatching grounds into springtime crèches. This gives weary parents time to get out and smell the wild roses, and proves what many cryptoherpetologists have long supposed: it takes a weyr to raise a Dragon.

Adrift through Summer Skies

Summer in a weyr is a time for Dragons of all ages to learn and grow.

Growth is the easy part. Warmth from sky and soil nourishes all, from egg to ancient.[19] The world abounds with plant and animal life—perfect for omnivores looking to add a few pounds and inches. While the entire weyr enjoys the season's bounty, the infants and juveniles show the benefits most dramatically, going through major growth spurts in anticipation of the late-summer molt.

When it comes to learning, from elementary lessons to advanced, summer school is in session.

For new Dragon parents, there is no such thing as a lazy summer day. Their brood has rapidly developed from awkward infants into curious, get-into-everything toddlers. In the brief halcyon weeks from June to August, the little Dragons must begin to find their place within the weyr structure and so gain a foothold on life that will help them survive into adulthood.

Hunting and foraging lessons are front and center when it comes to survival skills. These usually begin at about two months—the early days of weaning—and continue well into a Dragon's third year. While Western Dragons are not fully weaned until almost a year old, they begin to forage for fruits and veggies as soon as curiosity kicks in and their palates begin to mature. (Eastern and Feathered Dragons are eating on their own at about nine months.) It is a fallacy of mythic proportions that Dragons can eat anything. This is especially not true with hatchlings. To ensure against accidental poisonings, their guardians will take the youngsters on extensive field trips around their feeding range. They will teach them which plants are good, which dangerous; which roots and berries tantalize the taste buds and which

---

19. Hardy as Dragon eggs are, a Queen in summer must be careful her clutch does not get too hot. This is mostly a worry among desert Dragons, who will build their nest deeply as the surest means of having year-round control over incubation temperatures. A Dragon can always warm her nest up, but cooling it down is more difficult.

produce belly aches or flatulence or worse.[20] And they will show them where to find eggs and honey for easy snacks.

There will also be lessons in hunting techniques and the ways of local fauna. Though still landbound, Dragonlets can stalk and pounce and will be expected to catch small prey—rabbits, squirrels, etc.—by summer's end. While mature Dragons are quick and precise with their kills, these are not innate abilities. Young Dragons have to be taught how to hunt, and much of this learning occurs through games. Like felines, they will chase, catch, release, and catch again before going in for the kill. Not being great runners, grounded Dragons must be taught the ways of the ambush predator, lying in wait amongst the shrubbery for a hapless marmot or deer. They will also learn to hunt in groups, an essential tactic for those too young to fly. Fishing is another skill Dragonlets must master, though its demand for calm flies in the face of their less-than-placid natures. They would far

20. Colicky Dragons of any age can be a danger to both themselves and others. The same can be said of hallucinogens such as *Amanita* mushrooms and the buttons of *Lophophora williamsii*, aka peyote. While not exactly toxic, if young Dragons ingest them in sufficient quantities, weyr life will make Woodstock look like tea at Buckingham Palace.

rather chase each other through the shallows than hone their angling patience on a skittish salmon. Still, the rewards are many: easy to rend and digest, fish are a top treat on a weaning Dragon's menu.

Hatchlings spend much of their first summer exploring every nook and cranny of their weyr. They familiarize themselves with water sources, playgrounds, and sacred spaces, and learn the rules associated with each. While coddled by most elders as the cute new kids on the block, the spring's Dragonlets fall into a natural pecking order amongst themselves. Though the occasional scrap will break out—they are youngsters, after all—cases of actual bullying are almost unknown. This is assumed to be the result of either exceptional parenting or, as with modern courtship habits, self-preservation. Even a small Dragon is toothed, taloned, and very strong, so schoolyard scraps are too dangerous to be allowed.

Dragons in their terrible twos experience summer as a time literally ablaze. Fresh from cutting their permanent teeth—essential for grinding requisite fire fare—their pyronic sacs develop. After that, flaming is *the* thing to do. The metabolic changes Dragons go through to work with fire result in unusual dietary cravings, largely affecting their mineral intake. Any weyr with two-year-olds is sure to have the appropriate fare stashed away for the occasion. As a rule, their systems balance out within a couple of months and their diets return to Dragon-normal.

At the end of the day, fire breathing is a skill like any other and, as such, improves with age and practice. Once they are physically equal to starting a spark, young Dragons will be taught the weyr's rules of where and when pyrotechnics are allowed and then left to their own devices. It is logical for fire abilities to develop before flight. On a practical and social level, this gives impetuous young Dragons time to acquire control over their flame from the security of terra firma. When, in their third year, they take to the skies with fire skills in paw, they'll know how to handle backdraft and fire flow and be far less likely to set the weyr ablaze. And, from a purely physical perspective, well-balanced fire breathing produces the lighter-than-air gases required to get aloft. Quite simply: no fire, no flight.

If you are out in the field and come across a scorched quarry or glassy sandpit, chances are you've discovered a fire-practice site. It is wise to make all further observations from a distance, just to be safe.

Unlike Feathered Dragons, who are well fledged by the end of their first year, Western Dragons are not strong enough, nor their wings large enough, to get aloft until they hit three.[21] Thus, a Dragon enters her third summer aflutter with glee and trepidation: it's time to leave infancy behind and fly.

To prepare for this momentous event, a Dragon sheds the soft velvet from her wings in late spring, exposing sturdy, leathery sails beneath. Dragons will help each other in this metamorphosis, with patience and burnishing stones, rubbing each other's wings smooth. Such intimate grooming can be the beginning of many a beautiful friendship or even the first spark of later partnerships. Either way, it is quality time shared.

Velvet-free wings positively burst forth, needing a mere four to six weeks to reach proportionate size. Throughout this period, Dragons exercise their flight muscles every chance they get, paying specific attention to their *flexor alae major*, *pectoralus major*, and the *supraspinatus*. They also start to instinctively temper their fire, learning to adjust their bodily gases and fill their flight-sacs. While weyr elders oversee these activities, they seldom do more than gauge the young ones' readiness lest they overreach and injure themselves. Nature does the rest.

As the days slip towards midsummer, Dragons spend hours stretching their wings, growing accustomed to the sensation of them billowing flush as lateens in the wind. Then, when the time is right, they climb together to the top of a nearby cliff or tor. There, with the thermals churning from summer heat, they will spread their wings, and, with glorious yawps of success, let themselves be carried aloft. First flights are seldom more than semi-controlled glides from great

---

21. Flight and Oriental Dragons is still a mystery. Some scholars insist they can take to the skies right out of the egg; others say that it is a boon that comes to them only in extreme old age. Chances are, the truth lies somewhere in the middle, though research is ongoing.

heights. The thrill, however, is infectious, leading to repeat performances—this time with actual wing flaps—and followed by excursions of graduated longevity and daring. By their fourth summer, Dragons are flying like old pros, doing loops and barrel rolls, hunting on the wing, and making two-point landings and skyfire at will.

While the youngsters are busy becoming the best Dragons they can be, what occupies their elders during the warming days of summer? For those not mentoring the next generation, indolence can be a real problem, especially among adolescent males (ages 10–45).

Joseph Campbell observed about humans in peacetime:

> The male has to have something serious to do, that's all. …
>> every muscle has an impulse for action, and one is not
>> fully alive unless one is in action.
> So we have the invention, always in societies, of games.
> (Transformations of Myth Through Time, p. 4)

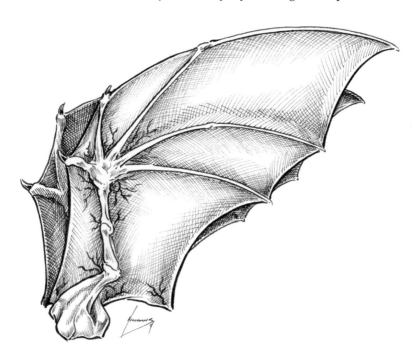

Dragons, like people, are great game players, especially in summer. It is time to get fit and sassy and prove their prowess before kith and kin. There are races and hunting contests, bouts of dodge fireball and aerial trials. Games keep enchantments busy, preventing boredom from erupting into brawls. Contests allow randy adolescents to show off to their prospective mates without killing each other and even shake up the weyr hierarchy a bit, which, as good ole Thomas Jefferson suggested to James Madison, can be a good thing now and then.

Older Dragons also use the summer to travel, scratching their wanderlust itch alone or with a companion or two. Some, perhaps with an eye to scouting new weyr locations, will just free-fly for a couple of months. Nothing dispels draconic ennui like new vistas to explore, and, blessed with navigational skills that would put a fleet of GPSes to shame, they never need worry about getting lost. Dragons always know which way is home. Less adventurous Dragons might opt to sojourn among neighboring enchantments—an excellent way to keep the wider draconic network humming. Visits are also a fine way to make inroads should a Dragon want to court a mate outside of his or her weyr. It should be noted that more than two Dragons on such an excursion is virtually unheard of. Another weyr would read such a sight as an invasion and respond appropriately. Where Dragons are involved, misunderstandings are best avoided at all costs: a bloody battle is hardly the way to end one's summer vacation.

When the sultry Dragon days of August return, all the wandering Dragons find their way home. Like an ouroboros nibbling her tail, the seasons come full circle. The enchantments are stronger and wiser. They've known passion, worry, joy, and triumph. They've celebrated new life and, no doubt, mourned the death of old friends. Next year will be much the same, and that is as it should be.

For Dragons know the wild ways. It is simple. As Thoreau suggested we all do, Dragons...

> Live each season as it passes; breathe the air, drink the drink, taste the fruit, and resign [themselves] to the influences of each.
>
> (*The Journals of Henry David Thoreau*, Vol. 2, p. 394)

*p*art II

The Long & Winding Road:
Dragons' March
Through Millennia

Nature does nothing uselessly.

—Aristotle

four

Dragon Evolution: Which Came First, the Ouroboros or the Egg?

It is spring. Deep in the bowels of the Arctic, on a fire-warmed bed of pyrites and precious stones, a clutch of alabaster eggs lies coiled in the protective tail of a maternal Siberian Firn Dragon. She has tended them for over a year, adjusting their temperature with scale rustles and Dragon blasts, and been tended in her turn by solicitous enchantment mates. Now, in the radiant glow of the quartz-lined chamber, they all gather, waiting. In a manner determined by Dragons of ages past, the mother-to-be plucks a note out of the air and holds it close, letting it vibrate low in her belly. The others follow suit, folding layer upon layer harmonically round her primal note. At just the right moment, she takes her tone and spins it into song. Her kindred lend their voices to hers until the lair trembles with a rising *carmina Draconium* (Dragon song). It is an old song, one they learned long ago when they were still in the egg. It is the song that calls through shell and infant scales to rouse the heart of all Dragons, the birthing anthem that pulls them into the world.

But when was this song first sung?

We can only speculate. Certainly we know that it is essential to examine Dragons of the past in order to understand the Dragons of today—to trace that most ancient incantation as best we can. For before Dragons could even imagine entering our human world, they had to first come into their own. We must track their evolution through the eons, going back to the Original Dragon—or at least as close as we can get.

Unfortunately, sorting fact from fancy is the eternal bane of serious dracophiles. The ardent cryptoherpetologist is hampered in this endeavor by a patchy—at best—paleontological record and myths and faërie tales which only serve to muddy already turbulent scientific waters. That said, there is much we know—and even more we can extrapolate—from modern Dragons and their more mundane kin.

At the heart of Dragon Studies is the desire to place our friends well within the larger cosmological picture. We're talking gods and monsters and the swirly bouillabaisse of primordial life. The rigorous efforts to bring a modicum of rational order to centuries of scientific chaos.

For somewhere in all that chaos, the first Dragon was born.

Dragon Footprints in Ancient Sands

There is a saying: Humans are new, Dragons are old. This is no draconic braggadocio replete with incised grins concealed behind folded wings. This is fact. Discovering precisely how old Dragons are is another matter entirely.

When it comes to ancient creatures, science has relied upon fossils and carbon dating to fashion at least an approximate evolutionary timeline. Until the nineteenth century, people believed they could do this with Dragons, too, particularly in the East.

During the early years of the Common Era, great caches of fossilized bones were discovered in central China's Sichuan Province. Long familiar with Dragons, scholars and peasants alike hailed these finds as rare and potent Dragon remains.[1] Pulverized for medicines and elixirs, they were touted across the known world as *the* panacea for everything from infertility to mortality. It was a logical conclusion at the time, one which devolved over the centuries into an annoyingly persistent muddle for cryptozoologists and mainstream paleontologists alike.

Everything changed during the nineteenth century. It was the dawn of the Modern Age. Charles Darwin and other naturalists were turning notions of natural history upside down and inside out. The demands of the Industrial Revolution, while taking an ecological toll on the planet, also led to the unearthing of fossil troves all over the globe. In this topsy-turvy environment, presumed Dragon/dinosaur connections fell under renewed scientific scrutiny. Many European scientists opted for an either/or scenario, gleefully discarding millennia of Dragon lore and history in favor of the new and improved "Terrible Lizards." It was clean, it was simple. These primordial saurian revenants were not burdened by the mythical and religious baggage thrust upon Dragons like an unwanted birthright. As the ramifications of the ever-expanding industrial/urban world—not to mention the increasing human capacity for mass destruction—drove diminished populations of wild Dragons farther from populated regions, the dinosaurs' ascendance in the human imagination was practically effortless. Dragon sightings became nigh on nonexistent, recounted in hushed tones and never in unfamiliar company. By the 1870s, save in the eyes, minds, and hearts of a few die-hard dracophiles, Dragons were all but relegated to the misty realms of legend and faërie tale.

It's been a long way back.

For better or worse—and there are arguments on both sides of the aisle—the popular cause of Dragons was hardly helped by the lack of even one definitive Dragon fossil find. No one could erect an ancient Dragon skeleton, jaws agape and boney wings unfurled, in the

---

1. The Tyrannosaurs and broad-headed Ceratopsid, cousin of the Triceratops, caused the greatest confusion. Big teeth and big heads naturally fit the classical notion of Dragon.

entryway of the Field Museum and say, "Yes! This is the being who pulled Medea's chariot through the heavens and warded the sacred Druid springs."

What a glorious sight that would be!

Unfortunately, we must instead offer up regret and ask, "Where have all the fossils gone?" The answers lie in legend and with anyone who has had the mournful misfortune to witness the death of one of these remarkable creatures.

Through the ages, signs have consistently led to the chemicals in draconic bodily fluids as the cause of the paucity of petrified remains.[2] Though the precise chemistry is still under debate, the most common theory goes like this: A Dragon's system produces extremely powerful vitriol—or sulfuric acid—as a byproduct of flight and fire breathing. Corrosive in and of itself,[3] it becomes even more so when combined with the salt, water, and other elements in a Dragon's blood. Elements which, given size and metabolism, are both more varied and more concentrated in Dragons than in any other known life form. Calcium, potassium, chlorine, magnesium, sulfur, and phosphorus, not to mention a broad spectrum of metals, are all in the mix. Add to this the extreme oxygenation of their blood resulting from flight and fight, and a host of volatile chemical reactions are just waiting to happen.[4] Thus, with a Dragon's demise—particularly

---

2. Gleefully embracing the absence of Dragon fossils is a vocal anti-Dragon minority in the scientific community. They see this as proof positive that Dragons are far younger than they would like us to believe, certainly younger than our most ancient human ancestors. Some would even like people to believe that Dragons are relatively modern beings emerging only within the last ten thousand years. This attitude is generally viewed as naive at best, speciesism at worst, neither of which has any place in rational scientific discourse.

3. Since Jabir ibn Hayyan in the eighth century, alchemists have used H_2SO_4 in their quest for the Philosopher's Stone. The presumed purity of Dragon vitriol put them atop these philosopher-scientists' most wanted creatures list.

4. Many cryptoherpetologists believe perchloric acid ($HClO_4$) to be one of the most likely compounds formed. It is extremely corrosive, and organic materials have a tendency to burst into flames when their paths cross. If the academics are right, it would make for a remarkable parting display.

a violent and bloody one—the fluids spewing forth decompose the body so quickly that little, if anything, remains to cart back to the castle as a trophy, let alone to fossilize. It also explains the reports of serious reciprocal damage visited upon even the most proficient of dragon slayers.[5]

Metaphysicians and poets espouse a slightly different take on the matter yet arrive at essentially the same conclusion. They propose that Dragon blood is so linked to Dragon spirit that when the spirit departs the blood is literally transformed. In that last expiring breath, Dragon blood goes from life giving to life taking.

From either perspective, Dragon's blood is an evolutionary marvel when it comes to (posthumous) self-defense. That said, it gives the fossil hunters fits and makes draconic autopsies near impossible. As human interest in Dragons turns from eradication to conservation, their complex blood chemistry leaves a considerable hole in the essential annals of Dragon anatomical and cryptoveterinary knowledge. It is a hole cryptoherpetologists are fast trying to fill.[6]

It is worth noting that time and rapid decay have not obliterated all Dragon remains. Every now and then people stumble across a dropped tooth or swath of sloughed skin, often failing to recognize it for what it is. It is easier to imagine these finds as bits of some heretofore unknown dinosaur than as the rare remnants of an ancient Dragon. We should not be surprised by this. While the notion that Dragons are simply dinosaurs in Darwinian drag has fallen out of favor in all but the most rigid academic circles, the ever-changing picture of dinosaurs and their ways still keeps Dragons in the deep shade

---

5. Dragon Hill, in the UK, is a prime example of this extreme Dragon decomposition. It is said that Saint George slew his famous Dragon there, and that the creature's blood so corroded the hill that it remains barren to this day. (Of course, everyone knows George was a soldier from Cappadocia, Turkey, and probably never set foot in Britannia, much less killed one of her Dragons on a hill in Oxfordshire.)

6. It was hoped that MRIs would help replace this void with hard, scientific knowledge; unfortunately the high metal levels in draconic flesh and blood make this a pipedream at best.

of the dinosaur family tree.[7] This is not always a bad thing, as some advances in saurian paleontology have actually helped flesh out the suppositions swirling around primordial Dragons and the origin of the species.

For many years, cryptopaleontologists tended to fall into one of three theoretical camps when it came to Dragon origins. Each of these theories—Dragon Drift Theory, the Rise of the Feathered Serpents Theory, and the Glacial Egg Theory—is valid in its own way and deserves examination. There are natural patterns in the trio, logical evolutionary progressions and survival adaptations which would serve the First Dragons well regardless of the period in which they emerged. In fact, the similarities are so glaring that, today, the scientific community generally views the three theories as a continuum: a draconic lifeline with breaks and setbacks—such as mass extinctions—each demanding a new and varied start, each providing results both comparable and widely divergent.

Singular theory or unified, when it comes to the First Dragons we are still dealing with conjecture, deduction, and outright guesswork—educated to be sure, but guesswork nonetheless. We must use our common sense and the wisdom found buried in layer upon layer of Earth's most ancient history. Then we open our eyes and leap.

Dragon Drift Theory

Chronology being the great organizer, it is only reasonable to start in the most remote past with the Dragon Drift Theory (DDT). DDT holds that Dragons—or their very, very distant ancestors—are among the earliest complex life forms on Earth, emerging from the antediluvian ooze during the late Paleozoic Era. Sometime in the Permian Period (approximately 250 million years ago [MYA]), they shed their primitive marine forms, exchanged fins for feet, and hauled

---

7. For a long time, Dragons were believed to be a direct raptor/pteradon offshoot, a notion which today seems patently absurd. Dragons are no more raptors than humans are pygmy marmosets.

Theories of Dragon Evolution

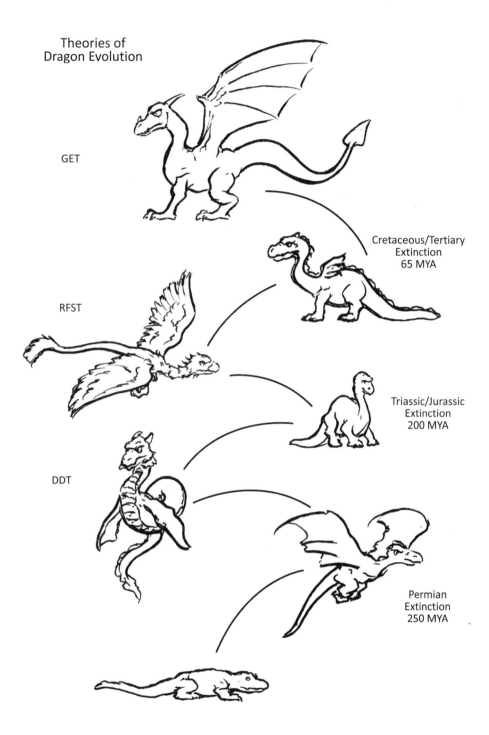

GET

Cretaceous/Tertiary
Extinction
65 MYA

RFST

Triassic/Jurassic
Extinction
200 MYA

DDT

Permian
Extinction
250 MYA

swim bladders from their fish days turned into fire sacs. Their diet also changed. Forced by the need for a more active metabolism, they began to eat insects as well as plants—the gargantuan bugs of the time made substantial meals, rich in vitamins and proteins. As the Dragons grew, small reptiles, fish, amphibians, sea bears, and the like would have been added to the menu.

The biggest evolutionary leap came in the form of the self-contained egg or amniote. Being able to lay their eggs on land freed DDT Dragons to wander as far from the seas as feet and wings could take them. In a geological heart beat, the Permian Migration was on.

It is important to understand something powerfully basic about Dragons: all Dragons and pseudo-dragons have a preternatural sensitivity to the planet. According to Dragon Drift Theory, this quality not only led them on their journey but also contributed to their evolution and survival. As elemental creatures, they tapped into the Earth and fed off her magnetic power grid.[9] One can reasonably hypothesize that the ley lines and their influences were proportionately more concentrated back in Pangaean days and would naturally have impacted the proto-Dragons to a degree we can only imagine. It is well within the realm of possibility that these planetary influences not only protected primitive Dragons from the extinction events that swept across both land and sea, but also aided early draconic evolution up to and including the development of wings. DDT suggests that the Permian Dragons let their instincts guide them along as they traversed the Pangaean landmass, the mandala-like energy lines serving as a map to future habitats and sanctuaries.

The planet's magnetic vitality likewise nurtured and strengthened the fledgling creatures. To this end, some of them grew heavy and sinuous, their body mass becoming too unwieldy for the densely forested and swampy land. Having no need for a strictly terrestrial existence, they slipped back into the sea. According to DDT, these

---

9. This is unlike any other creature before or since (with the possible exception of Unicorns). We humans have so much to learn.

elongated swimmers were the aquatic branch of the draconic family tree and, at least superficially, akin to the Eastern Dragons of today.

Beneath the waves they waited patiently until the land grew more forgiving. This took a long time. The great Permian Extinction decimated the Land Dragons, but made the Sea Dragons all the stronger and more resilient for the experience. Some cryptoherpetologists even believe that they were the direct forerunners of such notable Dragons as Raja Naga, the King of the Malay Sea Serpents, and Ryunjin, the Japanese Dragon God.[10] It is certain that their descendents ruled the oceans for millions of years and played major roles in the cosmologies and lives of coastal peoples around the world. When the time was right, their ancestors set claws again on land. And some of them stayed.

By the time Pangaea split and mammals ascended to global prominence, the ancient DDT Dragons were the among the prominent predators of the age. Though not numerous, by virtue of their size, cunning, and mobility, they ruled land, air, and sea.

The rest, as DDT advocates say, is prehistory.

The Rise of the Feathered Serpents Theory

Leap forward about 100 million years and you land gingerly on the cutting edge of the Rise of the Feathered Serpents. While agreeing that Dragons are ancient, the proponents of the Rise of the Feathered Serpents Theory (RFST) insist that the first Dragons on Earth did not appear until the approximately 100 MYA, during the early Cretaceous period. They thus avoided the cataclysmic Permian-Triassic Extinction which wiped out close to 90 percent of life on Earth (a good start by any reckoning) and the far less severe Triassic/Jurassic Extinction, which took a mere 50 percent of the emergent species. Even though some RFST proponents grant the feasibility of Dragon

---

10. Strictly speaking, this is an addled hodgepodge of fact and legend which only complicates an already obscure scenario.

Drift Theory, they insist that the great extinctions wiped out all the land Dragons, and so we must start from scratch.

Though cataclysms were in the past, Earth was still a rough place to live. The oxygen levels following the late Triassic Extinction fell off precipitously.[11] At the same time carbon dioxide was on the rise. A global greenhouse was in the making.

As Pangaea broke up, movement between the emerging continents became tricky. In the post-extinction world, the seas were one of the few places capable of sustaining large carnivorous life forms. Around every shore, the shallows were rife with ravenous Liopleurodon and Kronosaurs just waiting for an unsuspecting land rover to venture into briny channels.

Needless to say, diminutive, land-bound reptilians would not have travelled well under the circumstances.

What's a would-be Dragon to do?

Evolve, naturally, and take to the skies.

Let's take a step back. Unlike our friends in the Dragon Drift Theory, RFST proto-Dragons did not slog their way through a pseudo-amphibian inception. Rather, they were a distaff offshoot of the more upright and developed Thecodonts, evolving alongside the Archosaurs—or ruling lizards—of the era.

Small at first, these sharp-toothed omnivores were constantly scurrying away from the lumbering giants of the age. Over time, they grew and adapted to the changing landscape and hazards of Cretaceous life.

In this process, their bones became hollow, light, and strong. Their lungs developed into bellows-like organs to better oxygenate their blood. And, as the climate cooled, fine hair, then feathers

---

11. New evidence is suggesting that the low oxygen levels may well have contributed to the event.

covered their bodies for warmth. These feathers, layered over ultra-light bones, made flight not only possible, but natural.[12]

It was, however, their intelligence that gave them the edge they needed to survive.

It is believed that, pound for pound, the RFST proto-Dragons had the most highly developed brain of the age. Brawn went to the Sauropods, ferocity to the Theropods, armor and defense to the Cerapods. But smarts went to the Dragons. And it served them well. Recognizing that, when small, there is security in numbers, they formed tight family units to watch and ward. To survive the elements, they began to use burrows and caves for shelter, thus establishing what some cryptoherpetologists claim to be the first enchantments and, where the topography allowed, weyrs.

And, when the time was right, they went with the primordial flow and grew. A lot. Their necks became long and serpentine with flashy nape ruffs from crown to shoulder. Their bodies became well-muscled and svelte with long prehensile tails. As for their limbs, useful forelegs were as essential as wings, and strong, feathered hind legs were needed not only for flight stabilization but also for defense and den digging. These Feathered Dragons were monarchs of the skies. Faster and more agile than the giant, gliding Pteradons, they could hunt on the wing or wrap their tails around trees and dine on lush vegetation at their leisure. No ocean channel was too wide, no climate too inclement.

It is this versatility which made it possible for the Feathered Dragons to survive the Cretaceous-Tertiary Extinction and cross the evolutionary boundary into the Age of Mammals, continuing to grow, branch off, and evolve into the Dragons we know today. In that process, some shed their feathers for scales and some took to the seas, but all were magnificent.

---

12. A serious debate rages over the relationship—or lack thereof—between RFST newcomers and Microrapters/Archaeopteryx. Though arguments flourish on both sides, serious RFST devotees insist on only the most superficial of connections. One group became birds, after all, while the other, glorious Feathered Dragons.

The Glacial Egg Theory

The most contemporary of Dragon genesis theories involves another quantum leap onto the very threshold of modern times.

After the mass extinction at the onset of the Tertiary Period, all of Earth's large land animals faded from the scene. The asteroid-induced winter annihilated most of the plants upon which herbivores relied and, in turn, the scavengers and carnivores who relied upon the herbivores. Likewise, the loss of flora diminished the oxygen levels worldwide. On land, only small creatures could survive: early omnivorous mammals, primitive birds, and a very few reptiles and amphibians. It was time to start over again.

According to the Glacial Egg Theory (GET), it was out of this genetic ratatouille that a simple Dragonlike creature arose. Emerging from deep underground, like some hibernating Mongolian Death Worm, they set noses into the wind and tasted the air, strangers in a strange land. It was going to take all the tricks in their primordial arsenal to survive, to establish a foothold and conquer this new age.

Fifty million years later, during the Pleistocene Epoch, looking much like Dragons of today, they achieved their goal.[13]

These remarkable beings originally played in the shadow of the Megafauna: indricotheres and mammoth proboscidea, giant sloths and woolly rhinos, cave bears and dire wolves. They were muscular quadrupeds with strong reptilian aspects, omnivorous appetites, and rampant curiosity. Over time, small shoulder protuberances, or spurs, sprouted into wings, and their digestive system processed massive amounts of hydrogen for lift and fire. On wing and foot, they crossed the land bridges connecting East and West and partook in the Great American Interchange,[14] going from the Arctic to the tip of Patagonia. Endothermic and kleptothermic,[15] they were able to weather recurrent glaciations and adverse environments, their thick, layered

---

13. Thus proving that, even for Dragons, evolution is a slow process.

14. And similar continental migrations in the Old World.

15. Another advantage of enchantment living is having numerous bodies on hand to share heat in the most frigid of geological times.

scales adding enough insulation to let them live in the coldest ice cave or hottest desert. In the end, they covered the globe, cleaving to areas of intense electromagnetic energy and creature comforts sufficient for their evolution.

It is the GET Dragons who were coiled in the dark when shamans ventured deep into caves to leave pictorial invocations upon the walls. Their roars filled our distant ancestors with terror and awe. Their songs haunted Cro-Magnon dreams. Their descendents roamed through myths and legends from Lake Baikal to Tierra del Fuego.

Unity Theory

Sea Dragon and Land Dragon, feathered and scaled. Which came first, the ouroboros or the egg? We have three theories full of possibilities, ripe for merging into a truly Big Picture. The Unity Theory (UT) jumps at the opportunity to do just that.

Proponents of UT believe that Dragon genesis/evolution is a continuum, and that Dragons themselves are fiercely resilient. There is a fundamental thread of draconic DNA, nascent at times, struggling at others, which carries through despite mass extinctions, giant predators, and wayward asteroids. Even if there is only one strand of

Dragon DNA standing against all that potential death and destruction, it survives. It informs the next incarnation and, after the next grand extinction, it will still be there. Stronger, perhaps. A little more Dragonish.

UT posits that the glowing genetic memory of these proto-Dragons lingers, breaks through to the next age. Ultimately, around three million years ago, it branched off into the three True Dragon species we know today: the bewhiskered, serpentine Dragons of the Orient, the Feathered Dragons of Africa and South America, and the muscular, winged Dragons of Europe and North America.

This lattice of evolving DNA is a mirror of the Dragon's song. Like the more mundane humpback whale, Dragons spin their song, line upon line added and remembered over the eons. Fluid minor strains rise up from the sinuous Sea Dragons, refracted off wave and scale; light, avian trills come down from the aerie consciousness of the Feathered Dragons; and full-chested baritone laughs warm the caves of the familiar Western Dragons. The song is passed on and embellished, generation after generation. And so it will continue, with each enchantment's joyful incantation, each crack of Dragon shell, to the last syllable of recorded time.

So. Theories abound. Take your pick. And, no matter what, stand by it with the conviction of the best-educated guesser in the world.

Dragons expect from us nothing less.

What we call monsters can be seen as sublime.

—*Joseph Campbell,* The Power of Myth

five

First Encounters: Cosmic Dragons & the Origin of Our Species

In the Beginning there was Chaos. Out of Chaos, Dragons emerged to give shape and substance to the void. To create the Universe.

Or so it is said.

From time immemorial, Dragons have played decisive roles in cosmologies across six continents. They bound the world together with their scaly coils and drank the waters of the planet dry. They brought the rains, raised the mountains, and blocked out the sun.

They aided Creators, and were slain by Creators.

And they were themselves Creators.[1]

Tiamat, Aido Hwedo, Degei, Alklha, Vritra, Shen Lung, Quetzalcoatl, Ophion, the Fire Dragon ... such elaborate myths, every one—and totally logical given that Dragons are old and large and we are young and very small. But these tales are human, not draconic,

---

1. Dragons as Creators likewise bolster the veracity of a draconic manifestation in the world. For reason dictates that if God created people in His image, as Judeo-Christians and others hold, surely the Creator Dragons would have made Dragons in Their image. It keeps Them from being lonely.

illuminating the people who told them rather than the actual Dragons at their core. Still, they serve as steles of remembrance, marking the first Dragon/human encounters and laying the groundwork for how we of the world would ultimately treat our Dragons.

What sparked the veneration of Cosmic Dragons? Curiosity being hardwired somewhere deep in our DNA, we have a need to explain the inexplicable: birth, death, the sun, the moon, mountains, and seas. Or, as Douglas Adams put it, to answer "the Great Question of Life, the Universe, and Everything."[2]

Our early efforts at this monumental undertaking led us to look around and elevate the known to the unknowable. We stomped smooth the dancing ground of the gods, imbuing vast creative—and conversely, destructive—powers in heaven and earth, beasts, birds, and elementals with sacred worth. From whatever was at hand, we fashioned the gods who fashioned our world.

And who could possibly be more deserving of deification than a Dragon?

Of course, these are no ordinary Dragons—if there even is such a thing as an ordinary Dragon. They are larger, fiercer, wiser, more magical than their less-than-divine kin. Manifestations of strength, grace, courage, virtual immortality—all the attributes to which we aspire—they also juggle light and dark, good and evil, within themselves, in an almost human way. In culture after culture, the presence of Cosmic Dragons signifies those places in time and space where all our nascent fear, wonder, and desire run headlong into the transcendent forces of Nature. Wildness and Other, they speak to our need to revere something greater than ourselves.

Today, science provides many of the answers once relegated to the mystical. But the stories, the lure of genesis and our own "once upon a time" through which Cosmic Dragons fly, fascinate us still. They are the true testament of draconic perseverance.

---

2. Unlike the Magrathean computer, Deep Thought, 42 is not the answer we came up with. Yet.

Asian Dragons

Running the gamut from benevolent—if capricious—Creators to full-blown destructive forces, the Cosmic Dragons of Asia are as diverse and complex as the continent itself. Their heterogeneity has led many a cryptomythologist to view Asia as the draconic navel of the world, with Dragons and their tales flowing in and out over the millennia.

China

Though ancient people around the world knew Dragons intimately, some would argue that the Chinese knew them more intimately than most. It is certainly true that long before there was a Chinese nation, each tribe had its own tale of that first spark between Dragon and human. Later incorporated into Taoist and Buddhist cosmologies, some of the tales made the jump from provincial myth to more orthodox religious narratives, even spreading across China's borders into Southeast Asia, Korea, Japan, and beyond.

One such story is that of Pan Gu and the Cosmic Egg. It goes like this:

In the beginning there was Chaos. Out of Chaos came the Cosmic Egg in which Earth and heaven—yin and yang—comingled in balance. For eighteen thousand years, the egg nested in the void, all the while Pan Gu, the Creator, slept inside, growing. When at last he woke, he stretched and cleaved the shell in two, splitting yin from yang for all eternity. The light yang half of the egg floated up to form the heavens; the dark yin half settled below to form Earth. And in between, holding them apart, stood newly born Pan Gu. Some say he was a humanoid giant, all shaggy-haired and covered in skins. Others claim he wasn't human at all, but a great being with a Dragon's head and serpent's body.[3] Either way he was eager to make something out of the nothing around him, so Pan Gu took the next eighteen thousand years and tinkered with creation.

---

3. See Prof. David Chuenyan Lai, "The Dragon in China," Chinese Canadian Heritage Fund, http://www.cic.sfu.ca/cchf/ (accessed 2011).

According to some, he did not do this alone: The Divine Quartet—Lung Wang the Dragon, Qi-Lin the Unicorn, Gui Xian the Turtle, and Feng Huang the Phoenix—aided him in the endeavor.[4] Known as the Ssu-Ling, this original Fantastic Four were guardians of the cardinal directions, the seasons, and the five elements. Like Pan Gu himself, each of these auspicious creatures held within them a union of yin and yang. Of the four, the Dragon was the most exalted. Embodiment of positive, active yang energy, he was the guardian of the east, where the day begins, and of spring, when life begins.

When Pan Gu died, his body discorporated: his eyes became the sun and moon and his beard became the stars; the wind whistled from his final breath and his body became mountains and fertile plains. From his blood flowed rivers, from his sweat poured the rains. And the fleas on his fur became the fish and animals of Earth, from the tiniest mudskipper to the largest pachyderm.[5]

With the Creator gone, the sacred four became even more important to the continuation of life, the universe, and everything. Each was a pillar supporting their piece—their essential element—of the world mandala: Dragon, wood; Phoenix, fire; Unicorn, metal; and Turtle, water. Some insist there was a fifth guardian beast, the Yellow Dragon, at the navel of the world holding all together. Is it possible the Yellow Dragon—the fifth element—was a manifestation of Pan Gu himself?[6]

---

4. Busy though he was, eighteen thousand years is a long time to go with no one to talk to, even for a god. Though some modern populists have put a White Tiger in the Unicorn's stead, displacing Qi-Lin is cosmically ill-advised.

5. Millions of years later, two other draconic creators arose. Nuwa and Fuxi were the first woman and first man, but they were so much more. They were demiurges, half human and half Serpent/Dragon. And when they mated, their children were the first people, strong and draconic, who went out across the land and populated Earth. Thus Dragons created not only Earth but all upon her, including human beings.

6. The syncretic tendencies of the world place Pan Gu's four aides in consort with Ezekiel's four sacred creatures: lion, eagle, bull, and man. They were later associated with the apostles Matthew, Mark, Luke, and John, messengers of Christ. In *The Power of Myth*, Joseph Campbell speaks of the four apostles as the four directions of the compass with Christ at the centre, a fifth element, just like Pan Gu.

Each of the four blessed beings staked out his/her protectorate on the planet. The Unicorn ran off to the forest and its furry denizens, the Phoenix took to the skies filled with feathered kin, and the Turtle crept into the muddy marshes. The Dragon, favorite of Pan Gu, dove into the waters—blood and sweat of the Creator, and claimed them as his province.

As any agrarian people know—and as far too many modern people have forgotten—water is the life's blood of creation.[7] Without it, crops wither and people and animals die. Whole civilizations have crumbled for want of sufficient rain. It was only fitting that these people worship Dragons, just and fair and wise, when it came to all things water.

One particular legend tells of an ancient battle of wills between four Dragons and the Jade Emperor. Once upon a distant time, there were no rivers or lakes, only one great sea beneath the rising sun, and in the sea lived four extraordinary Dragons. Long Dragon, Yellow Dragon, Black Dragon, and Pearl Dragon played in the water and frolicked in the clouds, paying little attention to the comings and goings on Earth, for that was the province of the Jade Emperor and was—as he reminded them constantly—none of their business. One day, as they were playing tag among wispy layers of cirrostratus, Pearl Dragon pulled up short.

"Look," he said stretching his opalescent paw towards the land below. "Look at the fields, how brown and hard they are. I have never seen such a drought! Where is the rice? Where are the millet and beans? And look at the people gathering at the temple. Can you hear them?"

"Barely," said Black Dragon with his large ears. "They are so thin and weak, their voices hardly carry. But they are praying for rain, that much is sure."

Long Dragon had a soft spot for these humans; what he saw tore his heart. "Follow me," he said. "We will speak to the Jade Emperor for them. Entreat him to make the rains fall."

---

7. Our ancient ancestors clearly had a prescient understanding that life sprang from the seas.

They went deep into the clouds, to the palace of the Jade Emperor and laid the needs of the people before him. But the emperor's normally magnanimous self was under the spell of his new consort and though he promised to send rain then next day, it was more a dismissal of the Dragons than a ruler's pledge. As soon as the Dragons left the palace, his words vanished from his mind like so much morning fog. He only had thoughts of his lady.

Days went by and still there was no rain. The despair of the people grew so that it reached out into the ocean and touched the four Dragons deeply. Yellow Dragon suggested they go back to the Emperor, but Long Dragon would have none of it. "He did not listen the last time, what makes you think he'll listen now? No, we must take care of this ourselves. And quickly."

Then a burst of genius played across his eyes. "There is more than one way to make it rain," he beamed. "There is water in our sea. We can seed the clouds with our water, make them so heavy with it that they must pour it out upon the land!"

And so they did just as Long Dragon suggested, carrying great mouthfuls of seawater up to the sky. Then, with a flash from their tails, they cut the clouds with lightning and the rains streamed down to the ground below. The soil drank deeply, and the plants stood tall and green. Animals danced in puddles and the people sang with joyful thanks.

The emperor heard the song and turned livid. Who did the Dragons think they were? How dare they make rain without his permission? No one did that to him, not even the Dragons!

He ordered his warriors to arrest the Dragons and bring them to the palace. Loyal subjects of the Jade Emperor, the Dragons submitted without a fight, even when the emperor ordered them imprisoned beneath the largest mountains in the land.

"The emperor is not himself," Black Dragon opined.

"That may be," Long Dragon rumbled, "but if he can't keep the people safe and strong, then we must, no matter what." And in the shape-shifting way of their kind, the Dragons turned themselves into water and streamed forth from their rocky dungeons. The four great Dragons became the four Great Rivers of the land: Yangtze (Long), Huanghe (Yellow), Heilongjian (Black), and Zhujiang (Pearl).

The Dragons flowed back to the sea and, from that day on, they did their duty to the people, protecting them as only Dragons can, no matter how the Jade Emperor might rage.

However, not all the Cosmic Water Dragons were so benevolent. Long after the time of this heroic tetrad, when Pan Gu was all but a fading memory, the descendents of Long, Yellow, Black, and Pearl made a splash of their own. They were known as the four Dragon Kings: Ao Chin, Ao Kuang, Ao Ping, and Ao Shun. They lived in crystal palaces far beneath the ocean and ruled the rivers, rains, and bottomless depths, sans imperial interference.

In times of drought or treacherous seas, the people offered up prayers and oblations to the four Ao. If pleased, the Dragons would make the rains fall and calm the waves; the fields would flourish and fisherfolk thrive. If not, in due Dragon fashion, the four would raise tempests and tsunamis and dance on their tails so savagely that giant waterspouts would form round them, coursing through the land and leaving devastation in their wake. Like the water at their command, the Dragon Kings were fickle and would give or take as circumstances demanded.[8]

Japan

Water guardians are invaluable to the people of any island nation. Thus it is only proper that, from Hokkaido to Ryukyu-shoto, the ancient people of Japan knew in their souls that no sea-centric culture could survive without Dragon blessings.

Aside from being digit-challenged, the three-toed Ryu-jin (Dragon Spirits) of Nippon are very similar to the Cosmic Water Dragons who sported along the western shore of the Sea of Japan. This is to be expected: many of them migrated from the Asian mainland to the Japanese Archipelago thousands of years ago, tucked neatly into the tenets of Buddha and Laozi. Once there, they fell in with the other animistic spirits—or *kami*—of the islands and made themselves right at home.

The Cosmic Dragons of Japan break into two distinct groups. The inland needs for rain, clear lakes, and river runs are the purview of numerous fresh-water Dragon kami: the *tatsu*. Diligent but mercurial, the tatsu reside in spring and pool and lend ears to supplications from farmer and fisherman alike. But when it comes to the sea, a much more powerful class of Dragon rules. The tides must rise and fall with regularity, and storms and waves must be shaped with constraint. These are the tutelary duties of the royal Ryu-jin and his family. Living in a coral castle beneath the sea, with bales of turtles, jellyfish broods, and fevers of skates in attendance, they amass great

---

8. In his magnum opus, *The Golden Bough*, Sir James Frazer notes that, in 1888, there was a torrential downpour throughout Canton. The mandarins (bureaucrats) prayed to Lung-wong, the Dragon god of rains, to cease and desist, but he ignored them. So they locked him up for five days until he answered their entreaties. They would also, in times of drought, stake down the Dragon in the blazing sun until he conceded the need for showers. Interesting tales, though it's doubtful that any Dragon would allow him/herself to be so manhandled, even by mandarins.

stores of magical tide jewels and pearls of enlightenment, the perfect essence of the gods. Though not, strictly speaking, a Creator god, the Dragon King was the great-grandfather of the first Emperor of Japan.[9] Fishermen, divers, traders, and mariners all craved the boon of the Dragon King and feared the violent consequences of flood and typhoon should a battle arise between the Ryu-jin. Along every coastline temples, both Shinto and Buddhist, were erected in the Dragon King's name. Prayers were offered for bountiful catches and placid seas; festivals were held for inlet, shore, and tide, complete with rice dumplings, colourful kites, and rope Dragon effigies respectfully on display.[10]

Sumer

In the exploration of the vast panoply of Cosmic Dragons, travelling westward past China's setting sun is nothing short of stepping back to a more primitive and unruly time. Left behind is the elegant benevolence of the Far East in which Dragons held wisdom's pearls beneath their whiskered chins. The Cosmic Dragons of ancient Sumer and India are positively savage by comparison. They are chaos personified and chthonic to their core. That said, they are also beings outside the realm of oral narrative, their lives and deeds codified in the sacred texts of their people.

One of the greatest Creator Dragons ever known was Tiamat. She was the goddess of the oceans vast and wild, and comingling with her consort, Apsu, god of the freshwaters, made the heavens and the earth. They then brought forth a family of gods who named and refined the world.

> When in the height heaven was not named,
> And the earth beneath did not yet bear a name,
> And the primeval Apsu, who begat them,
> And chaos, Tiamut [*sic*], the mother of them both

9. See page 15.

10. Many of the traditions were adaptations from the Chinese Dragon celebrations, including fireworks and Dragon boat races.

Their waters were mingled together,
And no field was formed, no marsh was to be seen;
When of the gods none had been called into being,
And none bore a name, and no destinies were ordained;
Then were created the gods in the midst of heaven ...

("Enuma Elish: The First Tablet,"
The Seven Tablets of Creation)

Tiamat embodied creation in all its unbridled excess, and, as such, proved a problematic Cosmic Dragon. Her children and her children's children were a divine handful, and, as one might expect, there were cabals and battles, patricide and subsequent bloody revenge. In defense, she churned the seas into a flooding rage, giving birth to a new brood of Dragons ...

Sharp of tooth, and merciless of fang.
With poison instead of blood she hath filled their bodies.
Fierce monster-vipers she hath clothed with terror,
With splendour she hath decked them, she hath made
    them of lofty stature.
Whoever beholdeth them is overcome by terror,
Their bodies rear up and none can withstand their attack ...

(Ibid. "The Second Tablet")

It was up to Tiamat and these chthonic remnants of primordial Chaos to stand against the sky god Marduk and the rising forces of civilization, a scenario played out from India to Greece.[11] Unfortunately, the new world order had no place for them.[12]

---

11. See Chapter Six.

12. Some two thousand years after the Sumerians, Babylonian myth rewrote ancient history, claiming that it was actually Marduk who created heaven and earth, stars and rivers, from the dismembered body of the vanquished Tiamat. Try though they might to demote her cosmic importance, she remained a creative force even in death.

India

In Vedic India we find three-headed Vritra, a divine Chaos Dragon and, some would argue, a descendent of Tiamat; certainly a Dragon made in her wild mold. But where Tiamat was creative, Vritra was willfully destructive. A victim just waiting for a persecutor.

As is to be expected from a cosmological being, the details of his origins are murky at best. Some say he is older than the universe itself, a drought specialist, arising to give balance to Varuna, god of the Cosmic Sea. Others insist he was the first Dragon, son of Danu, goddess of the primordial waters, and of Tvastr, maker of men, animals, and divine weapons and guardian of *soma*, the intoxicant of the gods.[13]

Whatever his origins, Vritra threw his massive coils around the whole world and, in an early display of hoarding, greedily drank all the rivers dry.[14] With soma-induced Dutch courage and a thunderbolt crafted by Tvastr himself in hand,[15] Indra went forth to confront the great Dragon and return the waters to the world.

> I will declare the manly deeds of Indra, the first that he
> achieved, the Thunder-wielder.
> He slew the Dragon, then disclosed the waters, and cleft
> the channels of the mountain torrents.
> He slew the Dragon lying on the mountain: his heavenly
> bolt of thunder Tvastar [*sic*] fashioned.
> Like lowing kine in rapid flow descending the waters
> glided downward to the ocean ...
> (*Rig Veda*, "Hymn XXXII. Indra.")

And so the divine force of Indra thwarted a draconic power strong enough to destroy all mankind.

---

13. A later version of the tale states that when Indra, god of weather, killed his rival—and Tvastr's son—Trisiras, the heavenly builder fashioned Vritra as an instrument of his revenge. But that's a whole other story.

14. There are some who insist this was a perpetual conflict between Vritra and Indra, drought versus rain. Others say that it was a one-off climatic catastrophe.

15. Irony abounds in tales of Dragons and gods.

This is a precursor of the European evil dragon and heroic dragon slayer scenario. Given how well Indo-Aryan culture and language travelled, it is possible that Vritra's epic tale was a direct influence on later European attitudes towards Dragons.[16]

However, we would do well to remember that, in death, Vritra's release of the waters turned him from a destructive Dragon to a Creative Dragon, turning the world verdant and fruitful.

African and Austronesian Dragons

The deserts, jungles, and savannahs of Africa and Australia have known their share of cosmic beings, many of them lustrous Rainbow Serpents. Though not always active protogenic forces themselves, they were often invaluable right hands to the Creators, providing aid and even sacrifice for the sake of the burgeoning world.

Are the great Rainbow Serpents of the universe True Dragons? It is a good question, one worthy of a bevy of symposia at any cryptozoological conference. However, for the purposes of this study, let's put it this way: while perhaps not Dragons in a strict physiological sense, they are definitely Dragons in a metaphysical/cosmological sense. And that serves well enough.

Africa

Out of Africa two splendid Dragons came: Aido Hwedo and Minia. In the cosmology of the Fon people of Dahomey (present-day Benin), the great Rainbow Serpent Aido Hwedo was companion and aide to Mawu the Creator. In a manner reminiscent of a mother crocodile protecting her young, this great Cosmic Dragon held Mawu snug in

---

16. If the Kurgan model of Indo-European culture origins is accurate, many of the biases against Dragons in Europe and Western Asia may well have originated among the prehistoric people of the Ural steppes and been firmly fixed in our psyches long before any benevolent Chinese Dragons ventured westward along the Silk Road.

his mouth and transported her[17] across heaven and earth as she touched up creation. And when they stopped for the night, Aido Hwedo would hunker down, his sinuous bulk carving out valleys and river beds; in the morning, Mawu would turn the copious deposits of Dragon excrement into mountains, lush and fertile.

When Mawu felt she'd done enough tweaking, she stood back and admired the world. And it was good. But it was also heavy. Between mountains and forests and huge herds of animals, she feared the cumbrous weight of creation would make the whole thing implode. So she went to her draconic comrade and asked him for one last service:

---

17. Some insist Mawu and Aido Hwedo were both androgynous beings, combining male and female within them, not unlike Pan Gu's balanced combination of yin and yang. Given the Fon tradition of powerful females, the use of feminine pronouns here seems appropriate, but for clarity's sake we will split the difference and refer to Aido in the masculine.

would he wrap the world in his coils to keep it from falling apart?[18] Aido Hwedo assented and threw loop after scaly loop round the sphere of earth and sky, holding them together. And the power of the Dragon flowed through all creation.

In honor of the Dragon's cosmic gift—and in acknowledgment of the ease with which the sun burned his scales—Mawu placed the oceans about him to keep him cool and calm. Unfortunately there are still times when Aido gets heat-stressed and has to shift and shimmy to get comfortable, resulting in serious seismic disturbances. As for the Dragon's other needs, Mawu charged a tribe of monkeys with those ministrations. They tend him religiously, feeding him an exclusive diet of iron bars.[19] Recognizing the planet's limited resources, Mawu declared (with a farsightedness only gods and Dragons can claim) that when the iron runs out—and it will run out—Aido Hwedo will resort to eating his own tail. One after another, his coils will disappear until finally, in an apocalyptic end, the unsupported world will collapse in on itself. Fini!

Go north into the Saharan and Sahel dunes and you will find a Cosmic Dragon who gave her all that we might live. To paraphrase mythologist Joseph Campbell, in Goddess-centric societies, the world is the body of the Goddess. In the case of the Rainbow Serpent Minia, the world is the body of the Dragon. Literally.

Before the beginning, the legend goes, the Creator sat at the centre of the Universe surrounded by Chaos. Out of the swirling maelstrom, she pulled a thought, and the thought was Dragon. Minia, the Cosmic Dragon, grew and grew until her head was in the heavens and her tail buried deep beneath the waters under the surface. For eon after eon, Minia and the Creator kept each other company; together they were sufficient. Then, as is wont to happen in exclusive

---

18. It has been suggested that this was more of a command than a request, though the thought of commanding one's draconic colleague to commit to anything— let alone such an eternal sacrifice—seems uncivil at the very least.

19. Iron was once *the* resource of the region, though supplies have dwindled considerably since the apex of European colonialism.

relationships, there came a day when even a Dragon was not enough to keep divine loneliness at bay.

Minia then submitted herself to the Creator, who split her Dragon body into seven pieces. Out of the pieces, the Creator made Earth and all life upon it. Through the gift of herself, Minia achieved at-one-ment—the ultimate at-one-ment—with Earth and all creation. There is Dragon in the soil beneath our feet and in the waters that turn the soil to mud—in the grass and trees and streams feeding the oceans. There is Dragon in the smallest insect and the largest leviathan. There is Dragon in us all.

In *The Power of Myth*, Joseph Campbell wrote, "Somebody has to die in order for life to emerge." In this case, a whole world was born out of Minia's sacrifice.

Pacific Islands

Compared to their African cousins, the Rainbow Serpents of Austronesia are more Creators in their own right. Across the Indian Ocean, these cosmic ophidians are particularly prevalent as movers and shapers in the Dreamtime of indigenous Australian peoples. However, before we examine them, let's veer northeast some 2,000 miles as the Dragon flies and drop in at the islands of Fiji and a variegated Creator less familiar to the lay dracophile: Degei.

For thousands of years prior to their conversion to Christianity, the Fijians had an animistic pantheon, the Kalou-vu, the hierarchy of which Degei sat atop. It was a fitting position for her since she was Creator of All the World. A Cosmic Dragon so massive she filled the entire sky, Degei was also flexible enough to take up residence in a cave near the top of Mount Uluda on Viti Levu. Goddess of the firmament, she was generous enough to share the flight paths round the Koro Sea with the divine hawk Turukawa. One day, as she was flying high overhead, she noticed two eggs abandoned in the hawk's nest.[20] Fearing for their safety, she removed them to her cave. There she kept them warm and safe until they cracked open, hatching forth the first humans, a man

---

20. All Dragons have exceptional eyesight, but Cosmic Dragons even more so.

and a woman. Degei nurtured them and fed them on fruits and roots and taught them about fire, cooking, and language. And when they had grown, she sent them on their way to populate the islands.

It is said that many generations later, a hunting party shot a hawk out of the sky. The hawk was Turukawa. Degei was so furious she lashed the seas into a frenzy, flooding the world; but in the end, out of affection for the first humans she fostered long ago, she could not bring herself to annihilate the people. So she retreated back to her cave on Mount Uluda, where she lives to this day. And it matters not that few Fijians believe in her anymore:[21] when thunder roars or the ground trembles, it is the unrest of Degei being felt across the land.

Australia

Though most Cosmic Dragons are considered relics of a bygone age untouched by the harsh glare of modern science and belief, the Rainbow Serpent from Oz remains very much a part of the twenty-first century.

Powerful, creative, and dangerous, this primordial Australian being emerged from the Altjeringa—the Dreamtime—tens of thousands of years ago. One of the most important totemic figures of the continent, she is known to different Aboriginal peoples by different names: Andrenjinyi, Takkan, Kurreah Wawi, Wogol, Kajura, and Numereji, to name but a few.[22] In petroglyphs and cave paintings—works already ancient when the pyramids were just a glimmer in a megalomaniacal pharaoh's eye—her invocative image adorns the landscape from Bamaga to Manjimup. They are stylized, aesthetic limnings, not naturalistic, made in celebration of the draconic power within rather than the physical structure without.

Though some believe the Rainbow Serpent is the terrestrial offspring of the great Stellar Serpent who streaks through the Milky

---

21. Flat-Earthers do not make the world any less round.

22. "Rainbow Serpent" was a generic appellation contrived by British anthropologist Alfred Radcliffe-Brown in the 1920s. "The Rainbow-Serpent Myth of Australia," *The Journal of the Royal Anthropological Institute of Great Britain and Ireland.*

Way,[23] her precise genesis remains a mystery. We do know that, at the beginning of the Creating, she ascended from beneath the ground, where she'd been sleeping in the cool and damp. As she climbed to the surface, she nosed masses of dirt into ridges, palisades, and plateaus, leaving them to bake hard in the sun. Then she set out on the First Walkabout, wandering across the land, graving out rills and billabongs along the Dreaming Tracks, her Lines of Creation. But it was early days in the Dreamtime, and there was no water to flow through her landscape. And without water, there could be no life. So she became the water (here's yet another draconic water deity). She conjured the winds and rains, called up the tidal bores and first waves, filling stream and pond and estuary with the most precious resource in the world. And when the sun returned, she glistened all red and blue and golden as a rainbow and took up residence in permanent pools and deep rivers.[24]

The Rainbow Serpent's powers are life-giving and regenerative; with the gift of water, she became the Mother of Life. She was the maker of human beings and the law of the land by which they live. Those who keep her laws she blesses with the aegis of her totem, sharing the wisdom of plants and animals and bestowing upon them healing and rainmaking abilities.[25] Those who break her laws she punishes with illness and calamity, washing them away in floods or even turning them to stone. And the Dreaming Tracks she left across the landscape are her gift of songlines, the essential network linking the people to one another through time both spiritual and mundane.

It is perhaps the eternal nature of time in the Dreamtime that keeps the Rainbow Serpent so much with us. With her guidance and care, the rivers continue to run. And the world and all her children—on two feet, four feet, or even no feet at all—survive.

---

23. Paleontologists and naturalists lean towards the secular notion that she was a quite ordinary reptilian from the age of the megafauna, c. 60,000 BCE. This parallels the Glacial Egg Theory of Dragon Evolution. See Chapter Four.

24. Droughts, extensive farming, and global warming have, through the years, made such refuges harder and harder to find.

25. There are stories that the non-human animals who followed her proscriptions were rewarded with human form.

European Dragons

Greece

The Cosmic Dragons of ancient Europe wear their Indo-Aryan lineage with the panache of divine plumage. This is perfectly understandable given the cultural migrations radiating out from the Kurgan civilizations of Central Asia. Like Tiamat and Vritra, these Dragons come from the deeply dark, chthonic side of the cosmological order. They are the chaotic, dangerous shapers, guardians, and destroyers of the world.

This is particularly true of the Dragons of ancient Greece.

Long before Zeus and his dysfunctional family set up shop atop Mount Olympus, even before paranoid Cronus and his Titanic kin played with the Universe, there was Ophion and Eurynome.

According to the Neolithic story of Pelasgian Creation, Eurynome was the primal Mother, born out of Chaos, and Creator of the heavens (Uranus) and Earth (Gaea).[26] Her first task was to separate the water from the sky, and when she did this, she was so pleased with herself that she started to dance. She whirled across the ocean so fast that a great wind grew in her wake. She threw her arms around the wind and molded it into Ophion, a magnificent Cosmic Dragon and premier creature on this new world. Some say he lusted after the Goddess, others that she was enamored of the wild Dragon; perhaps they both simply fell under a spell of mutual seduction. Whatever it was, Ophion held Eurynome in his scaly coils and they made love. Out of their union came the Universal Egg, and…

> At her bidding, Ophion coiled seven times about this egg,
> until it hatched and split in two. Out tumbled all things that
> exist, her children: sun, moon, planets, stars, the earth with
> its mountains and rivers, its trees, herbs, and living creatures.
> (Robert Graves, *The Greek Myths*, p. 27)

---

26. Later myths place her as the daughter of Oceanus or as one of Zeus's many concubines, neither of which makes any sense whatsoever. See Robert Graves, *The Greek Myths*.

Despite their differences, Eurynome took Ophion as her consort and together they scaled Mount Olympus to watch their offspring grow and prosper. Unfortunately for Ophion, he was a braggart of a Dragon and couldn't resist claiming all of creation was his doing. Aside from being bad science, this was unbelievably disrespectful of the Goddess. When Eurynome had had enough, she kicked her consort squarely in the jaw, knocking all his teeth out and sending him reeling down the mountain to dwell in a dark, dank chthonic cave far below. Yet Ophion's role in this creation was not over. Along the coast, his teeth fell to the ground and human beings sprouted up. They were the Pelasgians, seafarers, like the Dragon, and the first inhabitants of the Aegean world.

Though the fractious Titans and their children supplanted Eurynome in the more patriarchal Hellenic myths, the motif of Dragons' teeth as the genesis of humanity remained, cropping up most notably in the story of Cadmus and the founding of Thebes.

By Cadmus's time, Dragons in Greek ethos had been demoted from Creator status to that of demiurge guardians and reluctant seers.[27] During the Bronze Age, they became expendable, pawns in rivalries between the gods and the objects/obstacles of heroic quests. Hera, for example, employed the Dragon Ladon to help the Hesperides guard Gaea's wedding present of golden apples. Wise, loquacious, and ever-watchful, Ladon enjoyed his pastoral warding until Hercules came along and, in the penultimate of his Labors, killed him and stole the auric fruit.[28] This act of wanton treachery exacerbated the already

---

27. This was, some will say, as it should have been, since Dragons are watchers par excellence. One has only to look at the etymology of the word to trace the logic in this: *Dragon* → Greek *drakōn*, the seeing one/the Watcher → *derkomai*, to see clearly → Indo-European *derc*, eye. With such linguistic pedigree, it is little wonder that, beyond their cosmological standing, the Dragon's historical position amongst humankind has largely been one of guard, counsellor, and observer from the shadows.

28. Some accounts insist Ladon survived the whole misadventure, being merely lulled to sleep by the sweet singing of the Hesperides. Though Dragons are known music lovers, it strains credulity to believe the nymphs would betray their patron, Hera, and their draconic friend for the sake of a hunky man's passing favors.

fever-pitch animosity between Hercules and Hera and, no doubt, that between Zeus and Hera, too. But at least Ladon merited a name; so many accounts of his kin list them simply as anonymous creatures doing a deity's bidding. Ladon was also gifted with the power of human speech, a rare trait harkening back to Ophion's time and signifying the high esteem in which he was held.[29]

And there was Aeëtes, son of Helios and king of Colchis, who had a Dragon guard the tree on which hung the Golden Fleece—the self-same fleece Jason and the Argonauts were tasked with bringing to his uncle, Pelias.[30] Hercules was party to that adventure, too. Some say the Dragon was slain, others that Medea used her herbalist's wiles and knocked him out with a sleeping dram. The latter seems the more likely since Jason was under Hera's watchful eye and she had a soft spot in her heart for Dragons.

Then there was the Dragon that was sacred to Ares and guardian of the holy spring in Boeotia. This is the Dragon with whom Cadmus crossed paths and who served as the generative force in the history of Thebes. The story goes like this:

Cadmus was a seafaring Phoenician prince sent by his father, Agenor, to rescue his god-abducted sister, Europa.[31] He sailed out of the Levant, searching for years the isles of the Mediterranean and Aegean seas to no avail. At length, like every good hero of his day, he went to Delphi for a little oracular advice. "Follow a moon-marked cow across the land," the Pythia said, "and where she lies down, there you will found a great city." Not one to ignore divine counsel, he followed a cow, given to him by King Pelagon, out of Phocis into

---

29. By way of explanation, some accounts say that he was Gaea's offspring, or even Hera's. In an ironic example of Divine Darwinism, these notable Dragons were the children of the gods no less—and sometimes more—than the heroes who slew them.

30. Dragons seem to have been plentiful in Colchis, for Aeëtes had a bag full of Dragon teeth he tasked Jason with sowing.

31. It can be argued that this myth is but another explanation for the Indo-Aryan invasion of the Hellenic world, dressed up in Olympian finery rather than the more visceral trappings of Eurynome and Ophion's Universal Egg.

Boeotia. There, exhausted, his bovine guide at last lay down to rest. Now came the time to sacrifice the weary cow to his patron Athene. Cadmus sent his men to a spring for water. Of course, the spring they chose was Ares's spring, protected by Ares's Dragon.[32] The Dragon killed the men, and then Cadmus killed the Dragon. Save for a half-dead cow

and a very dead Dragon, Cadmus was alone in the wilderness—hardly any position to fulfill the prophecy to found a city. So Athene instructed him to plant the dead Dragon's teeth in a procreative act. Up sprang a race of violent warriors—fitting children of a war god's Dragon—who fought among themselves until only five remained (echoing the tale of Jason in Colchis). This handful of men, the *Sparti*, or sown-men, helped Cadmus build Thebes, their bloodlines animating the noble families of the city.

Thus the sacred Dragon went from being a Creator of the World to creator of a local tribe. Quite a comedown.

And Cadmus still had god problems! You do not go around dispatching divine Dragons with impunity, even if you have the protection of a goddess. Complicating the situation further was the fact that Ares and Athene were not on good terms.[33] Cadmus had denied Ares proper deference and insulted him, to boot. Penance was due.

For eight years, Cadmus served the god of war; at the end of his indenture, Ares presented him with his daughter Harmonia's hand in marriage. There would be peace between them.

But the other Olympians were not through with Cadmus. The rest of the hero's life was far from peaceful, and the consequences of killing the sacred Dragon plagued him into his old age. In the end, believing that the gods favored Dragons over men, he wished—perhaps rhetorically—for a draconic existence. Immediately he began to sprout scales, wings, and a tail. Harmonia, in despair, prayed to join her husband in his new life; her entreaty was answered and they lived out the rest of their lives in spiky-wiky splendor.

Ultimately, despite the petty games of one-upmanship between gods and demigods falling across broad draconic shoulders and on ground sodden with the blood of Dragon sacrifice, there is a symmetry to all this. The meager human transforms: through expiation and supplication, hero becomes Dragon, and Dragon becomes hero. In

---

33. Though both war deities, Ares was raw, passionate violence and Athene was cool reason and detached strategy: the primitive Pelasgian vs. the more civilized Hellenic.

the end, the seafaring descendent of Ophion returns to the perfection of his progenitor's form.

The Norse Lands

In lands of long nights and bitter snows, the Cosmic Dragons of Northern Europe, though cut from similar Indo-European cloth, are expectedly darker and more menacing than their Mediterranean counterparts. These creatures are fearsome, baneful forces, and, to many, they are the personification of all that is evil in the world. A quantum shift from the Dragons not too far to the south and east.

While there are many lesser Dragons in Norse, Teutonic, and Celtic mythology, Dragons who come from natural beginnings and meet natural ends, there are really only two great Cosmic Dragons: Miðgarðsormr and Niðhögger. Destroyers rather than Creators, both of these Dragons literally hold the end of the world in their teeth.

Miðgarðsormr was the child of Loki, the malicious trickster and thorn in the side of his fellow gods. So appalled was Odin by the sight of the newborn Dragon that he hurled him into the ocean flowing around Miðgard, the World of Men. There Miðgarðsormr grew and grew until, circling the entire world, he was able to grip his tail in his pearly whites. As long as he stayed that way, all was well; but where is the fun in that? According to the *Poetic Edda*, when Ragnarök (the Norse End of Days) comes and gods and men are in a battle for their very existence, all the evils of the earth will rise up. This includes the Miðgard Dragon, who lets loose his tail and hurls himself up out of the sea, his great maw open wide enough to engulf the heavens. Thor, protector of men, slays the Dragon, but dies himself from the creature's venom. The sky turns black, the stars snuff out, and the world sinks beneath the swirling waters taking the old gods and men with it. A dramatic finish, to be sure. Fortunately for all of us, as with the Maya and Vedic cycles of creation, this was but an end leading to a new beginning.

Niðhögger is a different, yet no less dangerous, sort of Dragon. His existence was intricately bound up in the roots of Yggdrasil, the World Tree. With its branches in the heavens and its roots in the nether regions, the Cosmic Ash Tree, quite simply, holds the entire Universe together. Locked in its tangle of roots, Niðhögger whiled away eternity. There he slept. Some. And bantered snarkily with the sky eagle.[34] Some. And dined on the blood and rent flesh of the dead. A lot. But mostly he gnawed on the One Tree. Day after day, his appetite for ash root threatened the existence of the Universe; if ever he gnawed it away, the tree would die and the Universe with it. Fortunately, the Norns (Norse embodiment of the Triple Goddess and weavers of the destiny of gods and men) held the draconic damage to a minimum. With sacred herbs and incantations, water from the Well of Urðr (Fate), and tender solicitude, they restored the tree and kept the Universe together. For a time. It is absurd to believe that the weight of creation, good and bad, does not, over time, have a deleterious effect upon the Universe. But the Norns did the best they could for as long as they could.

With the Twilight of the Gods, everything changed. All Hel (pun intended) broke loose, just as the Norns knew it would,[35] and no amount of magic or care could protect the World Tree from the ravages of the last battle raging about it. While there are no accounts of Niðhögger playing an aggressive role in the ensuing mayhem, he is a prominent member of the cleanup crew, soaring over the battlegrounds, his mouth dripping with the flesh and blood of the newly dead.

> From below the dragon / dark comes forth,
> Nithhogg [*sic*] flying / from Nithafjoll;
> The bodies of men on / his wings he bears,
> The serpent bright: ...
>   (*The Poetic Edda*, Vol. I. "Voluspo." Stanza LXVI)

---

34. They did this by way of a squirrelly go-between, Ratatöskr, who raced up and down the great tree.

35. Not that they could do anything about it: they could see but not touch, proving once again that foreknowledge is a bitch.

With the advent of Christianity in Norse culture, the old gods faded into the obscurity of faërie tales; yet Niðhögger retained his underworld command with only minor variations. No longer having to obsess over the destruction of the Universe, he was given the task of serving Lucifer in the lower depths, dispensing punishment to the wicked with tooth and claw. Thus, while his less celebrated kin were targeted as the epitome of evil, after all the blood and gore, this

Dragon of cosmic destruction was reborn in the post-Ragnarök world as an instrument of divine justice.

New World Dragons

In the New World, creation was one of those monumental events happening somewhere between earth and sky with a healthy dose of water thrown into the mix for good measure. What an auspicious environment for Dragons!

North America

And yet, among the peoples north of the thirtieth parallel,[36] Dragons were surprisingly rare participants. There were, of course, familiar players: Bear, Buffalo, Wolf, Raven. Totemic figures, one and all. Even trickster Coyote got his paws dirty in the shaping and populating of the world. But hardly a Dragon in the lot.[37] The exception to this rule—and there always is one—is the Cosmic Fire Dragon of the Huron and Iroquois.

Long ago, during the before-time, in a Universe of water and sky, there was a young woman named Aataentsic. So beautiful was she that the Sky God, Chief-of-All-the-Earth, desired her to be his and his alone. This was quite an honor, to be sure, but one not without its perils. The Sky God had a fierce temper when riled and a jealous streak a mile wide. And desiring was not the same as having: there were tests and trials first. Aataentsic submitted to them all, proving herself worthy to be a divine wife.

For a time they were content, Chief-of-All-the-Earth and his young bride. But the Universe was young and the Sky God was often called away to tend this worry or that. In his absence, Aataentsic spent hours in the company of the Fire Dragon, a spirited and

---

36. Further south we enter the realm of the Feathered Dragons, and that is a whole different nest of basilisks.

37. There are some transplants, such as Aido Hwedo, who made his way across the Atlantic with the slave trade, taking up residence in certain corners of the Caribbean.

genial being who lit up the skies like a comet with breath and wing. They were close, though only they knew exactly *how* close. When, in the fullness of the seasons, Aataentsic became pregnant, her husband opened his ears to the malicious gossip drifting through the heavens. Scandalous chatter filled the air, recounting Fire Dragon's visits and the laughter heard in the Sky God's longhouse when he was away. Chief-of-All-the-Earth fumed and fretted, unable to block the slander from his mind.[38] Day after day he fixed green eyes upon his wife as she sat very still, her belly growing, her gaze stretching across the galaxy as if waiting for her scaled companion to return. He believed Aataentsic had been unfaithful and was carrying Fire Dragon's children, and nothing she said to the contrary could disabuse him of this conviction. Unable to bear the sight of her any longer, he ripped a hole in the sky and hurled her through it.

Down and down Aataentsic fell, tumbling through the firmament. She was divine, and thus would continue her descent until someone or something stopped her. Two loons saw her plummeting towards them and were dismayed. They rose up, flying close together, and caught her on their downy backs, breaking her fall. But she was heavy with child and they could not manage on their own. They sent a call for help out across the water world. Big Turtle heard them and rose to the surface of the Cosmic Sea; the loons gratefully set Aataentsic on his back.

"It is not right for her to live upon my shell," Turtle said. "She needs land to live upon." One by one the animals dove beneath the waters, looking for earth. All failed, and some died. Finally, lowly Toad returned, half-dead but with a tiny bit of mud in his mouth. From that little bit of mud, Aataentsic formed the world.

With land beneath her feet, she gave birth to the twins she carried. One good, Tijus-kaha; one bad, Tawis-karong. Again, this was a case of life out of death, for Aataentsic's evil son refused to come into the world the normal way. Instead (in a decidedly *Alien*-esque moment), he broke forth from her side and killed her. All was not

---

38. Othello had nothing on this guy.

in vain: out of her body came all the plants of the earth, maize and gourds, herbs and trees. She enriched the Earth that her sons might prepare it for the humans who were to come. But that is another story.

Did Fire Dragon sire Aataentsic's children as Chief-of-All-the-Earth feared? Is there noble Dragon blood coursing through the veins of the world makers? It is quite possible. In a cosmic heartbeat, the Dragon went from attentive intimate to fair-weather friend, an act indicative of a guilty conscience and/or dread at what the Sky God might do to him.[39] A further clue as to the twins' paternity can be found in a variation on the tale in which the good twin is known as Se' sta or Man of Fire.[40]

It gives one pause.

Mesoamerica

In the chronicles of truly great Cosmic Dragons, the Sovereign Feathered Dragons of Mesoamerica are in a class by themselves. A major player in the worlds of Pre-Classical Olmec (c. 1500–400 BCE) on through to the Post-Classical Aztec (c. 1200–1500 CE), the Feathered Dragon is found in religion, art, architecture, and literature throughout the region. From the primordial Dragon Campacti out of whose body Earth was made, to the shape-shifter of latter-day civilization, Quetzalcoatl, Mesoamerican life is steeped in the lore of these cosmic beings. Yet, no people were so thoroughly touched by draconic divinity as the Maya.

Literally set in stone, as on the balustrades of the Castillo—or Creation Mountain—at Chich'en Itzá, Feathered Dragons were an integral part of Maya life from the first world cycle to the last. They were also honored in the sacred texts of the people, most notably the *Popol Vuh*, or "Book of Council," of the Quiche Maya of

---

39. Or of what he'd already done to him. Chief-of-All-the-Earth might well have chased the Fire Dragon to the far ends of the galaxy. Or worse.

40. Much as the draconic qualities of courage and loyalty and wisdom are valued in people, their source is frequently kept in the closet. Dragons deserve better.

Guatemala.[41] Spared the Church's flames of purgation, a farsighted cleric transcribed this elaborate creation story out of glyphs and into the Roman alphabet during the sixteenth century. However, it is only recently, with an improved understanding of Maya linguistics, that scholars have been able to do justice to the text.

Though his power and purpose evolved with each world's coming and going, as the *Popol Vuh* makes clear, the Feathered Dragon figures into the tale of creation—the very planting and binding of the World Tree—from the beginning.

> There is not yet one person, one animal, bird, fish, crab, tree, rock, hollow, canyon, meadow, forest. Only the sky alone is there ... Only the sea alone is pooled under all the sky ... Only the Maker, Modeler alone, Sovereign Plumed Serpent, the Bearers, Begetters are in the waters, a glittering light. They are there, they are enclosed in quetzal feathers, in blue-green.
>
> Thus the name, "Plumed Serpent." They are great knowers, great thinkers in their very being ...
>
> (*The Popol Vuh*, p. 64)

As the story goes, Heart of the Sky, a divine triad, reached out to Sovereign Plumed Serpent—aka Gucumatz—to talk about making the world.[42] They mulled the situation over and, when they came up with a plan, they spoke their thoughts and brought the world into being: land and water, plants and animals, all formed on the breath of their word.[43]

---

41. Until recently, the mysteries of Maya cosmology were locked inside the seemingly indecipherable hieroglyphics adorning temple and tomb. There was no Rosetta Stone for these New World civilizations, in no small part due to conquistadors and their priests invading their lands in the fifteenth and sixteenth centuries and destroying a treasure trove of histories and sacred texts in codices that went back hundreds of years.

42. Creation to the Maya was always a group activity.

43. A concept not dissimilar to John's take on creation as set down in John 1:1.

That this first attempt at creation did not turn out precisely as expected did not deter them. They simply kept the good, and tinkered with the not-so-good, again and again, until they got it—especially humans—right. And they did, more or less. In this near-perfect world, the World Tree took root, binding the Universe—celestial arch, middle world, and underworld—together, and serving as the path of communion between those worlds.[44]

The Feathered Dragon, his procreative labors complete, opted for a change of job description, transforming into the Vision Serpent perched atop the foliated tree. From there he brought civilization and agriculture to the people, was the custodian of the winds and rains, and even acted as the god of war as needed. When summoned by blood sacrifice, it was the Vision Serpent's job to serve as a conduit between the Otherworld and the middle world of the living,[45] more specifically, between the shaman/king and the gods. In the stylized representations[46] of these Dragons, they often appear with mouths open, conveying the gods and ancestors from the other worlds to our own.

The Maya were a diverse people, each localized kingdom giving the myth their individual spin. In the Yucatan, for example, Gucumatz is replaced by Lakin Chan or Itzamna. This grand Feathered Dragon is honored as the maker of mankind and all life on Earth. He was also the inventor of writing—a monumental achievement!—and guardian of books (naturally), herb-lore, and medicine. Among the Post-Classical Maya of Mexico, the Vision Serpent Kukulcan was a distant incarnation of the Plumed Serpent. So wise was Kukulcan, so lustrous in form and manner, that a cult sprouted up around him like

---

44. The similarities between the Maya World Tree and Yggdrasil are curious to say the least, though their respective Dragons' positions and purposes are much different. For all the violence and blood sacrifice in their culture, the Maya had a less grim relationship with their draconic cohorts than did the Norse.

45. Some postulate that the Maya Otherworld runs parallel to our own, much in the manner of the Australian Dreamtime. Syncretic trends are everywhere when it comes to Dragons!

46. Portrayed aesthetically, like the Rainbow Serpents from down under, they are in this way transported out of the natural realm and into the sacred.

July corn, a cult powerful enough to turn cross-cultural. The Plumed Serpent, as a representative of the divine state, made his way north into the world of the Aztec. There, easy as molting, he sloughed his name once more, transforming into Quetzalcoatl, Guardian of the East and the Morning Star. But the glory of the Maya was not to last. This was the final such metamorphosis the Sovereign Plumed Serpent would undergo.

Years later, in a tragic misunderstanding of draconic nature,[47] Montezuma mistook the pale and puny Hernán Cortés of Spain for the great Feathered Dragon reincarnated. This blunder doomed the Aztec people and cast the Mesoamerican Cosmic Dragons deep into the mythic mists.

---

47. No True Dragon, let alone one of divine lineage, would answer tribute with wholesale slaughter. It's just plain bad form.

The glory of great men should always be measured by the means they have used to acquire it.

—*François de La Rochefoucauld*

six

Taming the Chaotic, Suppressing the Wild

Dragons did their bit for creation, and they did it splendidly, with grand ego, howling abandon, wry panache, and no small measure of sacrifice. Earth was on her feet, plants and animals were thriving. And people!—people were able to move beyond mere survival into the diverse pleasures of living.

For all their work, one would imagine the Cosmic Dragons had earned laurels and lauds; good long respites, at the very least. Unfortunately that was not in their stars, not even the stars they themselves set afire.

Oh, they were good enough to be Creators, to draw substance from the Great Void and weave it into Life's tapestry, but there were limits. As we left our Neolithic struggles behind, the very Earth they made was crumbling under their paws. A cultural/spiritual paradigm shift was occurring from which Dragons would never fully recover. In the West, in order for humans to rise, Dragons had to fall.[1]

---

1. Topography and the ethnographic disposition of the Far East kept their Dragons safe from the anti-Dragon malignancy that took hold of the Middle East and Europe.

The hub of all this activity was Mesopotamia, around 3500 BCE. The descendants of Marduk had crossed the threshold of creation, carved high-society out of the Stone Age wilderness, and complex civilization—with all its associate baggage—was oozing outward from the Fertile Crescent. Matriarchies fell to patriarchies; hunter-gatherer cultures gave way to the urbanized city-states; and tribal anthropomorphic gods and their hero/kings trumped the Mother Goddess, animistic deities, and their shamans at every street corner and ziggurat.

The effect on our scaly friends was devastating. Once immortal lords of creation, they were now the monstrous and mortal beasts dying on the tip of spear and sword. In the span of a couple of centuries, our ancestors proceeded to expel Dragons from the glorious garden into a dark, inhospitable wasteland, and no one bothered to ask if this was a wise move.

This was the Fall in all its manifestations. And Dragons were one of its first victims.

The reverence they'd inspired and enjoyed was supplanted by fear and a human desire to conquer and rule not only them, but the very wildness they personified.[2] The Indo-Aryans were embracing a new model for living, one in which sage and shaman no longer reigned. Their new gods bestowed kingship upon the worthy, and to be worthy, you had to be a hero.[3] You had to impress, to win your right to the throne with daring feats and legendary labors. How better to do that, to prove one's bona fides with the new political/religious world order, than by taking on a Dragon, the epitome of Chaos? How else could there be safety and social concord? How else could human

---

2. As Miss Rose Sayer erroneously pontificated in *The African Queen*, "Nature, Mr. Allnut, is what we are put in this world to rise above." This notion has led us down a multitude of disastrous paths. We would be better served listening to Chief Seattle's admonition that saying goodbye to Nature is "the end of living and the beginning of survival."

3. And if you could claim a little divine sap coursing through your family tree, the job was practically yours for the taking.

beings—and their human-faced gods—achieve the global dominion they so vehemently craved?

This was quintessential *apres-les-Chute* (after the Fall) thinking. In Nature/Goddess-based religions, the Earth and all her flora and fauna—including Dragons—were, as children of the Divine, divinely perfect. They may have been fierce, even deadly, but they were as the Creators intended them to be. With the Western notion of the Fall, those selfsame feral qualities became the vile opposition to the new creator God. Nature was no longer a wild "manifestation of divinity" but savage, violent, and at her heart, corrupt.[4] Consequently, Dragons (cosmic and otherwise) = Nature = Corruption. True heroes fight Corruption on every front, from the Mother Goddess down through her most awesome offspring. And so, what started with divine being (Marduk) vs. divine being (Tiamat) soon spread through Marduk's semi-divine descendant, Gilgamesh,[5] to every Teoma, Ardeshir, and Rustam who came along thinking they could slay a fierce-but-no-longer-invincible Dragon and win fame, fortune, and sacred honor.[6] In the process, these individuals took the Dragon's divine status onto themselves, meaning Dragons were no longer supernal, just big, frightening, and—to the ignorant—sinister threats to the established order. The true nature and purpose of the Cosmic Dragons got lost in the human-centric civilized world.

An historic blunder in this transformative chapter of Dragon metaphysics was the death of Gandareva,[7] one of the last Cosmic Dragons of Sumer, at the hands of the region's quasi-divine champion, Keresaspa. Gandareva was gargantuan even by draconic standards,

---

4. Campbell and Moyers, *The Power of Myth*, 98–99.

5. The paragon of heroic kingship, one of Gilgamesh's claims to fame was killing the Dragon who'd taken up residence at the base of a tree sacred to the Goddess Inanna. Parallels to Niðhögger are unmistakable.

6. It can be argued that modern humans, as descendants of Marduk, have Dragon slaying in their blood. An anemic excuse for heinous behaviour.

7. Also known as Kundrav in the Zoroastrian *Avesta*. He was a multi-cultural Dragon.

stretching from the heights of the heavens to the bottom of the sea. He had a terrible reputation for tearing up the land and dining on people as his appetite dictated.[8] Surely a Dragon at the top of any slayer's list. At least, that was what Keresaspa thought. He was a hero in the making and destroying the "monster" would be a milestone on his hero's journey. It was not easy, though. Only after an epic set-to full of blood, blindness, even family abduction, did man prevail over beast. Yet in his rush to be judge and executioner, in his arrogant specie-sist assumption that he knew evil when he saw it, he slew a Dragon who, for all his seeming ill-manners, was essential to the security of the Cosmos. Gandareva was warding an even more dangerous Dragon who was set on destroying the entire Universe. The exact name of this creature is omitted from the records, though one can hazard a guess it is Azhi Dahaka, the ravening beast who breaks free to run amok at the end of the world.[9] Good intentions aside, through his ignorance of the Cosmic Dragon, the hero hastened the world's end.

As is often the case with Dragon/human interactions, by focusing on the short-term gains, even a hero as exalted as Keresaspa wound up totally missing the big picture.

The murder of Gandareva was but the first in series of dracocides committed by Keresaspa. When the Cosmic Dragons were gone he moved on to their more ordinary cousins. He travelled throughout the region, from Ur to Armenia, setting the standard for generations of latter-day knights by "saving" people from a multitude of evil Dragons.[10]

And make no mistake: *all* Dragons of the time and place—regardless of actual temper or form—were considered evil. But how were they—once so divine and glorious—recast in such a negative light?

---

8. It is a curious distinction between the species that a Dragon meeting his dietary requirements is considered a murderer but the same is not said of a human dining on animal flesh, let alone of the human who then goes out and kills the Dragon. He gets a crown or perhaps sainthood!

9. Shades of the Miðgard Dragon and Ragnarök.

10. It is likely that many of his victims were pseudo-dragons; as long as they were a large, scaly threat to the human population, they fit the heroic bill.

The answer lies with two radical revisions in human thought and culture: one deals with war, the other with sin.

In simpler, antediluvian times, when life was tenuous at best, humans reserved war for rare instances of ritual and/or revenge, giving it an almost religious significance.[11] It was limited in scope and cost and allowed various peoples to live side by side with reasonable equanimity.[11] In the Bronze Age, with the domestication of the horse and the fierce mobility that engendered,[12] socialized aggression became the norm, demanding acts of sanguinary mass obliteration. This is the model we hold to still, the one which drove ancient Dragons to the brink of extinction.

Such modern warfare was not a matter of self-defense but of predation. Neighboring peoples were there to be conquered, their lands, stores, and herds—or in the case of Dragons, their purported treasure hoards—seized as victors' spoils. As Jacob Bronowski put it, "Organized war is not human instinct. It is a highly planned and co-operative form of theft" (*Ascent of Man*, p. 88). But being a thief was not as noble as being a champion riding out against one's enemies. So we engaged in a form of archaic double-speak that would make George Orwell blush, setting up an "us vs. them" dichotomy which we, as a species, cling to fiercely to this day.

No doubt Dragons would have been content to stay on the sidelines, as they had for centuries, and watch us go at each other. Unfortunately, we would not let them. For what could be less "us" than Dragons? What more worthy of our hatred?

But otherness alone was not always enough. For a hero to go against a Dragon, he had to believe he had Go[o]d on his side. This was where sin and divine judgment came into the equation. To frame the new world order for posterity and personal rationalization, sharp

---

11. See Campbell, *Transformations of Myth Through Time*, "And We Washed Our Weapons in the Sea," 49–71.

12. In his battle with Gandareva, Keresaspa had fifteen horses killed beneath him before destroying the Dragon. Despite so great a loss, he would have been Dragon fodder in short order had he gone in on foot.

cultural distinctions had to be established between good and evil. In simple terms, those of one's own tribe were good. One's own warriors were all virtuous heroes, one's kings wise and just, and one's priests all personal emissaries of the gods. (And the gods made this very clear.) Conversely, the tribes across the river—especially tribes deserving of conquest—were evil: savage, ignorant, devious, and godless.

The fact is, if one believes in it and looks for it, evil can be found most anywhere. In such a judgmental atmosphere, enemies abounded on every side. This thrilled heroes and would-be heroes to no end. An adversary-rich environment meant a plenitude of opportunities to prove one's worth, to increase one's wealth, and to rise through the social ranks. If one believed these foes were all sinful, one's heroism became a sacred act. After all, this was the gods' work one was doing, crushing the sinful, the "heathen" others. They deserved subjugation.

Just like Nature. Just like Dragons.

Both fell outside the grace of the new gods and were fair game. This was particularly apparent in the rising monotheistic faiths of the region which, in a wholesale eviction, threw Dragons out of the divine class and into a "minions of the Devil" category. In this changing climate there was no room for the embracing of Dragons; God and God alone had a corner on the wondrous. Even the Dragon who for centuries had guarded the Trees of Life and Knowledge was suddenly replaced by angels with flaming swords, and he was transformed into a legless serpent—the subtle agent of evil, the tempter most vile who led humankind astray in the Garden of Eden.[13] The later Gnostic spin to the comings and goings in the Garden[14] is remarkably pro-Dragon, representing the Dragon/Serpent as—naturally—the "wisest of all creatures," who encourages Eve's appetite for knowledge

---

13. See Genesis, Chapter 3. As is true of many of the myths of the time, even Genesis is a garbled patchwork of fact and contemporary legend. In particular, the apple part was borrowed from Ladon's life with the Hesperides. Eden was far too warm for apple growing, as pre-Fall nudity attests.

14. See "On the Origin of the World," *The Nag Hammadi Library in English*, 118–120.

that she might become more perfect, more godlike. In this version, the Rulers of Darkness—not God—prohibited the fruitful dining out of jealousy, not wishing to share their semi-divine state with lowly humans. Unfortunately, the Gnostics were considered heretics in their time,[15] and though sympathetic to Dragons, they were struggling for their own lives and not in a position to help the draconic cause vis-à-vis the religious powers of the day.

Dragons were also disadvantaged by the rising notion that those who were ugly or beastly were essentially evil; those who were comely were undoubtedly good. Just gods would not have made the world any other way, as the pulchritude of the local heroes so clearly proved. With such a decidedly human aesthetic at play, Dragons were readily tossed into the "ugly" camp. Though this reinforced the good vs. evil theme of the day, it was myopic, to say the very least. Had anyone bothered to open their eyes and examine the perfection of True Dragons, they would have seen their beauty. They would have realized that "There is only one world, for all of us"—even Dragons—"to live and delight in" (Durell and Durell, introduction). But then that might have given them cause to re-evaluate their anti-Dragon crusade and the history of the past five thousand years might have been very different.

In this growing "monomaniac culture of conquest," (Bronowski, p. 86) time and distance from their divine ancestry forced the hero-kings to reluctantly shed mythic status for more mortal trappings. It also forced them to prey on less-than-mythic foes. Not that this slowed the bloodshed. *Power* and *combat* were the watchwords of the day, drawing battle lines between nations and tribes.

To many, Dragons were just another tribe, dangerous, true, but mortal and open to conquest. They were a rallying point for aggressions, particularly once a nation's human enemies had been brought to heel. And, when bronze gave way to iron, violence against Dragons turned increasingly bloody.

As prosaic predators vied for champion status, every Dragon they slew was more frightening, more unusual than the last, edging

---

15. Early Common Era (CE) for us, late in the game for Dragons.

Dragons as a species deep into symbolic territory.[16] The chronicles of these confrontations wound up being a regular potpourri of fact and fancy, celebrated in art and literature for the ages. This was often easier than one might imagine. Out of half-knowledge and convenience, the Dragon Tribe was a mish-mash of True Dragons and pseudo-dragons. Couple that with a victor's tendency to exaggerate and the fact few commoners had ever seen a Dragon up close,[17]and you wind up with Dragons with numerous heads, scorpion tails, and spiky hides. For a time, being multi-headed was all the rage: the more heads a Dragon had the more dangerous they were, and thus the more valiant the slayer who took them down.

One of the most unique Dragons of the age's latter days was Asdeev. He was a prodigious individual residing in a cave in the remote hills of eastern Persia. That is, until he fell victim to Rustam, warrior-noble from Zabulistan and hero without peer. How many lesser creatures he destroyed during his lifetime is anyone's guess. It is clear that Asdeev was the climax of his dragon-slaying career. Like his Hellenic counterpart, Hercules, Rustam was set a series of labors by which to prove himself worthy. Going up against Asdeev was one of these labors. The details of the encounter vary from tale to tale. Some say he was a talking Dragon, as versed in the *lingua franca* as in pyrotechnics; others that he was a sorcerer trapped in a spell. All accounts point to one fact: Asdeev was one of the rarest of the rare: a pure white Dragon.[18]

Why this extraordinary beauty was chosen for elimination is a mystery. If we look at history, chances are he'd crossed a local

---

16. Depending on one's personal take on the religion of the day, it can be argued that the battles with Cosmic Dragons were purely allegorical. There were no records, no photographs or film, of the encounters, so we must speculate.

17. And lived to tell the tale, as the lofty dragon slayers would have us believe.

18. This was not Rustam's first run-in with a fair-skinned creature. When he was a young child, he killed the crazed white elephant of King Manchehr with one blow from his grandfather's mace. Though a necessary act at the time, and one which catapulted the lad to court stardom, slaying such a blessed being might just as easily have angered the gods and brought him only shame and sorrow.

princeling who, in turn, used Rustam to settle the score. Also a mystery is why, if Asdeev could communicate, the outcome of their meeting was so bloody. It's not like Dragons hadn't been reasoned with before. Buddha was reported to have not only dialogued with a Dragon but converted him to the Eightfold Path! Of course, that was on the other side of the Hindu Kush, where Eastern influences prevailed. It may boil down to cultural expectations combined with Rustam's inherent temperament: he was a warrior, a man more brawn than brain. He also claimed a direct line from Keresaspa, suggesting that his adversarial relationship with Dragons was as much a matter of nature as nurture. In the end, his actions were dictated by his strengths and his fears, and a noble Dragon fell.

———⌣———

Where did this cultural evolution lead Dragons? Briefly put, nowhere good.

The actions of Keresaspa, Rustam, and their ilk sent Dragons into flight. By the eighth century BCE, many a Near Eastern enchantment that weathered the excesses of the heroes' campaigns chose the better part of valor and discreetly migrated to Europe and the Orient, areas which remained (for the time being) Dragon-friendly. There they joined with indigenous weyrs, the European émigrés living fairly uneventful lives for almost five hundred years. Though travelling slower than Dragon flight, Mesopotamian culture and attitudes did follow their retreat. The creature lore of the Minoan and pre-Hellenic Greece shows this clearly, with the tale of Echidna, Mother of All Monsters, mirroring Tiamat's saga in virtually all aspects save places and names.

Despite past run-ins with local gods and heroes, Dragons had reason to believe they would now find refuge in the northern Mediterranean world. The scantly populated, craggy environment from the Caucasus Mountains through the Oneians to the Dalmatian mountains and Apennines suited their existential needs to a T. And classical Greek thinking seemed far more welcoming than that of the Middle

East. Where the finer minds of the Levant turned from mythology to theology, Greek intellectuals chose a more philosophical route.[19] Their approach to the colourful—but antiquated—mythology of the region veered off the literal path towards poetic allegory. Academic circles embraced science and naturalism, the notion of intrinsic good ruled in place of Edenic original sin, and mathematicians from Pythagoras to Euclid recognized the very Golden Ratio which points so clearly to draconic perfection.[20]

While this could not stop impassioned anti-Dragon sentiment from sweeping through Europe, the increasingly humanistic tilt did, for a short time, slow it down. It was a new facet to the transforming Dragon/human relationships, heralding a revolution in how we look into Dragon eyes and what they mirror back. For where the Mesopotamians made Dragons mortal, the Greeks made them personal.

Leaving primitive ways behind and becoming more complicated—at least thinking of ourselves as more complicated—Hellenic perception of Dragons revealed our own growing spiritual and intellectual capacity. An understanding and acceptance of the tripartite soul Plato discussed in his *Republic* was central to these changes in the wind.

In his exegesis on the righteous individual and the ideal city-state, Plato proposed, among other things, that the human soul is made up of three parts: the appetitive, the rational, and the spirited. The appetitive soul is linked to our creature-comfort cravings and needs, both essential and excessive. The rational soul focuses on truth and philosophy; it is the reasoning and intellectual part of our being. And the spirited soul is our brawny interior muscle, the part of us that makes sure we keep our appetites in check and follow our reason

---

19. Thales and the Pre-Socratic philosophers of the sixth century BCE viewed archaic pantheistic cosmologies as naive at best. That said, such high-brow views did not stop people from traipsing to Delphi for oracular advice or offering orisons and sacrifices at temple and shrine.

20. See Chapter One.

to honor.[21] If you transfer this from the soul to the psyche, you land in quasi-Freudian territory talking about the id, ego, and super ego. This was the template now imposed upon Dragons and used to justify our treatment of them.

In certain ways, we were making progress.[22] Science, natural history, and rational thought were beginning to triumph over superstition. This allowed Dragons to be viewed less as evil incarnate and more as the physical manifestation of the id (appetitive soul) run amok. True, such excess cast them in an ethically questionable light, but it did not carry the theological millstone of the Mesopotamian dualism.

By adopting a more intricate philosophical perspective, people were forced to look deep into the eyes of the Dragon—to see our hidden selves in their reflection. In keeping with the Platonic ideal, one's dominant nature—internal rather than social/class—would colour how one sees Dragons and what visions bounce back. The philosopher king might see the loyalty and wisdom of Ladon or Python; the warrior, the strength and ferocity of Ares's draconic familiars.

On the surface, this all seems to be reasonably advanced thinking, certainly evidence of our continuing maturity as a species. Unfortunately, the humanism of the central Mediterranean did not help Dragons as much as one might think. While Aristotle might look at a Dragon and appreciate his perfection of form and his essential place in the Universe, most people are not Aristotle.

Mammoth, elemental, unrestrained by convention or social mores,[23] totally eristic on bad days, Dragons were, to most, the manifestation of that bestial kernel every cultured human being carries

---

21. Plato went further, extrapolating that the aspects in our individual souls have counterparts within social structure of the ideal republic. Philosopher kings represented the rational soul; the military and law enforcement, the spirited; and the menial laborers and peasants, the appetitive.

22. Not that centuries of progress can't be wiped out in a moment, as the Christian persecution of Dragons and those who knew them attests. See Chapter Seven.

23. Aside from those within their own societal structures which, thanks to limited comprehension, would seem considerably unpolished to human eyes.

about but so very few acknowledge. Civilization may have begun to tame the natural chaos from which we were born, but what about the wildness in our own souls? How dare Dragons remind us of our atavistic pasts? Of the time when we huddled terrified against the dark, trembling at the vastness of the Universe? How dare they!

Evil or id, by whatever name, the fact remains that we are often far more threatened by the monster within than by the flesh-and-blood creature without. And, be it three millennia ago or yesterday, we are more willing to confront the Dragon, in all his lethal glory, than our own personal demons. That said, what follows is elementary: If we can control Dragons, we can control ourselves and beat back the howling night. We will be able to breathe easy in the conviction that we've finally risen above our animal passions, harnessed our savage appetites, tamed our id; the ego and super ego can relax in their supremacy.

By the time the Seleucid Empire capitulated to Rome in 188 BCE, we humans were patting ourselves on the back for the great strides we'd made in knowing ourselves and the world. Yet such strides came at the Dragons' expense, in the costly flow of Dragon blood.

Some might argue that it's the natural onus of symbology, pure and simple. To an extent, they would be right. Layer upon layer, we burden Dragons with more symbolism than any creature should have to bear. Time after time we ask—nay, *insist*—they hold all our fear and loathing, our wonder and desire. And even in such relatively enlightened times, we too often let our fear win out.

Fear makes us do unspeakable things.

For the symbols to take root and flourish there had to be sacrifice: blood to water civilization's soil. How else could the king absorb a Dragon's wisdom or the soldier, her valor? How else could we conquer our demons?

In the cultural hierarchy, Dragons were expendable. Was this an improvement over the indiscriminate slaughter they left behind in Mesopotamia? The point is moot. Either way, Dragons deserved better.

They deserved to be treated with less dread and more respect. To be seen through the prism of old shamanic awe as beings dangerous, yes, but glorious, too, just like the snow-swept mountains and the open seas. This was the beauty—the symbolism—our primitive ancestors saw in Dragons. The take-your-breath-away wowness.

But they couldn't go back. Neither could we.

Riding the increasingly bellicose tide of civilization, Homo sapiens staked their claim as the one and only alpha species in the world. To this end, we stole from Dragons their divinity and their ever-after immortality. Only by diminishing them might the mantle of superiority fall upon our scaleless, wingless, fangless, otherwise puny shoulders. With all-too-typical human parochialism, our actions drove Dragons into full-on survival mode. Fortunately, they're better at it than most.

Try though heroes and priests and philosophers might, Dragon wildness would not be suppressed.

We live, not as we wish to, but as we can.

—Menander

Jeven

Dragon Survival: Acts of God, Acts of Man

In the realm of natural as opposed to supernatural history, few creatures on Earth—humans included—are as adept at survival as Dragons. And almost none—humans included—have a need to be. Assailed on all sides by both nature and man, Dragons managed from the beginning by virtue of their physical prowess, intellectual adaptability, and sheer luck. Darwin would have been proud.[1]

Acts of God

It is a testament to their sturdy constitutions and elemental natures that Dragons have been able to weather climatic and geological forces longer and better than any other complex species. Whatever the planet threw their way, they not only persevered but came out the stronger for it. You might even say they had an "in" with Mother Nature.

---

1. If any species could prove Darwin's contention that, "those who learned to collaborate and improvise most effectively have prevailed," it's Dragons. (Attributed to Charles Darwin.)

When glacial epochs decimated lesser beings, Dragons simply hunkered down and endured. Dwelling deep underground, enchantments would huddle against the elements, their thick hides and internal "heaters" shielding them in their battle with the bitter cold. Many Dragons were also able to suss out geothermal pockets for that extra bit of comfort and protection. And, if things got tail-numbingly bad, they could slow their bodily functions to a crawl and hibernate until the world warmed up again.

Breadth and flexibility of diet have also been key to draconic survival. Being situational eaters, Dragons are able to travel as needs be, to dine on leaf and root when flesh is scarce, to forego foliage in desert or impenetrable snows and prey on whatever's at hand. Add to that unparalleled metabolic control, and Dragons can stretch the most paltry meal into a feast if circumstances so dictate.

When it comes to planetary upheavals, Dragons' finely honed instincts and sensitivities to land, air, and sea give them a preternatural heads-up about any approaching disaster. For humans in the know, this proved an invaluable early-warning system for unexpected "acts of God." Many a life was spared simply by being alert and able to read the behaviour of the local Dragons. Unfortunately the increasingly anti-Dragon attitudes polluting Common Era societies changed all that. One wonders how many more lives might have been saved had we not driven Dragons into hiding. Imagine the sight of the Campania enchantments departing the hills around Herculaneum and Pompeii days before Vesuvius erupted in 79 CE. Would the sixteen thousand citizens who perished have stayed at the heart of the impending doom had they been able to see Dragons fleeing, *en masse*, across the Sarnus Plain deep into craggy Apennine safety?[2]

Of course, it's not only volcanoes to which Dragons are attuned. They also act as barometers for earthquakes, tsunamis, floods, and

---

2. The naturalist Pliny the Elder, one of the few people of his generation who might have actually recognized and heeded Dragon warnings, was unfortunately so caught up in the possibility of observing Vesuvius going ballistic that he went right into death's path—a great loss for humans and Dragons everywhere.

most every sort of tempest imaginable. Their vivid displays could have spared the world so much pointless loss, if only we'd paid attention to them rather than trying to kill them. The death tally reaches easily into the millions. Even in parts of the world where Dragons receive traditional esteem, their influence has waned tragically over the years. Early weyr warnings went out before such natural disasters as the 1931 flooding of China's Huang He River and the 2004 tsunami that devastated the Indian Ocean nations, but the modern world failed to grasp their import.[3] We would do well to be more diligent in future. Messy though they might be, evacuations are much less painful than funerals.

Once Dragons pick up on adverse fluxes within the planet, they are uniquely equipped to take advantage of this knowledge. Capable of soaring into the upper troposphere and beyond, Dragons can, quite literally, rise above global cataclysms, experiencing most as temporary inconveniences at worst.[4] While blithely ignoring Dragon warnings, our fear-based need to lay blame for everything at someone's den-stoop was as prevalent then as it is today. This led our pre-scientific ancestors to assume that Dragons' survival of natural disasters obviously made them complicit in those disasters. Draconic indigestion caused volcanoes, their nightmare-tossed sleep made the earth quake, and their mercurial moods spurred every imaginable storm and its aftermath. While your rare Cosmic Dragons had influence over land and sea, it is pure pretzel logic to extend such powers to all.[5]

Of course, Homo sapiens have never been deterred by something as banal as twisted reasoning. We simply forge ahead, using it as yet

---

3. We seem more eager to spend fortunes on scientific gizmos than a little time learning the ways of Dragons.

4. Events occurring during nesting season produce the greatest difficulty for Dragons, particularly our feathered friends in Central and South America. Their size and integument leaves them more vulnerable than their Oriental and Occidental kin. Evidence of this is the April 1902 eruption of Gagxanul (Santa María) in the Guatemala highlands, which was particularly rough on the region's brooding Dragons; their numbers have only rebounded in the last thirty years.

5. See Chapter Five.

another justification for putting Dragons in the crosshairs and on the run. For though Dragons have seen the other side of fire, rain, and extinction-level events, the greatest threat to their survival is now and has always been Acts of Man.[6]

Acts of Man

Fear and inter-species misunderstandings have prompted various conflicts between people and Dragons since we were both sheltered in caves. That said, as a rule, the further back we go, the better was Dragons' standing in the world. Common hypotheses aside, this is not simply the result of increasingly lethal weaponry. In Paleo- and early Neolithic eras, the humans with authority were frequently tribal shamans. The moral and spiritual leaders of their clans, these people had personal relationships with all things mystical and rare and were wisely inclined to treat Dragons with respect. Attuned to the planet's ley lines, shamanic ritual spaces naturally intersected with draconic realms, especially the sacred caves in which holy men (and women) met elemental Dragons on their own terms. Those Dragons they did not deify, they saw as—to paraphrase poet Max Ehrmann—children of the Universe who had a right to be here. This went a long way towards the creation of at least temporarily amiable connections.[7] Unfortunately, such relationships did not last.

It should be noted that, left to their own devices, Dragons are basically nonaggressive towards people. Despite a well-oiled rumor mill spitting out misinformation to the contrary, "Live and let live!" are the words they thrive by. That said, they are the apex predators in their environment. In a pre-agrarian world, as people began to multiply, families grew into tribes and tribes into towns, and territorial disputes became inevitable. The Dragons were not wicked or

---

6. In this, Dragons are no different that the rest of us.

7. Cryptoherpetologists have speculated that Dragons were responsible for instructing early humans in the use of healing herbs and even with giving them fire. As Aristotle opined in *The Poetics*, "A likely impossibility is always preferable to an unconvincing possibility."

hostile; they were simply hunting the same herds and fishing the same streams.[8] Imagine the latter-day contention between American ranchers and wolves or Maasai herders and lions, then multiply it a hundred-fold with terror, ignorance, and our ancestors' abject urgency to survive. That was the situation facing Dragons. No shaman, no matter how silver-tongued, could hold back such a motivated—if rudely equipped—mob.

But the shamans could speak to the Dragons, apprise them of the growing discontent. And there was a lot of open land back in the day. Sadly, battles were not completely avoided and both sides took losses in the ensuing melees. Still, there was little taste for draconic retribution: most Dragons simply fell back to more remote terrain and lived.

This scenario was repeated numerous times over the years. Unfortunately, the definition of *remote* changed drastically as the human population started to explode. Land was appropriated for cities and fields, cattle, goats, sheep, etc., were domesticated. Turf wars between Dragons and humans escalated throughout the known world. In the human quest for global domination, these magnificent creatures were demoted to the status of pests to be exterminated or driven out.

Their numbers diminished. The Dragons retreated.

As discussed in Chapter Six, attitudes formulated during these territorial conflicts were augmented with deadly religious nuance as the human race marched towards the Common Era and the bloody Dragon Crusades. European Dragons and their struggles were a microcosm of the drama Dragons faced around the globe; different times and places, perhaps, but very similar stories. While Classicists treasure "the glory that was Greece and the grandeur that was Rome,"[9] for Dragons across the so-called civilized world it was little more than a segue from one dark age to another even darker. With empires grown about them and polarized monotheistic belief systems taking hold, survival-minded Mediterranean enchantments knew

---

8.   Given the millions of years' seniority they had on us, it would have been only
      fair to grant them deference. So much might have changed if we had.

9.   Edgar Allen Poe, "To Helen."

it was time to relocate. So, as Rome battered Carthage to a bloody pulp in the last Punic War (149–146 BCE), Dragons again took wing, heading north to Celtic lands.

Why Celtic lands?

For an answer to that question, we must again fall back on lore and speculation. There is a story of dubious origin about a sage and much-travelled Dragon from the Dardanelles, near ancient Troy (modern-day Turkey). All Dragons are farsighted, but this viridian beauty was more so than most. In 323 BCE—at the time of Alexander the Great's passing—she sensed grave danger stirring in the wind. She knew it was only a matter of time before Rome's adolescent martial ambitions would eclipse even Alexander's dreams, felling her kind as collateral damage. But that was not the worst she saw. The cults of the One God would soon drive out the many and irrevocably alter the rules for all Dragons in their purview. Hate would replace awe and, from wind-worn steppe to western sea, violence against her kind would rise on all sides.

Well, almost all.

This was where being a Dragon errant—though not a common life-style choice, especially among females—came in very handy. For this Dragon of the Dardanelles was not a provincial Dragon. Far from it. With all she'd witnessed in her wanderings, all the people she'd encountered, she believed down to the tip of her spiky tail that the Druids of the Keltoi were different from the rest. They'd lived with Dragons forever; they honored the old ways of wing and fire. And more than any other European people, they managed to see the visible and invisible as one. When, push came to gory shove, the northernmost Keltoi lands, inhospitable to thin-skinned, sun-loving Mediterraneans, could be a refuge of last resort. And so this scaled seer—who could have taught the Pythian oracles a thing or two—took up residence in a grotto on the deserted shores of Drakonisi (Dragon Island) in the Aegean Sea and waited. When the time was right, she emerged from her haunt and made the rounds of every weyr from Cappadocia to the Pillars of Hercules, telling each Dragon she met what she knew, urging them to go north.

Cryptoherpetologists refer to what followed from 147–50 BCE as the Celtic Exodus.

To fully grasp the importance of this migration, it is necessary to understand the position Dragons held among the ancient peoples of Northern Europe. This is not an easy task since there is virtually no written record, save that of a few Greek and Roman historians who definitely had their own agendas and were far from fair or balanced. As a rule of thumb, anything written before the sixth century CE about Dragons individually, Celts individually, or Dragons and Celts together (especially by the Romans) is a waste of parchment. As for the Celts themselves, unlike their Mediterranean counterparts, the learned people of the North wrote none of their teachings down as a matter of faith; such erudition was considered sacred and not for just anyone who happened to know his or her letters. While this did wonders for keeping a vigorous oral tradition alive, when it comes to their interaction with Dragons, we are better off looking to the art and tales of the time.

At the height of their influence, the Celts controlled lands from the Black Sea to the Atlantic and north to the British Isles. They were advanced farmers, traders, warriors, and, in the person of the Druids, mystics, artists, jurists, and philosophers. But long, long, long before the Celts, even before Neanderthal and Cro-Magnon eyed each other across Alpine chasms, the land belonged to the Dragons.[10]

Dragons knew Pict and barrow builder; they saw the rise of Stonehenge and danced along the Giant's Causeway.[11] When the Celts moved into the neighborhood, they found Dragons in the vicinity of every major power spot from La Mancha to the Isle of Wyre. This might have been a problem of apocalyptic proportions. The Indo-Aryan Iron Age battle ways of the Celts were a quantum leap ahead of the Neolithic people the Dragons were used to. Fortunately

---

10. As much as it could *belong* to anyone, that is.

11. Your more romantic dracophile might even insist they had a paw in the creation of both, though, as yet, there is no evidence on that score one way or the other.

for all concerned, these folks had more than forged blades and arrows—they had Druids.

Learned men and women, the Druids were the moral compass of the people. They were also blessed with the ability to converse with all manner of creature, including Dragons.[12] They looked into Dragon eyes and saw a part of the oneness of nature: as with tree and spring, deer and human, so too with Dragons. They recognized the Dragons were old before time with spirits "indwelling"[13] and immortal. Like the stones beneath their feet, they could roar with joy, speak, and sing. As keepers of their people's justice, faith, and wisdom, Druids formed an intimate bond with the Dragons of Prydain, Cymru, Brittany, and the outer isles, receiving both guidance and instruction from their long-lived associates. The Druids shared their knowledge with the people, and, in the process, Dragons became the most powerful creature in all Celtic lore. They represented the entirety of creation, from the rolling solidity of hill and mountain to the sinuous turn of river and stream.[14] To a people who honored the eternal unity of the universe, no being could be more magnificent.

These were the people who welcomed the Exodus with open, woad-painted arms. The oceans were full of fish, the forests full of elk and boar and wide-horned aurochs; there were resources enough

---

12. The Druids were believed by some to have brought the worship of Apollo with them from Greece, which would have given them a leg up when it came to Dragons anywhere thanks to Apollo's Pythian connections.

13. See Peter Berresford Ellis, *The Druids*, 157–246.

14. The tale of the Dragons of Dinas Emrys, though of post-Roman provenance, goes to the heart of this belief. King Vortigern, grandsire of Arthur, set about to build a great castle at Dinas Emrys, but the ground was so unstable he could not get its walls to stand. Merlin, still a beardless youth, was brought to the site and told the king the cause of his architectural misfortunes: Two Dragons, one red, one white, battled beneath the hill, sending fierce tremors through the land. Once freed, they took their battle to the skies, the red Dragon driving off the white. Merlin explained this was a portent of Vortigern's Celts besting the invading Saxons. The king was pleased, finished his castle without further incident, and adopted the red Dragon for his royal standard. Y Ddraig Goch is the emblem of Wales to this day.

for all and gratitude for assistance from any quarter. In short order, the newcomers made themselves as indispensable as the region's endemic Dragons. Without fanfare or fuss, they warded the sacred groves and lochs, oaks and wells, and portals to the Otherworld. In the mold of their Delphic kindred, they served as seers and teachers, bringing new plant lore and metallurgical expertise with them from the south. And, though neutral by preference, their long time observing our warring ways gave them much knowledge of military affairs, tactics, and strategy which they passed on when pressed. Though the times were hard and too often savage, Druid and Dragon tempered such lessons whenever possible, with liberal doses of ethics and justice in an effort to maintain a degree of civility in the world.

It is important to remember that, as integrated as Dragons became with Celtic life, they were rank amateurs at symbiotic living when compared to their Asian cousins. In Indonesia, for example, Barong and Bujanga not only protected the creatures of the forest but were brilliant at pest control and kept disease from the land. In China, the record of Dragons helping people is even more extensive. From Lei Chen-Tzu to Pai Lung and beyond, they were guardians, sages, and educators extraordinaire. Great Dragons all, with names and histories, they led the Chinese out of the semi-barbarism of the

Xia civilization (c. 2000 BCE), through the overtly moralistic time of Confucius and the late Zhou Dynasty, and into the glorious time of Laozi (c. 500 BCE).[15] They were instrumental in the development of art, literature, and medicine and were teachers by example in all manner of warcraft. Dragonfire taught metallurgists the finer points of tempering steel, Dragon teeth taught them how to keep weapons sharp, and the intense observation of Dragon scales even inspired the development of plated armour.

In the land of the Keltoi, the oral tradition of the Druids kept local Dragons anonymous, their contributions—especially in the areas of magic, astronomy, and even the bardic arts—going largely unsung. That said, they did not fly totally under the cultural radar. Though the common Celt may have been ignorant of the intricacies of draconic wisdom, they were certainly familiar with the natural fact of Dragons. Winged and fire-breathing, they were respected as Earth's untamable strength incarnate. Chieftains etched Dragons on shield and sword and inked them on their bodies. With such protection, they were invincible. The skies were kaleidoscopic with Dragon flight and everyone felt safe.

For a time.

In 55 BCE, Roman legions swept north on Caesar's ambition, targeting the Celts and all who stood with them, including Dragons. This first wave of what cryptoherpetologists refer to as the European Dragon Crusades was inspired (as were most Roman expeditions) by greed, lust for power, and vengeance for injuries real or imagined. The instinctive reaction of the northern enchantments was to take a step or two back and let the humans hash out their differences. Their pasts had shown them that, given their long life spans, intelligence, and cunning, they could keep low profiles during our intra-species hostilities and likely outlive whatever human unpleasantness was *en vogue*.

---

15. To this day, it is believed that no human had as draconic a world view as Laozi. Casting aside the conceited narrow-mindedness of his philosophical predecessors, Lao re-embraced that which was natural, i.e., Dragons: the embodiment of paradoxical Nature in all her chaos and harmony, power and stillness.

Unfortunately, the double-edged sword of draconic survival has always been their affinity for our kind. They'd built lives with the Celts and, though they refrained from actual battle on advice of Druid counsel, they held their ground at grove and spring. As nonaggressive as this posture was, it did not protect them from the advancing Romans.[16] To place a number on the Dragons lost during the Gallic/Britannic campaigns would be irresponsible history: we all know Dragons discorporate when they die. Nor are there records of how many people fell to fang and fire. It is certainly fair to assume that, though Celt and Dragon species survived the onslaught, losses were heavy on both sides.

It is also true that, as thick as the blood lay on Salisbury Plain, it was but a prelude of what was to come.

The Roman presence in Celtic territory continued to be a sporadic bane to Dragon, Druid, and ordinary villager for centuries. Every few years, the Latin hosts would return, collecting tributes and shoring up their garrisons. In 43 CE, with four legions at his back, Claudius finally succeeded where Caesar had failed, annexing Britannia from the Channel to Camulodunum (Colchester). A decade later, in a show of fear-base autocracy, Druidism was outlawed in the appropriated territories and its practitioners driven underground. Still, much of East Anglia, the Midlands, Wales, and all of Caledonia remained under tribal control. Plenty of room for Dragon and Druid—or so one would think. If only the Romans could have been content with their more-than-considerable holdings...but they were not. With each passing generation, the occupational forces increased in number, towns grew into Romanized cities, resources were sapped, and the old ways were lost along Roman roads from Dubrae to Vinovia.

The Celts were experiencing extreme hardships from exacted tributes both exorbitant and punitive.[17] Many a year, it was all they could do to keep life and limb together, even with help from the enchantments. The Roman occupation took its toll on the Dragons

---

16. In fact, aware of the value the tribes placed on their sacred sites, the invaders targeted them specifically as a means of inflicting grievous blows to Celtic morale.

17. This was particularly evident following the Iceni revolt lead by Boudicca in 60–61 CE.

as well. The desire for wealth, combined with persistent fictions about secreted stashes of gold and gems, led more than a few ambitious governors and foolish legionnaires to pursue Dragons when and where they could. They assaulted not only cave and den, but also the sacred sites Dragons shared with the Druids. This behaviour spread with devastating effect across all Celtic lands under the Roman eagle, plunging Dragons into a literal life-and-death struggle not of their choosing. To this day, in what remains of a *nemet* (sacred grove) outside of Locronan, Brittany, the echo of Roman atrocities can still be heard. During the Celtic month of Cutios, Time of the Winds, the boughs scream with the death throes of those ancient Dragons lost to alien greed and arrogance. Not a sound for the faint of heart, it serves as a timeless reminder: Never Again.

By the time Hadrian set the first stones in his Britannic wall (122 CE), hostility and loss of habitat had driven Dragons to the very verge of society. The actions of first-century Romans so grievously altered the nature of Dragon/human relationships that Dragons chose to take up residence on the hidden threshold between the material realm and the Otherworld. There they survived as best they could while, bit by bit, the stage was dressed for the "saintly" dragon slayers lurking just around the corner. It is encouraging to note that well-camouflaged Dragons—aided by likewise beleaguered Druid associates—were almost invisible to the ignorant or hostile. The art of hiding in plain sight is something Dragons share with Unicorns and other mystic creatures. Shamefully, we forced them to use this ability all too often during the next, more virulent phase of persecution. For, within a matter of a few generations, these magnificent beings, once seen as mere obstacles between Romans and their plunder, were re-imagined into the embodiment of Satan and servants of the coming Antichrist.

Not even the Druids could help Dragons out of this mess.

In the second to fourth centuries, the octopus arms of monotheism reached into Celtic lands via trade, conquest, and wandering evangelism. Yahweh, Isis, and Mithras all rolled out of the Middle East with varying effects. Ultimately, it was the dualism of

Christianity which not only travelled best but also had the most last-ing and, for Dragons, devastating effect.

In theory, the notion of the one God was not antithetical to Dru-idic beliefs, and the concept of resurrection fit them like a gauntlet: they witnessed it in the world around them every day. So it made a certain sense for the Druids to embrace the early Christians[18] and blend into their faith. But Dragons have no use of religion. They are all about nature and wildness and power, ethics, arts, and the mysti-cal. This new mania for building churches in Earth-blessed groves, alongside potent springs, only marginalized Dragons further. That the Druids would ever allow such things was beyond their comprehension

When Constantine embraced Christianity in 313 CE things only got worse. Church and state were one and there was no room for either Pagan or Dragon. Any previous *laissez-faire* attitude towards localized sects was abolished, and the notion that Dragons were demons straight from Hell was fine-tuned into the strictest article of faith. Horned and fire-breathing with leathery wings and spiky tails, they were the perfect models for Lucifer's minions. Add to such conspicuous physical attributes their association with the God-less Pagans, and they became the peerless targets of an increasing num-ber of fanatics. For centuries, little less than martyrdom got a person closer to being canonized than killing a Dragon.[19] From Saints Mar-garet and George in the third century to Saint Romain of Rouen in the seventh, the Catholic hagiographies are replete with bloody anti-Dragon—and anti-Pagan—deeds and propaganda.[20]

---

18. It is important to remember we're talking about the *early*, pre–Council-of-Nicaea Christians who were not yet bogged down by Church bureaucracy and, more importantly, still held to the tenets espoused in the Beatitudes.

19. Either True or pseudo, it seldom mattered, save to the Dragons in question.

20. In the litany of sainted dragon slayers, the most famous are: Michael, George, Margaret, Clement, Samson, Romain of Rouen, Philip the Apostle, Keyne of Cornwall, and those known in Dragon Studies circles as the French Quintet: Martha, Florent, Cado, Maudet, and Pol. "Slay a Dragon for God" was, quite simply, the catch-phrase of the day.

That said, not all early Christians, particularly those with strong Celtic ties, were keen on Dragon slaying. Seventh-century saint Adomnán of Iona chronicled his cousin, St. Columba, using only his devout words to convince the Loch Ness wyrm to leave a swimmer uneaten. Further south, St. Carantoc, a sixth-century Cymric prince, was known to tame Dragons rather than kill them, much to the local royalty's chagrin. And, in the tradition of Androcles, Carantoc's fellow countryman and contemporary, St. Petroc, Hermit of Bodmin Moor, treated a Dragon with a wood shard in his eye, to his everlasting appreciation. Their upbringing, rich in the ways of Dragon and

Druid, may well have inspired these three to deal with their ticklish interspecies troubles in relatively peaceful fashions.[21]

George of English fame, on the other hand, came from a Roman military background and so resorted to a military solution. It was what he knew. This leads one to believe that how we approach Dragons depends, in large part, upon how we approach the rest of the world. St. Francis, for example, would never walk up to a Dragon with sword in hand; far better a bushel of apples and a cask of pinot nero. Once again, Dragons teach us about ourselves even as we persecute them. But we digress.

With a largely illiterate populace, the Church relied on simple, familiar symbols to win converts and influence people. This was not the esoteric belief system of the Druids, reserved for the erudite few who studied for years before they could discern the subtle shades of the universe. The new religion was accessible to all. It was a dichromatic faith in which Dragons became emblematic of the Pagans and their pantheistic beliefs and, by extension, of all the evil in this world and the next. They were the reptiles Patricius supposedly drove out of Ireland (along with their Pagan cohorts). They were the Dragons who stared out from the illuminated pages of the Book of Kells and inspired writers from *Beowulf*'s scribes to J. R. R. Tolkien.[22] In short, for the past two thousand years, nothing has influenced the treatment of Western Dragons as much as the rise of Christianity and the fall of Paganism.

As with most things, the more powerful the empirical religion became, the more readily it was abused. Priest, bishop, and anointed warrior were not above using their faith as a smoke screen disguising what were little more than blatant land grabs from clan and weyr. The state Church was another wealth-hungry entity, and Dragons

---

21. Sadly, this does not explain St. Samson, a Welsh monk who slew a draconic creature tormenting the Isle of Dol. Reports are it was a "very venomous beast," which leads one to believe it was not a True Dragon at all but a hapless guivre with his back up against it.

22. Even the current spate of Dragon-friendly fantasy owes the Dragon's share of its underlying mythos to the dark times of the first millennium.

were targeted once more for their legendary hoards. Not that this was a cost-effective approach to filling royal coffers. For all the palaver about draconic riches in fact and fiction, there is little if any record of king, knight, or commoner—*anyone*—actually being enriched courtesy of a swiftly dispatched Dragon.[23] If there really were troves of gold, what happened to them? Logic dictates that the reports of draconic caches were exaggerations of the grossest kind. Unfortunately, like the lottery, not winning didn't keep people from playing—yet again, at the Dragons' expense.

In the tenth century, with the second millennium fast approaching, greed, fear, ignorance, and religious intolerance converged in a perfect storm of anti-Dragon zealotry. From egg to elder, it was open season on Dragons of every species, shape, and size. And, for the common masses, it was the heralding of the "end days" which proved the tipping point.

In the span of a few hundred years, thanks to the cunning words of monk and saint, Dragons had gone from being the dark guardians of Hell (the Otherworld) to the eternal minions of the coming Antichrist.[24] This might seem like a subtle distinction, and in the grand draconic scheme of things, it is. But while many concede there is darkness in the world as a matter of course,[25] to willfully serve an eschatological force is a different matter entirely. It is easy to see how apocryphal tales about the approaching end of days stoked the fears of the struggling poor beyond reason. To them, the Antichrist and his creatures were very real beings bringing very real torment. While this point of view is largely at odds with modern belief, back then it took

---

23. There is some contention on this score when it comes to the Merovingian dynasty of Gaul. Though their great plunder was recorded as the spoils of battle, speculation has run to Dragon gold as the source of their great wealth. This is in large part due to the extreme anti-Pagan/anti-Dragon religiosity of many of the Meroving monarchs, St. Guntram excepted.

24. The bestiaries of the day promoted this myth with the dove (Christ) having but one foe, the Dragon (Antichrist). There is little scientific truth here. A dove would make a poor mouthful for all but the smallest Dragon.

25. Even Dragons would likely be in agreement on this score.

only a little fine-tuning of Sabbath sermons and the "divine" law of the land to raise apocalyptic specters and make Dragons anathema to even their once-staunchest allies. Without friends, their choices in an increasingly hostile world became increasingly limited.

Dragons could either slip further into the mists or fight for their lives.

Most opted for the former course, notably a group of adventurous young Dragons from various weyrs around Northern Europe. Basically, sometime after the Saxon invasion of Britain in the fifth century, they decided they'd had enough and set off on an expedition to the New World. In Dragon Studies, this is known as the Trans-Atlantic Transmigration.

The rugged topography and temperate climate of the northern part of the New World was delightfully inviting to these exiles, and in a short time weyrs were established from Greenland south to what is now the Appalachians and west to the shores of Lake Superior. Cryptoarchaeological evidence shows that, in time, alliances were established and the indigenous Dragons—as well as the indigenous peoples—accepted the immigrants as an integral part of their world. One can imagine Leif Ericson spying an enchantment of Nordic Snow Dragons playing in the frosty shallows off Vinland. He and his crew, in their Dragon-prowed ship, must have felt right at home.

Some Dragons did fight: those caught with eggs about to hatch, or the righteous rogue who was tired of being pushed around. And a few even prevailed. For a time. But year after year, their position became less and less tenable. Extreme loss of habitat made them surly. And when the people thinned the forests of deer and boar and over-fished the lochs so that even kelpies had to labor through the winter, the most reluctant of Dragons came to embrace raiding domestic flocks and fields over starvation. As one would expect, this only made matters worse. Instances of lamb lifting, for example, were easily conflated into maiden kidnappings followed by *ad hominem* calumnies about wholesale terrorization of the shires. For Dragons who chose to hold their ground, their public images became so tarnished they were almost impossible to rehabilitate.

Aristophanes noted that, "The wise can often profit by the lessons of a foe," (Aristophanes, *The Birds*, Part 1) and Dragons have always—well, almost always—been wise. He went on to say that "caution is the mother of safety," and, in short order, the Dragons who made it through this turbulent time learned drastic caution. Weyrs were moved to more remote locations, far from the madding crowds and city knights; and when farm raids became necessary, hunting parties were strictly late-night affairs. For years, such survivalist behaviour gulled naturalists into believing Dragons were inherently nocturnal. In the best of all possible worlds, Dragons enjoy a romp in the sunshine as much as any of us.

Ultimately, the siege mentality we'd imposed upon Western Dragons was not sustainable. Though the new millennium brought neither a Dragon-mounted Antichrist nor the ensuing last days, it did mark the end of free-ranging Dragons throughout Europe. The Britain of Harold II—and, after the Norman Conquest, William I— was a Britain of few True Dragons and few Druidic Celts. [26] Both were in retreat, making their way as best they could in the distant parts of Wales, Scotland, Ireland, and the Isle of Man, the vestigial remnants of Brythonic and Gaelic lands. That no Dragons or weyrs were listed in the great survey of England, the Domesday Book (1086 CE), is indicative of just how far out of the mainstream they had been driven. Of course, some might argue that, since the purpose of the book was to ascertain the fiscal claims of the king, and since Dragons refuse the claim of any—even kings—there would have been no reason for Dragons to be included. They could have filled the skies like locusts[27] and still not been entered in the book. It is far more plausible that the *sidhe* and other ancient mystical folk, perhaps even a closeted Druid or two, joined forces to open the way for Dragons into the Otherworld.

---

26. A dearth of Dragons on the Bayeaux Tapestry depicting the 1066 ce Norman Conquest—save as minor border ornamentals—is a clear sign of their rare status in the natural world.

27. Which would have been a sight to see!

The fate of Continental Dragons was much the same, despite different players. As advanced and learned as they were, the Moors still drove the local Dragons out of Al-Andalus (Southern Iberia), first into the barren central plateau, and then across the Ebro River to the Pyrenees. The peoples of Central and Eastern Europe were involved in their own internecine struggles, leaving little to no room for Dragons in their worlds. The enchantments withdrew to Alpine heights and unpopulated woodlands, the better to survive the military turmoil around them. The Carpathian Mountains, largely unpopulated save for chamois, deer, bear, wolf, and lynx, were a veritable paradise for displaced Dragons looking to wait out the season of human discontent. That Vlad Dracul—Vlad the Dragon—and his son, Vlad "The Impaler" Țepeș, hailed from the region some four hundred years later is no small testament to Dragons' lasting impact on scarp and forest.

The Antichrist's no-show of 1000 CE was, for many, a letdown of cosmic proportions. For Dragons, it was reason to party like it was 999. They were, at least temporarily, off the hook. The Church fathers began to take a less literal view of the Book of Revelation, internalizing evil in such a way that most anyone—from pauper to prince— was quite capable of embodying attributes previously reserved for the harbinger of the Second Coming. In this climate, the figure of the Antichrist became increasingly political.[28] Secular wars and the Great Schism that divided the Eastern Orthodox and Roman Catholic Churches kicked up any number of candidates from the ranks of both profane and holy orders. Artistically speaking, the depictions of these potential fiends, draconic cohorts included, became more and more fanciful. Painters and illustrators were not above putting the face of some power-hungry despot or the local foe *du jour* on both Dragon and rider, not to mention giving the former unnatural forms with multiple heads, great protruding tusks, and seldom a wing in sight.

---

28. An attitude propagated in certain circles to this day.

Renaissance naturalism changed this, of course,[29] but until then, the absurdity of these images would have doubtless caused great relief around the weyrs. No rational individual could possibly mistake such blatant caricatures for the real thing; no educated individual could see the theological bane of Dragons as anything other than symbolic.

Lamentably, medieval Europe was not always rational and, aside from the clergy and a few aristocrats, far from educated. Add to that a dwindling number of people who could attest to firsthand Dragon experiences and you still had an extremely hostile environment..

---

29. While the Dragons portrayed by Carpaccio, da Vinci, and Raphael, to name a few, are certainly more realistic, they are also clearly pseudo-dragons, not True. Anyone with a proper familiarity with the species would know this.

As the centuries rolled by, True Dragons continued to lay low. The everyday world became the province of native pseudo-dragons: loch wyrms, marsh draks, wyverns, gargouilles, nikyrs, et al. Less well mannered than their True kin, they gave townspeople fits and Dragon hunters the excuse they needed to sharpen steel and venture forth to glory. This may have provided humans with a passing sense of security, but ultimately it's a little like nabbing a cartoon Nemo and calling him Moby-Dick. That said, in the world of Dragon Gestalt, what happens to the least of their kind happens to the greatest, for they are all children of the Cosmic Dragon. (Worth remembering, that.)

It is also worth remembering that, entering the twelfth and thirteenth centuries, the use of gunpowder took human violence to a whole new level of carnage, well beyond Iron Age basics of sword, bow, and spear. Not that the long bow wasn't as effective against Dragons as against the French at Agincourt. It gave slayers a safety of distance not to be underestimated, and an expert archer—someone on a par with the Earl of Huntingdon, say—could pierce the rare chink in draconic scales with a well aimed shaft. But Dragons had been evading archers since the days of Arjuna and the Indo-Aryan hordes. These new explosive armaments simply proved what most Dragons already knew: there are no bounds to the human capacity for useless slaughter.

While such brutal activity tormented the medieval enchantments of Europe and the Near East, Dragons in other parts of the world were, to the best of our knowledge, faring quite well. The Western Hemisphere was enjoying the heyday of the Feathered Dragons. In Africa, which had yet to feel the constraints of colonialism, the desert and jungle Dragons still roamed free. And the Dragons of the Far East were thriving, with individuals such as Chang Lung making names for themselves as protectors of land and people. One can but hope that the intrepid Polos of Venice—Niccolo, Maffeo, and young Marco—left the court of Kublai Khan with not only silks, spices, and missives for the Pope but also a more liberal appreciation of Dragons.

In his *Epistles*, Horace wrote, "You may drive out Nature with a pitchfork, yet she still will hurry back." Of all that is Nature, Dragons could certainly be no less persistent than the meanest weeds. In the fertile calm after the Hundred Years War (1337–1453), they returned to the human world—at least around the edges.

It did not hurt that, come the fifteenth century, the narrow-mindedness of the Middle Ages was flowering into the Renaissance. After the fashion of long-ignored Græco-Romans, scientific curiosity began to cast a long shadow over superstition. From artist to zoologist, the minds of the day turned to the world about them, rediscovering and expanding upon knowledge long forgotten. Mathematics, natural history, medicine, astronomy, engineering, the practice of arts fine and liberal—in virtually every field, it was as if eyes shut tight were suddenly opened to the bright light of day.[30] Inquiring minds wanted to know everything. Especially the alchemists.

They even wanted to know about the Druids. They were fascinated by the mysticism and lore of the ancient Celts, their knowledge of metals and stars, herbs and animals. Sadly, there was a tendency to romanticize them and get many of the details wrong. This was to be expected. They could only go on Roman accounts, second-hand Roman accounts, and Celtic tales—myths and legends—filtered through Church dogma. Druidic oral teachings were long lost in the miasma of conquest and conversion. But the fact remains: an interest in Druids meant an interest in Dragons. And, like applause for Tinker Bell, interest brought them back from the brink of oblivion.[31]

---

30. Some areas of study were more progressive than others. Despite the invention of the microscope and major advances in the understanding of human anatomy, the healing arts were hampered by the Church's insistence on adhering to Galen of Pergamon's second-century Roman ways. It took many years for the practice of medicine to catch up to the research and theory.

31. The impact of belief on existence was not limited to European Dragons. The conquistadors and their priests, by decimating the New World peoples with sword and Bible, did grievous harm to the New World Dragons who counted on their belief and protection. Hernán Cortés and his ilk brought the golden age of the Feathered Dragons to a crashing halt.

It also put them square in harm's way, yet again. As humanistic as certain Renaissance intellectuals strove to be, the Church was still the preeminent power on the continent. And where the Church ruled, Dragons maintained their medieval standing as emissaries of evil. This arcane prejudice might have amused them were it not for its attendant dangers. Still, Dragons could not be other than they were no matter what mud symbologists with agendas might sling.[32] Worse than being demonized by the foes they knew was being hunted by those who, under other circumstances, should have been friends. Alchemists, apothecaries, and venomologists all looked to Dragons and the lore swirling about them and saw a veritable smörgåsbord of parts and products to be used for everything from talismans and elixirs to poisons and panaceas. Alkahest, for example, the universal solvent as elusive to alchemists as the Philosopher's Stone, might have been locked up in the mysteries of Dragon blood. And powdered Dragon horn might have been the magic bullet for everything from plague to dyspepsia. If only these Renaissance men could tap the source as they believed the Druids had.

It was a blessing for Dragons that the intellectuals of the day were less adept at dragon slaying than the knights and warrior heroes of eras past. Less-than-reputable individuals likely surmounted this obstacle by employing mercenary hunters. Others, like the physician/occultist/astrologer Paracelsus, opted for more humane studies of living Dragons.[33]

The fashionableness of Druids and Dragons ebbed and flowed through the years. They were big up to Jacobean times, then came such a dry spell during the eighteenth-century Enlightenment that, aside from the occasional missing cow, the general populace hardly noticed Dragons at all.

---

32. If we manage to survive as long as Dragons, we may claim license to hurl epithets. Until then, we'd do better folding back time to build on the wisdom of the Druids and see them as they are, in wonder and glory.

33. Paracelsus travelled across Europe, the Middle East, and into Asia. Oh, the number and variety of Dragons he must have seen!

Most people assumed they were beings of fancy rather than fact, and so they became just that. For centuries.

With magic fading from the Old World, there was little room or need for Dragons save as legendary curiosities, much like the faërie folk, silkies, and Unicorns. As the years passed, Dragons retreated deeper and deeper into civilization's background. Soon they truly became William Butler Yeats's "wizard creatures of hope and fear," appearing rarely and then only to those open to the experience.

A nineteenth-century Druidic resurgence brought Dragons into the post-Industrial world. Hand-in-paw with pre-Raphaelites, occultists, and nascent Darwinists, enthusiasm for the Druids softened public attitudes towards our winged friends,[34] proving, once more, that the storied Dragon of the Dardanelles was right: time and again, the Druids made European Dragon survival possible.

Which brings us to modern times.

Dragons are back in the world, for sure, but at what cost? Life on Earth has gotten complex and technical in ways none of us—not even Dragons—could have possibly imagined a mere thousand years ago. In the name of progress, we felled the blessed groves and bottled the sacred springs. We have fouled Dragon skies and waters, exterminated much of their natural prey, and left them but a fraction of the land once theirs. Even in the Orient, Dragons long spared the prejudice inflicted upon their European cousins have begun to feel the bitter sting of lost belief and drastically depleted habitat. Like so many other species hanging on by the skin of their teeth, modern Dragons are in need of our sufferance and protection, though chances are they will endure without.

Charles Darwin observed, "The most powerful natural species are those that adapt to environmental change without losing their fundamental identity which gives them their competitive advantage."

Dragons are Dragons. Fundamentally.

They defy the odds of nature and man. They live.

---

34. While Victorian Europe wasn't exactly pro-Dragon, it could be viewed as neutral towards them. A draconic Switzerland, if you will.

*p*art III

The Care & Feeding
of Dragons

Does anyone think it's easy
To be a creature in this world?

—Kenneth Patchen, "Perhaps It Is Time"

eight

Wild Dragons
Near & Far

Over the last century, the wilds of Earth and all who live in them—including Dragons—have been under assault. According to United Nations figures, the world's human population has leapt from 2.8 billion to over 6 billion in just fifty years,[1] and some suggest it will reach 10 billion by 2050—a prospect that has Dragons shivering from nostril to spade. Year after year, humans gobble up more and more land and resources, and, in the process, we push all other species out of our way.

Dragons do not take kindly to being pushed. They will not simply disappear because the human race operates under a delusional sense of global manifest destiny. This naturally puts them at odds with corporations, governments, and individuals. It has also been the impetus behind major Dragon conservation efforts around the world. In turn, the work of dedicated cryptoherpetologists and lay dracophiles makes it possible for us to experience Dragons, both near and far.

---

1. UN DESA report, "The World at Six Billion," UN DESA, http://www.un.org/esa/population/publications/sixbillion/sixbillion.htm (accessed 2011).

Dragon Sanctuaries: Keeping Your Distance

Strictly speaking, all Dragons, large and small, feathered and scaled, are on the worldwide endangered species list.[2] Of course, this does not automatically protect them from poachers, developers, and even the well-intended but monumentally ignorant amongst us. To further protect them, the World Association for Dragons Everywhere (WAFDE) has been working with governments and international conservation organizations to make every known weyr a designated Dragon Sanctuary.[3] Despite pockets of dracophobic sentiment, WAFDE's efforts have been met with increasing support, an encouraging sign that the wonder of Dragons continues to outweigh our fear of them.

The history of Dragon Sanctuaries is an ancient and distinguished one, harking all the way back to Delphi and the golden days of Olympian Greece. As patron and overseer of Delphi, the god Apollo was responsible for guaranteeing the prophetic veracity of the oracle. To this end, not only did he place his sibylline priestesses over the Omphalos—or "navel of the world"—in which he buried the mystical Dragon Python, but, perhaps as a hedge against having done wrong by killing the great Dragon, he preserved a clutch of her precious eggs. These he took to a remote part of the Pindus Mountains, where, legend has it, he built a great garden enclosed in walls of gold. In the garden, he placed Epirotes, a wise and capable Dragon, and charged her with hatching and raising Python's prophetic children. It was a sweet sinecure she could not refuse. For centuries, they stayed safe in the garden and the Pythia of Delphi retained her oracular reputation. Python's offspring were fruitful and multiplied until, it's said,

---

2. Pseudo-dragons also make the list, though this is a pro forma classification. For many species, exact population counts are near impossible to come by—some are regretfully assumed to be already extinct. Still, if they were not listed, there would be no legal redress for their killing or capture. It seems a small thing, but for many creatures, it is all we have to offer.

3. Naturally, this does not cover solitary Dragons or pairs, or any as-yet-unregistered enchantments or weyrs.

Epirotes watched over the greatest multitude of Dragons in the Mediterranean world—a true feat of draconic conservation.[4] No one is sure what became of this first Dragon Sanctuary, though it is a curious footnote to history that the people of the region—now split between Greece and Albania—are known as Epirotes to this day. A sure sign of Dragon in their blood.

Modern Dragon Sanctuaries are not as ostentatious as Apollo's gilded garden, but they serve the same purpose: to keep their rare residents safe. Wherever possible, a Sanctuary's aegis covers not only immediate weyr lands but also vast tracts of surrounding hunting grounds. In this way Dragons are contributing to the protection of whole ecosystems.

From a human and scientific perspective, one of the great things about Dragon reserves is the access afforded to enchantments. Much like Serengeti National Park or the Arctic National Wildlife Refuge (ANWR) or any number of national parks from Tierra del Fuego to the *zapovedniks* of northern Russia, Sanctuaries are a bonanza for cryptozoologists, allowing them to study Dragons *au naturel* and the biological complexity of the habitats themselves. The recent treasure trove of verifiable information about these extraordinary creatures can, in many cases, be directly linked to methodical preserve research.

As for civilians, Sanctuaries give them the opportunity to indulge their love of Dragons from the security of strictly regulated treks and guided photographic safaris. These excursions have been instrumental in enlightening the public, promoting wonder and goodwill between humans and Dragons, and the money they generate goes to support educational and anti-poaching efforts around the globe.

The Dragon Conservancy Program has recently started the Adopt-a-Dragon (AAD) initiative, a project modeled after the U.S.

---

4. Local lore is full of questionable tales of virgin offerings. It was said a maid refused meant a year of calamity; a maiden accepted meant great good fortune. As the records are light on daughters lost to anything but natural causes, one is led to believe either the people of the Pindus Mountains were decidedly luckless or the stories are dismissible flights of fancy.

Bureau of Land Management's National Wild Horse and Burro Program and the American Bear Association's Friend of the Cubs package. For a modest annuity, Dragon-loving individuals can "adopt a Dragon" anywhere in the world. You get a photo of your Dragon, certificate of fosterage, and a weekend pass to the Sanctuary of your choice. Not only does AAD channel much needed funds into conservation efforts, it provides dracophiles around the world with a rewarding sense of chipping in. In this age of rampant species extinction, every little bit helps us all.

Despite best efforts and the latest surveillance equipment, the sheer size of protected regions makes monitoring all human traffic impossible. This is the great outdoors, after all. It is a harsh reality of the world that poachers and latter-day St. Georges thinking to bag a wild Dragon or steal eggs from an enchantment do find their way onto Sanctuary land.[5] In the past such encounters would have been weighed heavily in the Dragons' favor, yet modern weaponry has stripped them of much—though not all—of their natural advantage. Recognizing this increased danger to our enchanted friends, it should be said that trespassing on Dragon territory with malignant intent and no proper introduction is still apt to result in blood, pain, and loss of human life. For this reason, it is important to use only Sanctuary-approved tours and travel with personnel who are trained in Dragon science, lore, and etiquette. They know how to keep you and the Dragons as safe as possible.

Anyone looking to spend their next family vacation exploring a Dragon preserve should remember three things:[6]

---

5. The newest, most despicable threat to the enchantments is a zealous band of dracophobes who seek nests for the sole purpose of destroying the eggs and annihilating the next generation of Dragons. If any such people are reading this, know that Dragons have the right to use whatever means necessary—up to and including lethal force—to protect themselves and their offspring, in egg or out.

6. These rules—especially #3—apply to all Dragons whether in Sanctuary bounds or out.

1) *Here Be Dragons!* You are in their home; act accordingly.
2) Never wander off on your own, especially during mating and hatching seasons.
3) The law *always* favours the Dragon should anything messy and unpleasant occur.

Keep these caveats in mind and venture forth. You will be rewarded with an experience not soon forgot!

Dragon Lay-Bys:
Inviting Enchantments to Your South Forty

One of the conspicuously modern problems facing Dragons on the wing is where to touch down for the night. Field and forest were once the rule rather than the exception, but no longer. Pole to pole, humanity is sprawling across the globe.

What's an itinerant Dragon to do?

A growing cadre of individuals dedicated to Dragon preservation has addressed this problem by creating what is, essentially, an international network of Dragon lay-bys. Registered with WAFDE, the rest stops make it possible for a savvy Dragon to travel around the world without risk of setting down where she's not wanted. Naturally, such undertakings are not for your urban, or even your suburban, dracophiles. The space is simply not there. But, for those who live in the country and have a spare thirty or more acres, setting it aside for wayfaring Dragons can be an enticing idea.

If you are up for such a project, draconic needs must inform all planting and landscaping of the site: water, food, and shelter.

Dragons coming in after a day on the wing will be both thirsty and grimy, so a fresh water source is a no-brainer. This can be a lake or a stream, or, best of all, a stream-fed lake which keeps the water moving, clean, and vital.

Where available, sea access is always appreciated but should not be seen as an alternative to fresh water: not all travellers will be marine Dragons able to process the brine into a potable libation. If you are digging a lake from scratch, be sure it is big enough to accommodate a self-sustaining amphibious ecosystem, frogs, snails, water plants—cattails, duckweed, papyrus, etc.—and, of course, fish. A well-stocked lake or river is as welcome to wing-weary Dragons as a Ho-Jo's to I-90 motorists outside of Deadwood, South Dakota.

Which brings us to food. Traveling Dragons prefer frequent snacks to one or two heavy meals. They are less likely to feel weighed down or have to worry about air sickness (not a common ailment but very unpleasant if it occurs). When they stop for the night, however, they are inclined to want a moderate-sized well-balanced—flesh and foliage—repast. To this end, lay-bys should have ample hunting grounds. A nice forest replete with deer, boar, and fowl works very well. For a time, people were providing livestock as an alternative to wild prey, but this has been discouraged in recent years. It gives Dragons a taste for domestic meat which leads them to raid neighboring farms and stir up unnecessary anti-Dragon sentiments. After all, the farmer and the Dragon should be friends. If you happen to be squeamish about Dragons dining on warm-blooded prey, you will need to have ample fish available to meet your guests' protein requirements.[7]

Planting for Dragons is a multifaceted endeavor in which nutrition, shelter, alchemy, and aesthetics collide. First and foremost, be sure to plant within your ecological zone. While a lush stand of painted bamboo might look like home away from home to a wandering Szechuan Dragon, it is a far from practical choice for a rest stop in northern Vermont. And cacti are seldom appropriate in all save the driest habitats. If you want to branch out from strictly indigenous flora, contact your local horticultural college or arborist. They will be able to steer you towards exotics which will thrive in your area.

Dragons, as discussed previously, are both elemental and, as the Chinese appreciated, yin and yang—masculine and feminine—together. They naturally enjoy a comparable symmetry in their surroundings. Alchemists and herbalists will tell you flora (like fauna) is divided according to gender and the prime elements: air, earth, fire,

---

7. You might also want to reconsider the whole lay-by situation. Dragons are not for those with delicate dispositions.

and water. Planting with an eye to a male/female and elemental balance is not only good for the land, but also seen as an open invitation to Dragons to drop in. Say, for example, you have ash trees (masculine/fire) you might want to plant some birch (feminine/water); slippery elm (feminine/air) can go nicely with honeysuckle (masculine/earth). If you're uncertain how to proceed, consult your local alchemist or check out the library. There are several excellent books out there, including Scott Cunningham's *Encyclopedia of Magical Herbs* and Sandra Kynes's *Whispers from the Woods*. If you feel horticulturally challenged, the following suggestions give you a good place to start:

Planting for Dragons by Zone			
(Some species are multizonal)			
Taigia/ Subtundra	Temperate	Subtropical/ Tropical	Desert
• Black spruce • Red cedar • Rowan • Larch • Paper birch • Mosses & lichens (very nutritious) • Bilberries • Coudberries (yummy!)	• Smoke trees (an obvious choice) • Copper leaves • Rhododendron • Ferns & bracken • Honey locust • Goldenraintrees • Beech (the chantrels that grow under them are a real plus) • Chestnut • Hardy fruit trees—apples, pears, etc. • Dogwood • Willow (esp. pussy willow) • Ninebark • Serviceberry (beautiful and fruity!)	• Monkey puzzle (great for Feathered Dragons) • Flame trees • Dragon trees (of course) • Jacaranda • Gum trees • Cacao • Mahogany • Bald cypress • Butterfly bush (also good for Unicorns) • Bamboos—including blue, thorny & dragon's nest species • Citrus trees • Tipu tipuana (fast-growing shade tree)	• Tuna trees • Saguaro • Queen & date palms • Olive • Spiny smoke trees (desert variety) • Bottle tree (great for shade & drought relief) • Chaste tree • Joshua tree • Acacia

Since variety lends spice to life, your standard lay-by should have a potpourri of thickly boughed conifers and deciduous trees. As foodstuffs, hardwoods—nut and fruit trees—are prized for the sweetness of their leaves and twigs, not to mention their windfall bounty. However, they are, as a rule, slow growers. For quick shade and windbreaks, you'll want stands of trees like aspen, poplar, and eucalyptus. If you are looking to attract Feathered Dragons, be sure your trees are sturdy enough to allow them to roost in comfort.

Along with fruits, nuts, and woody fare, Dragons are appreciative of a wide variety of berries, grasses, and wild herbage. As a matter of landscaping, you might consider such perennial favorites as juniper, gooseberries, wild sage, ginseng, mullein, hawthorn, ginger, and, of course, dragon's blood. On-site vegetable gardens are ill-advised. Not that Dragons don't appreciate more traditional veggies—they love them. But draconic palates are as individual as humans' and a Dragon eager to feast on pigeon peas might inadvertently trample the Brussels sprouts planted beside them. If you wish to share your garden's bounty with sojourning Dragons, set up a feeding station near their shelter.[8] These are also excellent spots for mineral licks, a little salt bringing out the flavor in any dish.

Lay-by shelters need not be luxurious; Dragons are just passing through, not taking up residence. Still, they do enjoy a place to get out of the burning sun or pounding rain.[9] If a site does not have any natural caverns, there are several reasonable substitutes available. Those looking for something quick to set up and durable will find that Quonset huts make excellent all-weather retreats. Simply place them against a hillside, cover with sod, and landscape inside and out. Add a charming stone or two, and a Dragon will feel right at home.

---

8. Though Dragons seldom travel during the inclement seasons, such stations can also be used as food drops for the rare winter guest.

9. Or, in the case of taiga retreats, the blinding snow. For those intrepid few who dwell in and around the Arctic Circle, ice caves make wonderful Dragon shelters.

On the other hand, if you have patience and a green thumb, you might opt for the organic route and grow what's known as a quick bower. For the closet arborist, training supple vines and saplings into rustic abodes is a creative adventure limited only by the scope of one's imagination. That said, bowermaking is labor intensive and the resultant shelter will tend towards the drafty, especially when the leaves fall. Still, Dragons on the wing have a penchant for roughing it and will certainly appreciate your efforts.

Now that you have your Dragon rest stop prepared, you must register it. This is a simple matter: fill out a few forms with WAFDE, pay a modest fee—which is funneled back into Dragon conservation efforts—and have an on-site inspection just to make sure everything is up to draconic snuff. After that just sit back and be patient. It may take weeks, months, even a year or two for Dragons to find you. But they will. And once they do, if the room is pleasant and board plentiful, word will get out and Dragons will beat a flight path to your door. No one is quite sure how, but Dragons always know the best places to stay. They couldn't do better if they followed a Baedeker.

A word from the wise: As mentioned in Chapter Three, most Dragons travel during the balmy summer months. This does not preclude visitors throughout the year—especially in tropical climes—but your lay-by's going to be busiest from May to September (November to March in the Southern Hemisphere). During the on-season, it is not unusual for Dragons from disparate weyrs to share a bower and a meal without the slightest trace of territorial hostility. It has been suggested—and the empirical evidence bears this out—that the enchantments have an unspoken agreement to treat lay-bys as mini-Switzerlands. It would be the height of bad manners to break the spirit of neutrality with a dust-up.

While a *pax loci* is in force for the Dragons, do not trust that it extends to Dragon/human interactions. True, it is bad form to bite off the hand that feeds you, but these are wild Dragons we're talking about.[10] Respect that wildness, use your head, and keep your distance. In time, particularly with Dragons who are repeat guests, you may develop a moderate rapport and be allowed to fraternize with them. Listen and watch carefully. Never presume. Never push.

Dragons will not be pushed.

---

10. A bear may dine at your bird feeder, but you would be a fool to treat him like a stray cat with a pat and a chuck under the chin.

To Whomever
These village fires
Still have meaning
O may your own most secret
& beautiful Animal of Light
Come safely to you.

—Kenneth Patchen, Wonderings

nine

Coddled Eggs & Orphans: Welcoming a Dragon to Your Table

Ever since a scraggly jackal cub mooched scraps from our prehistoric ancestors, human beings have felt the need—the compulsion—for animal companionship. For pets. Dogs, cats, rabbits, birds, horses—some work with us and some keep us from being lonely. In return, we are bound by a solemn covenant of affectionate care and respect, even defense against extinction. We keep them alive and they lower our blood pressure. That is the altruistic, sanitized way of modern pet keeping. But deeper down, in places we are not always comfortable visiting, it's something quite a bit more primal: Pets remind us, in the light, of the eyes that once watched us in the dark. They give us the illusion of superiority, of being able to master the wild and rule the world.

But why settle for a tabby if you can have a tiger, or an anole if you can have an alligator? The bigger, the better; the more exotic, the more your neighbors will drool with envy. And what could possibly be bigger or more exotic than a Dragon?

If this train of thought appeals to you, stop.

Dragons are not pets. Never have been, never will be.

You can't go to your local fur-fin-and-feather emporium[1] and pick out a cute little blue Dragonlet to set off the lapis streaks in your new carpet. So don't try.

That said, every so often forces in the universe conspire and a fortunate few topple into the unique world of Dragon keeping. Rather than have you stumble about potentially doing more harm than good and putting yourself and your charge in danger, we offer the following chapters. Combine them with what you know about Dragons in the wild, stir in a healthy dose of empathy and common sense, and you will have a first-rate education in the care and feeding of Dragons.[2]

Remember: At heart Dragons are realists. They don't expect perfection from us. But they do expect us to keep them safe and well, body and soul. This is the contract between a person and any creature in their care.

As long as you are a Dragon keeper, the monsters of Want and Neglect are yours to slay.

First Things First

Dragon keeping is not for everyone.

No matter how much you consider yourself a Dragon person, believing it's so does not make it so. For starters, it is a major commitment. You need space and wherewithal and lots of both, even if you are only fostering a Dragon until she is mature enough to be returned to the wild (ten or fifteen years old). As anyone with a cat or dog knows, the cost of food and vet bills is rapidly making even the most mundane pet ownership a luxury. While standard veterinary services are usually wasted on Dragons, the food bills can be exorbitant, especially in the early going before they learn to hunt for themselves. You must also prepare for the fact that a Dragon will outlive you many times over. This seems obvious, but you'd been surprised how many people get caught up in the moment and fail to think ahead.

---

1. Or black-market Dragon poacher or Dragon mill.

2. As the saying goes, chinchillas may be rodents, but treat them like rats and they'll die on you every time.

If the sight of a cat feasting on a still-warm chipmunk turns your stomach, or you change the channel away from *Wild Kingdom* when the cheetah rips into a gazelle, put all thoughts of Dragon keeping out of your mind and get a goldfish. Dragons are predators, and no amount of contact with humans will change that. And, unlike captive big cats, they are not content to dine on butchered fare, even if it's warmed in the microwave. They must hunt, especially if they are going to have any chance of fending for themselves.

Most experts agree that the best training for a Dragon keeper is to first be a lay-by provider. You can get your feet wet with relatively minor consequences should things go less than swimmingly. Assuming everything goes well, you will have a Dragon-friendly environment all set up, not to mention much needed experience up-close-and-personal with our friends. You will also be known to The Powers That Be (WAFDE, etc.) as a reputable Dragon caretaker. This makes it much easier for you to be approved and licensed by the appropriate local, provincial, national, and humane authorities, a deal-breaker when it comes to keeping Dragons. Licensing is as much for your protection as anything else. Whether for cause[3] or on "principle," there will always be people who disapprove of Dragons and the people who care for them. Some of those people might just be your neighbors. Having all your paperwork and credentials in order can help defuse tense situations, particularly if the police are called in. When it comes to Dragon keeping, ignorance of the law is never an excuse. Since Dragon regulations are both site-specific and in a state of cultural flux, be sure to bone up on all pertinent codes and ordinances. Keep in mind that local constabularies are often less than thoroughly versed in draconic statutes, so politely share your expertise—and the name of your attorney, for good measure.

With people and Dragons, civility counts.

---

3. What passes for "cause" these days is usually some unfortunate misunderstanding over lost livestock. In the heat of the moment, Dragons make easy scapegoats.

An Egg in Your Basket

There are essentially two ways to become a Dragon keeper: find an egg and hatch it, or adopt an orphan. Each route has its own unique set of challenges. With an egg, such hurdles are largely physical, revolving around the need to create a proper nesting and hatching environment. With an orphan, behavioural and psychological issues are, understandably, paramount.

Dragon eggs are seldom lost or abandoned, a fact which makes finding such treasures the veritable stuff of legend. That said, *seldom* does not mean *never*, and, if you live near Dragons, do not, to paraphrase Tolkien, leave this out of your calculations. Should you be blessed to know a hatchling from her first breath, the Cosmic Dragon is surely smiling upon you.

When walking through woods or along cliffs, keep your eyes open, especially in autumn or late winter/early spring.[4] If you discover an egg—or a whole clutch—the first thing you must do is note the location. Not only does this guarantee you'll find it again, but it serves as valuable information for conservationists. That done, keep your distance. Watch and wait for forty-eight hours.[5] There are times when a Queen, particularly a young Queen alone through no fault of her own, will nest in the open. Her needs for sustenance will force her from the nest on occasion, but she will return. If, however, there is no sign of Mother—or Father—Dragon[6] after two days, something untoward has definitely happened. You can assume the egg is bereft of parental care and proceed to take it into custody.[7]

---

4. No one is sure why these times of year, but data from the latest survey of Dragon keepers bears this out.

5. Some people insist you should notify the authorities right away, but this is not absolutely necessary. Yet.

6. A Dragon Sire rarely incubates eggs on his own. If something happens to his Queen, a Sire, likely overwhelmed by grief, is apt to abandon her clutch.

7. If you come across an egg but are not looking to be a Dragon keeper yourself, call the local authorities. They will come out and collect your find.

With the greatest of care, remove the egg to a secure, warm place. This is not always easy: your find is heavy, not to mention that chances are it's not just lying by the side of the road awaiting rescue. To keep the jouncing and bouncing to a minimum, you will need block and tackle and a sturdy, well-cushioned sling, cart, or travois. In ultra-remote locations, a helicopter is indispensable. For a nesting chamber, a large shed, barn, or even a garage will do in a pinch as long as it's weatherproofed and temperature controlled. Ideally you will want to use a portion of what will ultimately be your Dragon's lair—a cave, dome, or hangar-like structure—so that, once hatched, your infant is not overly confused by moving into yet another new habitat. She may not have seen the space, but a Dragon has extraordinary powers of sense memory and will pick up on residual nesting scents and be comforted by their familiarity.

Though you will want to reproduce a Dragon's nest as best you can,[8] you're not expected to have access to the sort of rare minerals and gems found in a wild weyr. Use instead a fine silica-sand base mixed with organic material—straw, loam, branches—and copper

8. See Chapter Three, Dragon Days of Autumn.

shavings. "Copper!?" you say, having just cringed at the estimate from the plumber scheduled to replace your old pipes. Yes, copper. At roughly $0.20/ounce, it is relatively inexpensive and conducts heat about as well as silver ($36.67/ounce) or zirconium ($5.00/ounce).[9] Place the egg in the nest and cover it completely. Every second day, you will want to uncover it, check its progress, rotate it a quarter-turn counterclockwise, then cover it again.

Depending on the egg's stage of development, you will need to keep it between 98 and 120 degrees F. An examination of the shell folds will help you determine the appropriate incubation temperature. If they are 2 or more inches deep you have a young egg, between 6 and 8 months old, and must keep it at a steady 98 degrees; when the folds go under the 2-inch mark, increase the temperature by five degrees per week until they smooth out and you hit 120 degrees. Though you can heat the whole nesting chamber, an ambient temperature of 120 degrees is, at the very least, uncomfortable to most

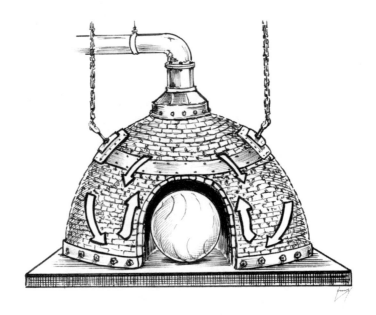

---

9. Don't even ask about gold ($1,543/ounce). It bears repeating: Dragon keeping requires deep pockets.

people and will dissuade you from spending long hours of quality time with your charge. A series of directed heaters—propane or natural gas—spaced evenly around the nest can warm the egg in its sandy casing and leave the surrounding area cozy but bearable. Excess heat can always be funneled via a hypocaust to your home, greenhouse, or other buildings, making them nice and toasty while cutting down on your personal utility bills. When faced with the costs of Dragon keeping, sharing resources where you can is a real boon to the coffers.

You should spend time with your egg every day. Talk to it as much as you can so the Dragonlet inside becomes familiar with your voice. Since you won't be able to do this 24/7, it's advisable to make recordings and play them when you get hoarse or can't be physically present. It soothes the embryonic infant and mitigates any number of behavioural problems later on. If you're stumped for conversation, try reading to it, preferably something with a good plot and not too much gratuitous violence. There is anecdotal evidence that, as the weeks wear on, Dragon literary leanings veer from Chaucer to Edmund Spenser to Jacqueline Susann. Though some scientists insist this is due to inter-shell hormonal shifts, chances are it's as simple as there's no accounting for taste, even among Dragons. Enthusiasm being contagious, start with personal favourites, something you can recite with gusto. Appreciative shell rumbles will let you know when you've hit on the right tome.

Remember that Dragons are gregarious, even in the shell, and thrive in an animated environment. Do not hesitate to bring friends around, the more the merrier. And play music. Most any kind will do. As with their literature, Dragons appear to be very eclectic in their harmonic likes. And when you can't be there, leave the music on. It won't replace the comforting touch of maternal scales, but it will reassure your developing Dragonlet that she's not alone. If you are going to be absent for more than six hours at a time, use instrumentals not vocals. This prevents your Dragon from hatching forth convinced the original Broadway cast of *Into the Woods* is her weyr.

As the egg matures, you have time to put the finishing touches on your Dragon habitat. Landscape it with boulders and dirt mounds, places to dig and places to hide. And plants. Lush plant life will not only give your charge the illusion of being in the wilds, but also provide her with hours of diversion—peek-a-boo being a favourite pastime of young ones. Plant with an eye to variety, size, colour, even fragrance. Just be sure all flora are Dragon-safe, as a hatchling will be curious and nibble where she can.

The minute your egg starts to harden, you can begin counting the days until you have a bouncing baby Dragon on your hands. The tricky part of these last few weeks is finding a way to replicate hatching fire. Short of convincing a pair of Dragons to help out,[10] what is a person to do? Some people have tried flame throwers. It seemed a logical idea, but in actuality the flame was neither hot enough nor uniform enough to crackle the shell. One of the more practical alternatives is a domed kiln with forced-air gas burners blasting down from the top and a wide flue at the bottom to pull the flame flow down and around as uniformly as possible. You must fire your kiln, fast and furious, until it reaches an internal temperature of 2,000 degrees F.[11] The best way to gauge this is by placing pyrometric cones strategically around the egg.[12] Once you attain the desired thermal reading, shut the burner off and force-cool the chamber. As soon as it is physically possible, you will want to break down the kiln so the egg is open to the air. The temperature should return to 120 degrees within five hours, tops. This will produce requisite shell crackling and allow your Dragonlet to emerge as nature intended.

Thanks to modern audio technology, replicating the birthing anthem is a less complicated, less expensive endeavor. Excellent

---

10. The problem here is not draconic willingness to help but the fact that few people have extra Dragons just hanging around.

11. Unlike a potter's firing, you don't have to worry about hairline cracks resulting from a lack of patience. Shell crackles are good.

12. Do not be snowed by people trying to sell high-tech gadgets which are more bells and whistles than anything else. Pyrometric cones are not only simple— some might say idiot-proof—but inexpensive and much more accurate than any other product on the market. And they're readily available online or from your local ceramics supply store.

recordings have been made of draconic natal song which, when played at the appropriate time and volume, have proved capable of rousing an infant Dragon and encouraging her to break forth. Naturally, your timing will lack a Queen Dragon's elegant precision, but count sixty-eight hours from egg firing and you will be close enough to do no harm. Volume is another matter. Inside of sixty minutes, you will have to crescendo from a barely audible whisper to a deafening 110–120 decibels, then maintain that for a full half hour before cutting to silence. This requires a state-of-the-art sound system and earplugs for yourself and any human family and friends in attendance.[13]

In anticipation of the blessed event, the following preparations are a must:

Have a stiff scrub brush and warm water on hand to remove any egg residue. Not only is this a bonding experience between you and your Dragonlet, but it helps to physically stimulate the infant's system, much like a cat licking her newborn kittens. You will also need the fixings for your Dragon's first meal: 2 pounds of finely ground fish and meat, 2 pounds of shredded greens, 2 ostrich eggs, and a pound of honey. Mix together on the morning of the hatching and keep at approximately 100 degrees F—warm, but not cooked. Newborns must never eat a cold meal no matter how hungry they are; it gives them colic.

Once all is in readiness, plug your ears, pump up the volume, and let your infant Dragon do the rest. Should something go wrong and the need arise to actively play midwife, keep a hammer at the ready. Just in case.

Still shell-sticky and wobbly, your Dragon's first move will be to taste the air about you and get a firm sense of your essential smell. If you happen to be partial to a particular perfume or cologne, be sure to wear it. This will help the Dragon distinguish you from others in the great herd of humanity. Then comes a bath, then a meal. Then a party. Despite having your hands full, never forget to celebrate. Dragons

---

13. If you have any other four-legged companions, keep them clear of your hatching ground, as the acoustic levels will be very painful and make them apt to be hostile towards the Dragon before she's even born.

expect it. In the words of the immortal Horace: "Now for drinks, now for some dancing with a good beat" (*Odes,* I, xxxvii, 1).

There is currently a great deal of debate among cryptoherpetologists over the role imprinting plays in a hatchling's life. An old Dragon keeper's tale insists the only guarantee of a connection between a Dragon and her person is to be *the* first thing she sees when she chips her way into this world. At best, that is a simplistic take on a complicated subject and totally negates the evidence of remarkable relationships between people and orphan Dragons, some as old as a year, even two, before they meet their first human. True, weyr studies show that Dragonlets are bound to their parents from the get-go. Given the communal aspect to hatchings, however, most

scientists believe these ties are more a function of scale-on-shell nesting contact combined with Mother Dragon's birthing song than any love-at-first-sight imprinting. Remember, we're talking Dragons here, not geese. Unfortunately, there is not much a person can do about nesting contact[14] and you will obviously be using a hatching anthem not your own. It is therefore vital to give prenatal care due diligence, especially talk time.

That is not to say vocal habituation is the only way into a hatchling's good graces. Food equals concern and affection in any newborn's life, and a Dragon's primary guardian should, whenever possible, be the one who feeds her for the first month or so. As between Dragons, so between Dragons and people; grooming also builds trust and reinforces bonds. We shall go into detail on both these subjects in Chapter Ten.

An Orphan in the Storm

People who take on the challenge of orphaned Dragons must be generous, patient, and empathetic in the extreme. They are championing the problem children of the Dragon keeping world and deserve our respect and admiration for their efforts.

Orphan Dragons are one of the great tragedies of Dragon/human relationships. Accidents and natural disasters take their toll on Dragons of all ages, but clashes with people persistently tear enchantments asunder and leave hatchlings destitute. Back in the days of questing heroes and would-be saints, swaths were cut through the ranks of Dragonkind with total disregard for the families. The notion of Dragons as solitary creatures led slayers to ignore the possibility that they were less than cordial because they were protecting their children. Consequently, no consideration was given to what might happen to those orphaned children in a Dragon-hostile world. Of course, any naturalist with a dram of common sense could have set them

---

14. Though people have tried various contraptions and costumes, they're just not the same.

straight on this. Though not as helpless as baby gorillas or wolf cubs, most orphans would die; a few would be adopted by dracophiles and alchemists;[15] fewer still would make it on their own. But those who did survive would harbor grave antipathies towards people, perpetuating the adversarial Dragon/human relationship *ad extremum*.

Today, the number of orphan Dragons in the world is on the rise. Wars, mercenaries, and poachers stand in the errant knights' stead and show just as little regard for the hatchlings their venal crimes leave behind.

True, some bereaved Dragonlets are captured for quick cash sales on the black market, but ninety-nine times out of a hundred, this only postpones the inevitable. Like baby alligators in the 1960s or exotic wild cats in the 1990s, black-market Dragons are purchased by individuals more interested in novelty and status than being proper caretakers. Such people are ill-equipped to deal with any Dragon, let alone a frightened infant in need of extra patience, guidance, and affection. These traumatized hatchlings have been ripped from the wild, their parents, nestmates, and everything they've ever known. Stress and acting out are virtually inevitable. While they may be treated well at first, chances are they end up dumped by the roadside the minute they nip a finger or break a bed.[16] That anyone would discard their Dragon rather than take her to a sanctuary or, at the very least, call the authorities, speaks volumes about their character.

No animals are disposable. Anyone who believes they are deserves the full and swift judgment of the law.

---

15. This was not always a good thing, as some alchemists were more concerned with Dragon parts than with Dragon lives. Not only did they lose a font of knowledge through such short-sightedness, but they made Dragons increasingly wary of all people, even those who might have been their allies.

16. Of course, any proper Dragon keeper would know not to let their charge on the bed in the first place.

So, what should you do if you find an orphan Dragon—or, as is frequently the case in the wild, a brood of orphans?[17] First, remember she is apt to be shy, scared, and starving. Her previous experiences with people have put her instincts in conflicted overdrive: she doesn't know you or trust you—in fact, she'll be tempted to take a bite out of you—and yet she's compelled by hunger and loneliness to risk approaching. It makes for a potentially volatile situation. Proceed by mixing up a savory meal and placing it and fresh water in a quiet location. Then, holding to the eloquence in stillness, sit back and do nothing. Given enough time and space, the need to feed will eventually overcome her fears.

While your waif is dining, observe her for signs of injury or illness. Lameness, weepy eyes, difficulty breathing, dull or broken scales, not to mention open sores and/or wounds can usually be spotted from a distance. If any of these signs are present, or you just get the feeling something is not right, call a professional right away. More than a few Dragon keepers—experienced, well-intentioned, and thinking they can handle anything—have been rushed to the emergency room after trying to tend a wounded foundling. Of course, as with all Dragon-related mishaps, it's not the orphan's fault. We should know better. So, don't be foolish. A vet will be able to do a closer examination with minimal risk to Dragon or humans, and treat as necessary. It's why we pay them the big bucks.

Though each case is unique, in three to four weeks, all but the most severely abused orphans will start to feel at home in their new environment. By this time, they should be eating on a schedule, using proffered shelter at least in severe weather, and accepting human companionship, even enjoying shared swimming or playtime and

---

17. This is a situation seen more and more in war-torn parts of the world where it is not unheard of for Dragons to become collateral damage. Whenever possible, parentless siblings will stick together. They should be allowed to stay together until they choose otherwise. Something to remember. If you can't accommodate more than one orphan, call the authorities. They will find someone who can.

affectionate rubs under the chin. If you make it this far, pat yourself on the back. You're off to an excellent start.

Now prepare yourself: there's likely to be turbulence ahead.

It would be a gross generalization to say that all orphan Dragons have behavioural problems; likewise, you don't have to be a genius to realize that the potential is there. Considering what they have gone through, it is frankly amazing they don't all have raging PTSD, a fact which speaks to the high level of dedication and care provided by Dragon keepers around the world.

Forewarned being forearmed, there are a few common problems you should watch for. Orphans, especially solitary dumpees, are prone to abandonment issues which make returning them to the wild difficult if not impossible. Usually slow to trust, once a connection is made, they will stick to you like honey to a bear. Orphans usually outgrow the most cloying of dependent behaviours by late adolescence, though a few remain firmly attached their whole lives, which can make planning vacations a bit tricky. Resorts may welcome ferrets and Afghans, but they tend to draw the line when it comes to scaled beauties lounging poolside. More importantly, to Dragons so grievously lacking in self-reliance, the death of their person can be a crushing, even mortal blow. Remember, the sooner she starts to feel confident in her Dragonhood, the better. Do not hesitate to get outside help if, as the years pass, your concerns grow.

Though they may be great with you and your immediate family, orphans are apt to distrust strangers with a vengeance. This makes for an excellent home and family guardian but can get dicey when the relatives you haven't seen in a decade decide to drop by. Dragons are smart, intuitive, and loyal. They will pick up on your emotions and act accordingly. Take precautions, make introductions, and maybe think twice before leaving them alone with the in-laws.

Dragon Despondency—or Weyrsickness[18]—and nightmares are also prevalent in young orphans. Though there are no sure-fire remedies, spending a lot of time with your charge, even bunking down with

---

18. See Chapter Eleven.

her at night,[19] can work palliative wonders. If such woes persist past weaning, consult a Dragon behaviourist.

When all is said and done, with proper care and guidance, you should have every reason to expect as long and happy a life with an orphan as with a fresh-from-the-egg hatchling. Just follow her lead and don't move too fast.

---

19. At her place, not yours, of course. As much as you might want to welcome a Dragon into your house, free-swinging tails and the concomitant home repairs make this ill-advised for all concerned.

It should be mentioned that radical conservationists insist Dragon keeping, while a necessary evil in the grand scheme of species survival, should be a stopgap at most—a means of transitioning wayward hatchlings into adulthood and then ushering them back into the wilderness. This is a noble sentiment but not always practical. There are orphan Dragons, for example, so battered and bruised by the world that they simply can't bear to return to living wild. There are even more who hover in an intermediate place between free weyr life and human companionship.

No matter what the ideologues say, in the end, we can only do our best. The Dragons must decide the rest for themselves.

Who can believe that there is no soul behind
those luminous eyes!

—Theophile Gautier

ten

The Early Years

Whether she crawled egg-sticky into your arms or out of the wilderness, you have suddenly become guardian/parent/companion to 200 pounds of irrepressionable baby Dragon. As you adjust to your newly assumed mantle of Dragon keeper, a slightly sick, anxiously overwhelmed sense of panic is no doubt settling deep in your stomach.

Not to worry, it happens to the best of us.

Take a deep breath and relax in the certainty that you are going to make mistakes. That's just the way it is with people. And with Dragon keeping. Fortunately, blunder as you might, it's very hard to actually kill a Dragon with TLC and good intentions. Odds are your hatchling will survive your time together more or less intact.

Still, odds can always be improved.

Attend!

What's in a Name?

It is said that, long ago, Dragons taught the ancient peoples of Earth that great power lies in names. Names can summon and control, charm and destroy. Names are magic strong as Dragons themselves.

Growth Rate for the Average Western Dragon

3 weeks

18 months

11 years

50+ years

Now, you will likely feel a wicked inclination to hang an appellation on your hatchling's egg-encrusted horns.

Don't.

Every Dragon is born with a name and they will tell you what
it is as soon as they are old enough to remember. Calling an infant
anything other than Dragon or, if you must, Draco, will only wind up
confusing you both.

The Remembrance of Names usually occurs when Dragons turn
three—sometimes two, if they are precocious. It is a rite of passage
no less than first flight or breathing fire, and an important step across
the threshold between infancy and adolescence. Since it's believed
most Dragon names are passed down through the generations, this

joyfully solemn occasion establishes a link—particularly for Dragons who have only known the company of humans—to ancestors heretofore only dreamt of. It gives them the sense of draconic continuum so essential for a youngster's self-esteem. A Dragon secure in self is able to stand tall and proud amid the maelstrom of the modern world.

It should be noted that Dragons do not share their names with just anyone. This is a survival instinct honed in more hostile times when evil men used the power of names as a lash to break Dragons, body and soul. Though the world has grown considerably more Dragon-friendly, it is recommended you use only nicknames in the company of strangers. You never know who might be listening. An adult Dragon is strong enough to resist the most nefarious *nomen* incantation, yet many still choose to keep the relative anonymity of their soubriquets. This is easier on us, too, as the majority of Dragon names are near impossible to wrap our tongues around. When the time is right, work out a suitable nickname with your charge, something sufficiently draconic she can live with and use in public.

The Way to a Dragon's Heart

As you plunge into the daily nitty-gritty of Dragon keeping, know this:

First, last, and always, an infant Dragon is hungry.

Feeding four to six times a day, a hatchling will almost double in size during her first three months. During this time, you are her link to food, to her very survival. The perfect opportunity to form a deep connection with your new companion has just been handed to you on a platter. Don't blow it.

Though even the youngest of Dragons will put on a great show of self-sufficiency, like the rest of us, they enjoy company when they're feasting. Just put down their food, pull up a chair, and relax. They will do the rest. Messily enthusiastic eaters at the best of times, it is wise to give hatchlings their own dining area, preferably one easily hosed down. This not only allows for the uninhibited expression of their wilder ways, but also keeps your housekeeper from quitting in disgust because the breezeway looks like a Roman orgy exploded all over it.

On those rare occasions when a hatchling refuses to eat on her own—usually a call for a little extra attention—you will have to play Mother Dragon in earnest and hand-feed her. Do remember that hungry Dragons are not always careful Dragons, and watch your fingers. If your charge does not return to her old eating habits within a week, contact your vet or qualified cryptozoologist. Something serious might be going on.

In their quest to grow, newborns will easily consume 30–40 pounds of ground flesh, greens, honey, and ostrich eggs per day. Some whole grains can be added but only in moderation: 3 percent of the total is more than enough. Since it all goes into the food processor, frozen meat and fish are acceptable provided they're well warmed before feeding. For the remainder of their diet, however, access to fresh supplies is essential. Many Dragon people have extensive gardens and keep herds of ostriches and vast apiaries for just this reason. In the absence of a green thumb, try working out an arrangement with a local Dragon-friendly farmer. You might, for example, offer Dragon dung in exchange for vegetables. Before you laugh at the prospect, consider that Dragon dung is not only 100 percent organic, but also more nutrient-rich than any of the commercial fertilizers on the market today.[1] Churn Dragon dung into the soil and a bumper crop is virtually guaranteed.

At two to three months old, your Dragonlet should start foraging, even hunting a bit for herself. A squirrel or a vole, that little extra crunch in a meal, is just the thing to tickle her gastronomic fancy. While no one expects you to be able to teach her as an elder Dragon would, you can show her where to hunt and fish, play stalking games, and generally encourage her from the sidelines. In this as with so much else, rules are very important. Dragons must be taught the difference, for example, between the lake and the backyard fishpond, lest your prized koi quickly become mid-morning sashimi snacks. If you intend to return your Dragon to the wild, you might want to contact

---

1. Not to mention that you don't have to worry about people using it for home-made explosives.

someone with an older Dragon and invite them over for hunting sessions. Acquiring skills is essential for survival and there is nothing like learning from a real pro.

A fully weaned Western Dragon's diet should be 50–65 percent animal proteins, preferably fish and/or fowl, 40 percent vegetation, and 5–10 percent minerals. These numbers even apply to Polar Dragons who, though situational carnivores in the wild, thrive on a more balanced diet when it's available. Red meat is all right now and then, but far too rich as a regular menu item. This may explain why Dragons, sensible eaters as a rule, do not care for it much. For Eastern and Feathered Dragons, the more veggies the better, and they only touch red meat under duress. Though you can raise livestock to meet your Dragon's needs, it is far better for all concerned—especially your bank account—to have well-stocked woods and waters at their disposal.

A word of warning: young Dragons have been known to turn territorial around their lake or stream, so be careful. For a long time this was interpreted as a creature simply guarding a food source. Of late, there's a growing belief that it's actually a matter of race-memory harking back to the days when Dragons watched over sacred springs. Whatever the cause, you'll want to discourage—or at least temper— such behaviour for everyone's well-being.

How much Dragons ingest is contingent upon age and activity. In their first few years, when growth is paramount, they can eat as much as they want as long as their diet remains balanced. Like people, the older they get the slower their metabolisms are, and though they'll naturally cut back on their intake, activity is crucial to keeping trim without having to enforce any dietary restrictions. For European and Feathered Dragons, daily flights usually do the trick, while Asian Dragons are partial to swimming and kicking up earthworks to work off those extra pounds.

Vitamins and minerals are a vital part of any creature's daily fare, and Dragons are no exception. Left to their own devices, they usually manage quite well, yet there are times when even the most conscientious eaters need a little help. During molting season, for example, many Dragons crave extra root vegetables in response to increased keratin production. Also, be sure your charge's diet is always rich in antioxidants, particularly L-ascorbic acid, or Vitamin C. Like people and guinea pigs, Dragons do not synthesize C and so must get it from external sources. Feathered Dragons out of their native habitat are particularly vulnerable to C deficiencies, indicating that their natural regimen is high in citrus fruits and rich leafy greens. While supplements can be used, studying the flora of a Dragon's place of origin will not only point to nutritional needs but also to indigenous means of meeting those needs.

Dragons are true individualists when it comes to their menu choices. A clutch may share certain vague genetic predilections, but ultimately each Dragon acquires tastes all her own. Palate preferences may be influenced by a food's colour, texture, fragrance—even the company your Dragon is keeping when she takes that first bite might make a difference. That said, bold flavors are usually well represented: juniper, cacao, horseradish, spices from agrimony to zedoary root, and, of course, the whole spectrum of chiles, especially when Dragons start playing with fire. As long as you make sure she has a nutritionally complete and balanced diet, your Dragon should be able to find her own epicurean way. Pay close attention to her evolving likes and dislikes. This will show your Dragon you care about the little things in her life as well as give you ideas about the best treats to use in training.

Connecting: Touch, Boundaries, and Saying "No!"

You cannot tame a Dragon.

Understand that from the start.

No matter how affectionate they may be, when around Dragons you must always remember they are wild and potentially dangerous. This does not mean it's impossible to have close and rewarding relationships with Dragons. They are bright, sociable, and, if given no cause to the contrary, actually like our company. You just have to be careful and connect.

The key to safe, joyful Dragon keeping is proper socialization. From the moment you and your Dragon meet, your actions and attitude inform her behaviour around people, other animals, even other Dragons. Each day, your little Dragon looks to you for nourishment and comfort. Each day, your affection and care reinforce the bond between you. It lays a foundation upon which all further socialization and training will stand; the stronger the foundation, the better. This is a long-term relationship you're building, so being thorough is more important than being fast.

Dragons are very tactile creatures, and, aside from feeding, grooming is one of the best ways to connect with your young charge. Since care of scale and horn is an essential, even ritualistic, part of their existence, it's advised you set up a daily schedule and stick to it.[2] This will give your Dragon a sense of continuity leading her, bit by bit, to not only endure your attentions, but look forward to them.

You don't need fancy tools: good quality curry combs and scrub brushes suffice for everyday, and wing burnishers are little more than large, Vulcanized-rubber scrapers. Remember, it is your time together which is most important. Whether scouring embryonic membrane off a newborn Acadian Trihorn or combing the ankle tufts of a sinuous Mongolian Red, every moment you spend helping them primp and preen is a moment spent cementing your position *in loco familia*. Not only is your Dragon growing accustomed to your touch, she is also recognizing you as kin. The more you're accepted as family—the more your Dragon believes she is part of *your* enchantment—the less likely accidents will be.

This familial relationship extends to your pets, as well. Dragons are companionable creatures, and, in the absence of their own kind, they tend to be surprisingly inter-species friendly. They've been known to display a specific fondness for cats, birds, and chinchillas, while dismissing horses as dense and dogs as infuriatingly dependent. However, as with most things Dragon, common-sense precautions are a must. Make formal introductions all around and never leave a Dragon under a year old alone with Toto—the temptation to play toss the terrier is more than any hatchling should be asked to resist. Once

---

2. A postprandial bath is always a good place to start.

your charge is aware that the other non-humans in the house are also members of the family, there is little danger of a late-night culinary misadventure which leaves you one tabby short and trying to console a remorseful Dragon. A little effort up front leads to easier sleep for all down the road.

Beyond basic socialization, formal training of young Dragons is considered a quixotic endeavor at best.[3] They are, after all, large, willful creatures who, like small children, delight in testing their people, in seeing just how far they can push the limits, how often they can bend or even break the most reasonable of rules. They are also uncanny milquetoast detectors, capable of sensing vacillation in an instant and, given the slightest opportunity, exploiting it to the fullest.

This doesn't mean you should just let your Dragon do as she pleases. That would be the height of carelessness and folly. Remember: as a Dragon keeper you are responsible not only to your individual hatchling, but to Dragonkind as a whole. You and your charge are ambassadors to the world, great sections of which still view Dragons with fear and suspicion. To those people, first impressions count, and while it's said there is no such thing as a bad Dragon, only a Dragon with bad manners, bad manners can get a Dragon in a lot of trouble.

Working with Dragons is more a matter of art than science. That said, a few simple guidelines never hurt.

Be firm—Dragons admire strength—yet loving. Be mindful of the fact that, as cheeky as they get, Dragons are also loyal and eager to please. And they understand our language demonstratively better than we understand theirs.[4] Talk to them. Explain what you are doing in a clear, reasonable fashion. Make sure they grasp the concept of boundaries and respect yours as much as you respect theirs. Not only

---

3. They are not dogs or parrots to be taught tricks, so don't even try.

4. No one knows exactly how much of what we say translates into Dragonish, though if historic reports are any indication, the Druids and mystics had no problem communicating with them. It is believed that Dragons not only understand simple words and commands—be careful when commanding a Dragon—but also complicated concepts, even abstractions. That, of course, is no more than one would expect from Cosmic Creatures.

does this prevent serious disciplinary problems come adolescence, it also goes a long way towards building the trust between you. As rebellious as your youngster gets, somewhere deep down, she will know that your rules are not capricious or punitive. They are for your mutual welfare.

Your hatchling should be taught immediately that "No" means "No." This goes for not jumping into the Jacuzzi or playing on the patio furniture[5] all the way to not raiding the neighbor's hen house. Remember: you are the parent in this dynamic. Once rules are established, make sure they are followed; if they are ignored, be sure it's an affirmative choice on your part and not a matter of caving in to a petulant Dragonlet. By the same token, you don't want to be a killjoy, straitjacketing her natural enthusiasm. This can be a delicate balancing act, especially with troubled orphans, but if you approach it from a place of respect and fun rather than domination and control, and lavish her with praise when lessons are learned, that's half the battle won.

Be aware of any bad habits creeping into your Dragon's behaviour. Bad habits breed like lemmings and are harder to break than a four-minute mile. If you're not careful, in a few short years you'll wake up and find you have an uncontrollable fire-breathing delinquent on your hands, which is not good for either of you. Again, diligence and patience early spare you trouble later. You will also want guard against your Dragon becoming a one-person Dragon. This can result in her being overly protective of you and jealous of other members of your family, a scenario which can get very messy very quickly. While only one person should be the voice of training—it keeps confusion to a minimum—do have other members of your family present and involved as much as possible. Especially children. Dragons like children.

Clearly and concisely, teach your Dragons where they can and can't go, what they can and can't get into. Since fences, even moats, around a Dragon habitat are both cost prohibitive and quite useless, you must appeal to draconic intelligence and good sense to keep them at home. When you feel confident your charge will not bolt from your

---

5. Though they may manage both well enough as newborns, their first growth spurt will lead straight to expense and embarrassment.

side as soon as you open their lair door, take them on a walkabout. Every day, for as long as it takes, show them the limits of their range and make sure they understand, "This far, no farther." If your land is vast, the prospect of tracing its entire purlieu is apt to be daunting to your little one, so take it in incremental steps. Start with a circle a quarter-mile radius from her den and increase it as she is able. Be sure to feed her right away upon returning home. This is positive reinforcement of the highest order, and will serve you in good stead should your Dragon ever wander off.[6] All Dragons have excellent internal compasses—not to mention noses—and will find their way home for dinner from most anywhere.

It is not unusual for little ones to be less than thrilled by the prospect of daily lessons. In the face of such Dragon-headedness, treats can be great motivators. A pouch full of salmon-wrapped habaneros or ginger fingers should be a standard part of every Dragon keeper's gear. For best results, do not schedule training sessions immediately before or after a meal. If they are ravenous, they won't be able to concentrate on anything other than food; if they're full, the most savory treats become gratuitous.

Beyond Fundamentals

By the time your Dragon is a year old, the basics of living with people should be as natural as breathing. This does not, however, mean your job as a Dragon keeper is done.

In their second year, Western Dragons will start experimenting with fire, a definite teaching moment for all. If ever there is a time for rules to be followed to the letter, this is it. First, make sure your fire insurance is up to date. Set up a flame-friendly practice area—a fallow field or abandoned quarry will do nicely—and restrict your young firebrands to that space only. Explain the vagaries of the winds—a

---

6. When this happens, as it surely will, do not panic. Put out her dinner as usual and remember the Tolkien maxim: "Not all those who wander are lost." If you have kept faith with her as a Dragon keeper should, she will come home.

strong fan and a flame thrower make excellent demonstration tools. Finally, make "Not near the house! Not near the woods!" your mantra. Say it loud, say it often, until it is etched into your Dragon's memory. Only when you are confident they've got it—really got it—should you let them play with fire.

If you haven't done so before now, this is an excellent time to start networking with other Dragons and their people. Aside from the company they provide, other Dragons can educate on matters about which we humans can only guess. Draconic body language, for example, or the art of hurling fireballs (though studies indicate the latter is more of a natural talent than something which can be taught). Visiting Dragons also help alleviate boredom, which can be a real problem for Dragon and Dragon keeper alike. A bored Dragon is a restless Dragon, inclined to act out just for the hell of it. If your neighbor reports his prize heifers loose three days in a row or neatly dug craters crop up overnight making your driveway look like half a mile of Swiss cheese, you know you've got a problem. Call in reinforcements, fix your neighbor's fences, and give your Dragon something to do. Fast.[7]

Year two is also when Dragons begin to get a taste for hoarding— or, if you will, personalizing their living space. If you find yourself suddenly missing hubcaps, mirrors, door brasses, and the like, check with your Dragon. Ask politely and she'll probably give them back, especially if you give her a bauble of her very own for Summer Solstice. In fact, as Dragons get older, the proffer of sparkly treasures is a better incentive for training than the most succulent morsel.

Many people are convinced life with Dragons doesn't hit full stride until the third year. First comes the pomp and circumstance of the Remembrance of Names, reinforcing the ties between Dragon and person, not to mention being a great excuse for a party. Honor the day with feasting and music, dancing and games. Funny hats are optional.

---

7. Keep her away from the cows; though, if you can turn it into a game, you just might inveigle her into repairing the mess she made of the drive.

As important as her Naming is, from a human standpoint a Dragon's first flight is far more spectacular.[8] Daedalus to da Vinci, Montgolfier to Goddard, in fact and fancy, we have looked with envy upon the creatures of the sky. Now we are no longer limited to the inelegance of airplanes. Now we have Dragons!

Of course, not all Dragons consent to being ridden, as is their right. A great deal depends on their individual temperament and, beyond that, how well they've been accustomed to human touch. Proper respect and appreciation on a keeper's part are also essential. In the past, riding Dragons meant to be returned to the wild was not advised, the idea being that it makes them too comfortable around people which, in turn, makes them vulnerable. While this is a wise approach in principle, most experts today hold that such beliefs seriously underestimate our scaled friends. They are far too smart not to readily tell friend from foe regardless of circumstance or surroundings. Perhaps the surest path lies somewhere in between.

Naturally, the entire matter is moot until your Dragon gets airborne. In spring, you will want to assist in removing the fine velvet

---

8. Which doubtless shows Dragons just how little we know.

from her wings. This is not a simple afternoon's chore, but one which can take up to a week of meticulous scrubbing and burnishing. Still, it's time spent together and should be cherished as such.

When it comes to actual flight, there is little you can do save keep an eye out for wing sprains and lend your full-throated support from the peanut gallery.

Dragons need a full year—even two—of flying solo before being approached about giving lifts. This provides them with time to not only gain skill but develop physically. Despite their great size, remember that they are still young and growing. This makes them fragile. By age four or five, they will be sturdy enough to give rides without fear of injury.

Saddles—even saddle pads—are anathema. If you wish to know the joys of Dragon flight, you must get accustomed to riding bareback. The natural place to ride a Dragon is sitting between the last two neck ridges just at the withers, ahead of the wings—this affords reasonable support without interfering with wing movement. Approach your Dragon with deference, gift her with a sparkly or a treat for her palate, then, if she permits, clamber aboard. No flying yet; just let her get used to the feel and weight of you. If you are less than comfortable holding on with only your knees, a neck strap can be used. This is not to be confused with a bridle (never!), but is simply a soft leather band which fits round the Dragon's neck and is for your sense of security only. Curiously, many Dragons actually enjoy neck straps—multicoloured or elegantly embroidered, they are regarded as marvelous bits of fancy dress. The most festively inclined love the addition of bells. In the tradition of elaborate harness brasses, such finery is particularly appreciated around Yuletide.

Appropriate attire is essential for Dragon riders, too—speed and altitude will give you frostbite before you know it. Standard flying togs used to include leather or sheepskin dusters with lined gloves, boots, and protective headgear. This made for a warm, if cumbersome ensemble. The advent of silk micro-fleece and polypropylene fibers have led to lighter, cozier flying apparel, reminding us that just because something is modern doesn't mean it's anti-Dragon. Like most animals but more so, Dragons pick up on their people's anxiety, so you might also want to pack a parachute, at least until you are secure in your seat.[9]

When first astride your Dragon, remember that she is still in her early adolescence.[10] This may make her mischievous at best, rebellious at worst. Make sure she understands that joint flights are intended to be fun for both of you—no fancy aerobatics or buzzing the neighbor's livestock. If you've done a proper job with early training, there should be little trouble getting her to adhere to basic flight safety and etiquette. If not, keep your feet on the ground.

Navigating the Sea of Ennui

As the years go by, the rough-and-tumble part of Dragon keeping fades into familiar routines punctuated by unexpected thrills. This is the season-to-season wonder of raising a Dragon.

The most immediate—and persistent—challenge before you is to keep your charge mentally and physically stimulated. Games are always distracting—king of the hill, dodge fire, air soccer, etc.— though in the absence of other Dragons, you are apt to be run ragged or worse.[11]

For the long haul, nothing holds the draconic imagination like travel. As Dragons hit their sixth year, they put away their childish, get-into-everything ways for a more studied curiosity. Flyabouts— exploring the world and, in the process, hobnobbing with others of their kind—are the best education a Dragon can hope for, as well as being sources of perpetual delight. Not that you should just send your charge off on her own. It is considered the height of negligence for a kept Dragon under eleven to wander unattended, no matter how

---

9. Be sure to take fluids, too, as a preventative against altitude sickness.

10. This may last for a while. Dragons have been known to maintain their youthful rambunctiousness well into their second decade.

11. Yet another reason to cultivate your Dragon keeper's network.

mature she might seem. So keep your summers free. Though Dragon people are hardly parochial by nature, an annual Dragon keeper's holiday can be a broadening experience for one and all. It is also invaluable if you plan to release your Dragon back into the wild. Like a senior's habitual college tour, your Dragon can get a feeling for weyrs and their residents, even make connections for the future.

Liberating as a flyabout is, there are certain restrictions you must bear in mind. Travelling by Dragon does allow you to bypass the hassles of tickets, boarding passes, and airport security, but you will still need a passport and applicable visas if you plan on crossing international frontiers.[12] There are no such demarcations in a Dragon's view of the world, so be sure to keep a map with you. Ignorance of borders is no excuse in a combustible world. You will also need your Dragon

---

12. You might want to keep your trips local at first, perhaps limit yourselves to a long weekend at a nearby sanctuary. As your Dragon gets stronger and more adventurous, she'll no doubt want to expand her horizons. Take guidebook in hand, hold tight, and enjoy the ride.

keeper's credentials; this prevents you from having your legitimacy questioned or—heaven forbid!—your travel companion impounded.[13] The State Department has enough on their plate without worrying about Dragon-sparked incidents. On the upside, thanks to their resistance to most disease, Dragons needn't worry about immunizations or time spent in quarantine.

"Work," Voltaire noted in *Candide*, "saves us from three great evils: boredom, vice, and need." To the best of our knowledge, Dragons don't have to worry about vice, but the other two ...

As much as they thrive on just "being," Dragons are not all-play-and-no-work creatures. Uncannily cognizant of their precarious place in the modern world, they seem to grasp better than most the truth in the onerous axiom, "There ain't no such thing as a free lunch" (TANSTAAFL). It helps immensely that, like Border Collies and Alsatians,[14] they enjoy tasks challenging to mind and body.

As Dragons become settled—as settled as Dragons can be—they are more than willing to be helpful to their people and community. This is not only an essential weapon in the ongoing battle with ennui, but it can markedly offset the financial burden all Dragon keepers face. When it comes to Dragons and work, most anything is possible as long as it's interesting, non-repetitive, and properly appreciated. Strength, keen senses, and flying abilities, for example, make one Dragon better than a whole pack of Lassies when it comes to search-and-rescue efforts in the wake of avalanches and earthquakes.[15] Dragons also have a natural affinity for earthworks. They are adept at geomancy as well as construction, and will eagerly pitch in for the construction of fire and sea walls, dikes, and roads—all those essential

---

13. It is ill-advised to test a Dragon's loyalty; this doesn't mean bureaucrats don't do it.

14. Apologies to Dragons everywhere for comparing you to canines, even intelligent ones.

15. Some people refuse to use Dragons in the mountains, insisting that the slightest ill-timed roar could strip Mont Blanc bare. Though there is truth in that, the general consensus is they are more help than hindrance, and not availing ourselves of their proffered aid in times of disaster is nothing less than the rankest dracophobia.

bits of our infrastructure we have let fall into such egregious disrepair. If you and your Dragon are assisting the community at large, be sure to be properly compensated for your time and effort. TANSTAAFL applies to humans, too, though we conveniently forget the fact if we can get away with it.

Remember this above all: you are dealing with creatures who delight in problem solving far more than labor, the latter without the former being mere drudgery. The more work is fun for Dragons, the more Dragons make life a joy for their humans.

The art of medicine consists in amusing the
patient while nature cures the disease.

—*Voltaire*

eleven

Wellness in a Dragon's World

As a rule, Dragons require very little veterinary care. The usual litany of health woes which plague other companion creatures stand little chance against a hale and hearty Dragon.[1] They are all but immune to salmonella and stomatitis (mouth rot), not to mention a slew of parasites and amoebic and fungal infections to which captive snakes and lizards are prone. Rabies, cancers, most viruses—even anthrax and foot and mouth—are completely foreign to Dragons, wild or kept. Conversely, the chance of zoonotic contagion is so slight as to be considered a statistical impossibility, which should reassure us all. Cryptoveterinarians tend to attribute this hardiness of constitution to their ancient lineage, and that may be; of course, lately that's become their catchall response whenever they're stumped on the science and do not wish to appear ill-informed.

---

1. As with all creatures, wounds, malnutrition, old age, and other stressors can make Dragons vulnerable to opportunistic infection or disease. It's not likely, but it can happen.

A Pound of Prevention

Though a well-kept Dragon needn't worry about serious illness, there are still a few health matters of which you ought to be aware.

Proper hygiene and diet go a long way towards keeping Dragons fit. Scrub down their eating area daily to prevent the proliferation of unwanted bacteria. Check their water sources, making sure they do not become stagnant and foul. As for the rest of their habitat, Dragons are, by and large, neat creatures. They keep their dens clean and have been known to incinerate excess slough, dung, and unwanted nesting materials as needed. When it comes to battling germs, not even a high-tech autoclave can compete with a good blast of Dragonfire.

Walk your woods and fields frequently. Get rid of any noxious greens or fungi. If you are unsure what something is or how it will affect your Dragon, remove it. You can always plant something you know to be safe in its stead. This is particularly true of mushrooms, toadstools, and certain orchids. They look good but can have serious psychotropic effects. Trying to handle a tripping baby Dragon is one of the more dangerous aspects of Dragon keeping and should be avoided if at all possible.

Watch out for overeating. This can become a problem after weaning when young Dragons begin to explore the vast variety of soporific delicacies available to them. The best remedy for a tummy-sore Dragon is to keep her on her feet, walking, and let nature do its thing. Stay away from all over-the-counter treatments; these are designed for people and will only make your Dragon feel worse—not to mention that proportionate dosages would make them cost prohibitive. If you start feeling helpless, a liberal draught of warm snapdragon/peppermint tea with honey and a dash of basil will prove palliative with minimal side effects.[2] Some people prefer ginger to basil, which, while fine for Asian Dragons, can give Western Dragons excess gas—a dangerous prospect when they reach their fire-breathing years.

---

2. Try a dram yourself to ease anxiety.

In recent years, acute gout has become a problem for older Dragons (150+ years). This is attributed to dietary imbalances causing accretions of uric acid in their joints, most frequently the wing carpals. If your Dragon displays a marked stiffness to her movement and a sudden dullness to her hue, all else being equal, gout is a logical diagnosis, especially if her diet has been rich in game. Cut red meats out of her daily fare immediately and increase her vegetable and fluid intake. Some people have gone so far as to enforce a 30 percent fish/70 percent vegetable regime with excellent results. Don't permit flying until joint inflammation has subsided and she can move without pain. Given that Dragons tend to put a brave face on any discomfort, you might want to insist—as best you can—on a couple of extra days' down-time, just to be sure.

Bodily wounds—cuts, scrapes, broken bones—are rarities in a modern, well-kept habitat. Draconic integuments can withstand the roughest everyday wear[3] and, for all their honeycombed lightness, Dragon bones are very strong. Which is not to say accidents don't happen. A tree might fall, a youngster might get in a scuffle with a playmate. Or, violating postings and the law, a poacher might come after your Dragon. Poachers are hardly knights, but they are treacherous. Though a Dragon's blood is only lethal if her wounds are lethal, it does have a corrosive potency which makes any first aid tricky. For starters, you will need industrial-strength, Neoprene-coated gloves—18-inch gauntlet style are best. Fortunately, most scale injuries Dragon keepers see can be treated with a thorough cleansing and topical application of lavender or tea tree oil. A liberal sprinkling of powdered cayenne promotes blood clotting, and calendula or comfrey compresses are excellent for drawing infection out of puncture wounds. On those occasions when you're looking at a major laceration, use heavy-duty surgical staples rather than sutures. Limit your Dragon to water baths—no dust—until healing is well under way— usually in a day or two.

---

3. Except immediately after a molt. See *Molting Balm* in the next section.

Broken bones should be lightly splinted and your Dragon's movement restricted as much as possible. Plaster over scales itches something awful, giving you a miserable—even dangerous—Dragon hell-bent on ripping her cast to shreds. Keep her warm and quiet against the risk of shock, and be sure her diet is extra rich in easily digested proteins and minerals until she's healed.

Dragons have remarkable recuperative powers, as long as they don't overdo it. To this end, nothing is quite as salubrious as music. Dragons love music—lyric, guttural, raw, visceral, sometimes painful, always soaring music! They especially love music when they're under the weather. It needn't be baroque, just something simple with a steady rhythm—flutes or lutes or Aeolian harps, euphonious but not too New Agey—to help them relax and not fight nature's healing ways. This is particularly beneficial when, for example, an overeager young Dragon gets a wing sprain and only time and utter indolence will get her back in the air.

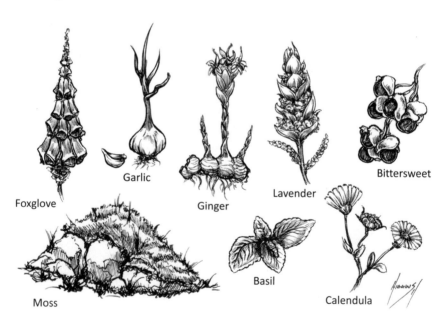

Foxglove

Garlic

Ginger

Lavender

Bittersweet

Moss

Basil

Calendula

Caring for your Dragon's external needs is also important. Claws should be trimmed on a regular basis, though a good farrier is better suited to this job (and usually a lot cheaper) than your local vet. As your Dragon enters her second century, you may wish to have her teeth filed on occasion. Good dental hygiene never hurts any of us and she will certainly enjoy the attention. Again, as with talon trimming, a competent blacksmith is as good—if not better—than a vet.

Dragon Pharmacopoeia

Though Dragons seldom require medicines as we humans know them, there are a few standby remedies which should be in every Dragon keeper's pantry. A helpful hint: Brewery vats and paraphernalia are ideal tools for preparing your own tonics. Anything smaller simply can't accommodate the quantities of ingredients required for draconic cures.

Weyrsickness Remedy

Every so often, no matter how attentive you are to hatchling or orphan, a heavy melancholy will settle over a young Dragon and just refuse to lift. This is post-egg Dragon Despondency, or Weyrsickness. If you've tried everything else to draw your Dragon out of herself to no avail, Weyrsickness Remedy might just do the trick.

In a 100-gallon copper vat, place:

- 1 hundredweight crushed bittersweet berries
- 40 pounds honey (clover or wildflower preferred)
- 14 pounds forget-me-not petals (or 1 quart extract)

Fill the vat with fresh spring water and bring to a boil. Simmer uncovered for 8 hours. Let cool, then decant into 10-gallon kegs.

At the first sign of post-egg depression (look for weight loss, inability to sleep, and general malaise) administer twice daily, 1 pint for each 100 pounds of body weight, in your Dragon's food. If the depression persists, double the dosage and spend *lots* of time with your little one. You might also arrange play dates with other young

Dragonlets in your area; occasionally the companionship of a more mundane creature—cat, burro, etc.—works wonders. On the off chance the symptoms linger for more than four to six weeks, contact a professional. A chronic condition may be developing and relocation to a rehabilitative environment might be the best thing for the little one. As hard as it may be to say good-bye, sometimes it's the only thing to do.

Molting Balm

Young Dragons grow so fast in their first few years they seem to be in a state of constant molt. This is, of course, perception rather than truth, but still...To protect those tender patches of new skin exposed by a good Dragon shedding, you should always have a batch of Molting Balm on hand.

In a 50-gallon copper cauldron, melt:

- 20 pounds cocoa butter
- 20 pounds almond oil
- 8 pounds of beeswax (Proportions of balm softeners [oils] to balm hardener [wax] may vary depending on how hot or cool your Dragon's temperature runs. Do not hesitate to tinker with the proportions until you have a compound right for your Dragon, one which applies with a minimum of elbow grease; excessive rubbing makes for a very unhappy hatchling.)

Add to the mixture:

- 10 pounds bruised lavender
- 10 pounds pot marigold (*Calendula officinalis*) (Be sure to harvest the calendula at noon under a bright, hot sun for peak potency.)
- 2 quarts lemon oil
- 8 ounces ylang-ylang

Simmer for at least 4 hours, then strain off the lavender and calendula solids and put the balm in oaken containers to cool and solidify. You can also press the herbal residue to extract residual oils. They are both aromatic and efficacious in treating minor wounds and scrapes.

Molting Balm should be applied liberally immediately following shedding, particularly in tropical and subtropical environs where the risk of sunburn is high.

Flying Ointment

Every now and then a Dragon has trouble taking wing and is in need of a little extra lift. Flying ointment was devised for this purpose. *Warning*: Do not confuse this with what used to be known as Witches Flying Ointment, or aconite; the two are very separate and *very* incompatible treatments. Actually, Flying Ointment is something of a misnomer in that it's less an ointment and more a highly concentrated herbal extract which you dilute and use as a spray. Remember: this is potent stuff—prepare and handle with care.[4]

Infuse in 2 gallons of cold spring water:

- 3 quarts foxglove blooms (*Digitalis purpurea*)
- 2 quarts windflower (*Anemone*) (Gather the windflower in the spring when the blooms are just coming out. Dry or fresh anemone can be used, but remember that the dried are more concentrated: use only 1 ½ quarts of dried blooms.)
- 1 pound mugwort (*Artemesia vulgaris*)

Let it stand for 12 hours in the sun, then distill, slowly. You should wind up with approximately 1 quart of concentrated essence.

Add to this:

- 3 ounces basil oil (Witches' Herb)

---

4. A cautionary tale told in Dragon Studies seminars relates how an overeager Bavarian Dragon keeper forgot the first rule of flying ointment—dilute!—and applied it to his Dragon's wings full strength. That young Dragon took off like the proverbial bat out of Hell—an expression Dragons grasp in full—and wasn't able to land for three days. The steward was much more careful after that, heeding the cheeky caveat his Dragon was said to have nailed up in the supply shed: *Schwach Oder Sterben* (Dilute or Die). Though surely more fiction than fact, it's a fable from which we all can learn.

Stir gently—*never shake!*—and decant into a dark, airtight glass bottle. Allow to age in a cool place—basements are good, caves are better—for at least three months.

When needed, mix one (1) ounce of concentrate with one (1) gallon of spring water in a large plant sprayer. Spray your Dragon's wings—top and bottom—20 minutes before flying exercises. Do not use for more than 10 days as it has a cumulative effect, rapidly becoming more than a young Dragon can handle.

Though herbalists swear to the efficacy of Flying Ointment, there are certain members of the Dragon community who insist it is no more than a sweet-smelling placebo for diffident three-year olds. Of course, this theory has yet to be tested under either double- or single-blind protocols; and, while everyone concurs that a Dragon's mind is a powerful thing, in the end, it matters more *that* it works than *how*.

Medicine Chest Staples

For those just-in-case times, it's always good to have sufficient supplies of the following around:

- Spanish or Indian moss: Excellent as poultice mediums, especially for bruises acquired during those first awkward flights.
- Snapdragon tea: Good for upset tummies and insomnia.
- Honey: To help all medicines go down.
- Lavender and tea tree oils: Excellent topical antiseptics.
- Mint and mustard: Excellent for poultices if your Dragon should catch a chest cold.
- Mullein (*Verbascum thapsus*): Mix with warm milk and honey for congestion.
- Garlic: For those rare times when an antibiotic is needed.
- Ground cayenne: For use as a blood coagulant.

Having a large herb garden on site, though helpful and certainly enjoyable, is no longer essential. If you are short on time or an herbalist's inclination, there are some excellent mail-order/online herbariums around the world which provide ready access to essential pharmaceuticals. You are sure to find a reasonable source for the requisite supplies.[5]

If you are going to plant for yourself, a solid herbalist's book is a must. Among favorites used by Dragon keepers are Matthew Wood's *The Book of Herbal Wisdom: Using Plants as Medicines* and Dian Dincin Buchman's *Herbal Medicine*. For those who have Eastern Dragons or are simply interested in alternatives, Dan Bensky's *Chinese Herbal Medicine: Materia Medica* and its companion volume, *Chinese Herbal Medicine: Formulas & Strategies,* are a bit pricey but about as comprehensive as they come.

———————

When all is said and done, nothing benefits a Dragon's health as much as a vigilant Dragon keeper. Know your Dragon. Know her habits of eating, exercise, and sleep. Know her colour and her temperament. And know when she strays from her draconic norms.

There is an old Irish proverb, "Every disease is a physician." It was surely coined with Dragons in mind. Every day we learn more and more about our friends, in good health and poor. That we don't know everything yet is far from a shameful admission. It simply means we must study harder, observe better. For now, short of prevention, common sense, and a few tried and true treatments, simply aim to care for your Dragons and keep them amused when they are ailing. Nine times out of ten, nature will take care of the rest.

---

5. The one thing of which you can't truly be sure is harvesting method, so essential with marigold and windflower, for example. This fact alone has kept many a Dragon keeper in the herb business.

What shelter to grow ripe is ours?
What leisure to grow wise?

—Matthew Arnold, "In Memory of the Author of 'Obermann'"

twelve

The Turns of Mortal Coil

And so the years pass. Your Dragon has left cuddly infancy and rowdy youth behind. By the time she's midway through her second decade, she will be nearly half her adult size and ready to take on the whole world. This is a transitional time full of joy, worry, pride, sorrow, and choices which will affect both of your lives for years to come.

Flying Free

Ask any Dragon keeper and they will tell you one of the hardest decisions they've ever made is whether or not to release their grown charge into the wild. Of course, if you could ask the Dragons, they'd likely say the decision was entirely out of human hands. Somewhere in between lies the truth of the situation.

Temporary guardianship is the aim of most Dragon keepers: to foster their Dragons until they're big enough to thrive amongst their own kind, then send them on their way. In the footsteps of rehab-and-release experts through the ages, they raise their nestlings to be as fearless and wild as they can be.

As anyone who's worked with Dragons knows, you can do every-thing by the book, but, in the final analysis, only the wishes of your ward truly matter. To shove a Dragon out of the proverbial nest is cruel—not to mention physically impossible—if that Dragon pre-fers to stay. Luckily, by the time she is free flying, you should have a clear idea how she is disposed on the matter and can shape the next decade of her care accordingly. If she tips her horns in the direction of enchantment life, the best you can do is teach her to hunt and forage, to forsake livestock for game and people for other Dragons. Nurture independence and a healthy suspicion of strangers, and trust that mil-lennia of draconic instinct, evolution, and luck will do the rest.

There is considerable disagreement on how best to introduce Dragons back to the wild. In the past the standard was to make a big deal of flying to the weyr of their choice and saying formal good-byes. Some keepers would even linger for a month or two to monitor their Dragon's integration. While this approach sounds all very heartfelt, even sentimental, it creates serious logistical problems (how ever do you get home?) and, ultimately, is more for your sense of closure than your Dragon's welfare. Today, most releases are more modest affairs. Often, a Dragon will simply wake up one lazy-hazy midsummer day, taste the wind, and without bother or breakfast, spread her wings and be gone.

Abrupt? Certainly.

But, if you've been paying attention, it's not shocking. Dragons always leave signs, subtle, even enigmatic, but signs none the less. When your Dragon joins you unexpectedly down at your favorite swimming hole and shows more than usual patience with your Shel-tie, when she leaves all save the crème de la crème of her hoard under your front porch and gets a far-away, restless cast to her eye, you'll know her departure is imminent. Don't make a fuss or get teary: Dragons shun the maudlin. Just spend a little extra time with her, perhaps linger over grooming—you'll want her dapper as Y Ddraig Goch for her new "family." An impromptu picnic is never amiss and will let her know that you have, indeed, been attentive.

Don't think for a second that returning a Dragon to the wild means you will never see her again. For one thing, you can visit her new environs, possibly catch a glimpse of her cavorting through the mist.[1] And even if you don't spot her soaring free, be assured: you are not forgotten. Dragon memories put elephants' to shame. It may take her five years or ten—factor in a sufficient period for acclimation and draconic time sense—but one day you will be walking through the woods, perhaps rock-hunting around the lake and, *voilà*! There she is, basking in the morning sun, drowsy-eyed and nonchalant as if you'd seen each other only yesterday.

It should be noted that some animal-rights ethicists claim it is inherently immoral to release any wild/exotic creature raised by humans back into their natural habitat, insisting time spent intimately with people ill-equips them for the rigors of life on the wild side. They contend that a Dragon fifteen years in the company of humans is a tragedy waiting to happen. To bolster this conviction, they point to studies showing odds stacked as high as the Great Wall against the efforts of even trained conservationists. And they're right: the statistics are grim. Predators, in particular, often lack the fine-tuned hunting skills essential for survival. According to research out of the University of Exeter, for example, among captive-bred carnivores over two-thirds of the study's subjects fell prey to starvation, hunters, or automobiles within eighteen months of their release.[2]

Can Dragons do better?

We believe so.

As well-intentioned as the anti-release folks may be, they seem to forget that Dragons are not your usual mundane rehab-and-release subjects. While you can't free a Dragon disinclined to go, neither

---

1. It is advised you stay away for at least a year. Your Dragon needs time to settle in without distraction or reminders of the cushy life.

2. See Kristen R. Jule, et al. "The Effects of Captive Experience on Reintroduction Survival in Carnivores." *Biological Conservation* 141 (2008): 355–363; and "Revisiting the Effects of Captive Experience on Reintroduction Survival in Carnivores." *Current Conservation*. Issue 3.4. (2009).

can you hold one who has the purr of enchantments rumbling in her blood. Not to mention that, compared to hapless bunnies, ocelots, or monkeys dumped back into the wild, Dragons are positively brilliant—and a match for any car on the road. If you have raised her right, not only will she be hale and hardy—an asset when presenting to a foreign enchantment—but she will know that, should things go terribly wrong in the great world beyond—she always has a safe haven to which she can return. She will always be welcomed back home.[3]

Staying Close

Of course, not all Dragons are disposed to going native.

For a long time, the prevailing theoretical winds swirled around the idea that those Dragons hatched into our world and imprinted from day one could never make it among the weyrs. In the last fifty years, this strict Lorenzian[4] notion has faded by the scientific wayside. Statistics show as many orphans as hatchlings are embracing life amongst humans; even a few older Dragons are opting to carve permanent arrangements out of lay-by sojourns. The truth is, there are myriad reasons Dragons elect to remain with their people, most of which we shall never know.

For those who stay, day-to-day routines won't change much from ages ten to thirty and thirty to fifty. This creates a comforting sense of continuity, and your charge's growing self-sufficiency leaves more free time for you to plan excursions and Dragon amusements. Of course, should your Dragon choose to take a mate, all bets are off. An expanding family requires shelter renovations, extra plantings of garden, field, and orchard, even the occasional delicate negotiation with the people next door. Fortunately, the winning ways of well-mannered

---

3. As Robert Frost wrote, "Home is the place where, when you have to go there, / They have to take you in" (*The Death of the Hired Man*). Curiously, though boomerang kids are becoming legion in these financially strained times, since statistics have been kept, the number of Dragons who return to the company of their people has held at a steady 10 percent.

4. See Konrad Lorenz, *The Year of the Greyleg Goose*.

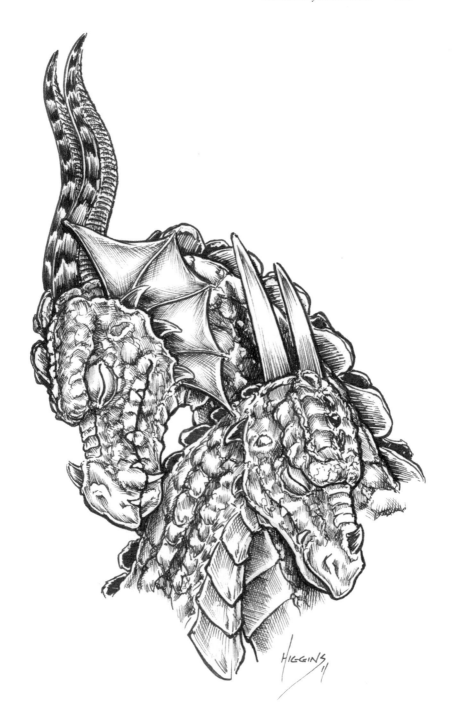

Dragons can usually charm acceptance from the sourest of neighbors: prejudice crumbles under the weight of so much splendor.

For you and your Dragon, the companionship of one of her own kind, while labor- and cost-intensive up front, more than returns the investment in dividends of future Dragon delight. Remember to take your time, work with—not against—your Dragon(s), and there will be fewer do-overs in the end.

Studies of Dragons who pair off in kept environments are wafer-thin, at best. Most reports are of nonbreeding pairs who met and grew acquainted on Dragon keeper jamborees or lay-by parleys.[5] Accounts of captive breeding were, until the turn of the century, considered little more than faërie tales. The space and resources required were simply far beyond the means of most individual Dragon keepers. Of late, large-scale conservation projects have had a few successes with pro-creating pairs, though, much as these consummations are devoutly to be wished, they remain at the emotional discretion of the Dragons. No amount of human cajoling will make a difference one way or the other.

For Dragon and Dragon keeper, "time is the fire in which we burn," as Delmore Schwartz wrote. Information on Dragon longevity is largely anecdotal and properly suspect. According to the Chinese, for example, a Dragon is nothing more than a sea snake for her first 500 years, then slowly acquires horns, limbs, whiskers, ankle tufts, etc., until, in her third millennium, she finally enters her fully Dragonish adulthood. If she makes it to her 3,000th birthday, she is able to fly and mate and produce a new generation of baby Dragons. This long, slow lifeline is a clear offshoot from the age of Cosmic Dragons and accounts for tales of individual beings so old that they are considered

---

5. Occasionally a kept Dragon will bring home a mate green to the ways of people. Give them plenty of time and space to settle in. Your Dragon is the best teacher under these circumstances. Though he will likely never be as comfortable around people as she, if treated with deference and care, he should let you keep all your fingers and toes.

immortal. Of course, it also flies in the face of everything we know from modern cryptoherpetology, natural law, and just plain Dragon sense.[6] In Europe and the Americas, Dragon lore, while slight on actual numbers, speaks of creatures who have menaced villages and wilds for centuries. Given that the regions were rife with dragon slayers for so long, it is far more likely the locals, ill-versed in distinguishing one Dragon from another, simply assumed the son to be the Sire. It makes for a better story.[7]

We may not yet know the exact count of a Dragon's days, but if an Aldabra tortoise can make it to two hundred, Dragons, in this age of conservation, can surely see their fourth century with little more than silvered whiskers to show for their troubles. Advances in modern medicine aside, you and your Dragon must accept that, barring an unexpected tragedy, you will be playing Yorick to the worms when she's still in her prime. This creates a host of issues for you both should your Dragon choose to stay in your care.

Despite their own longevity, Dragons seem to have a keen awareness of the frailty of human existence. As we hit our seventies and our thinning hair whitens and our laugh lines remain long after our laughter has faded, we tend to slow down. While this doesn't mean time with your Dragon is suddenly reduced to evenings sharing Bosco (cocoa) and counting fireflies on the front porch, she will instinctively know that the exuberant excursions of your youths must give way to more sedate outings. Quiet ambles by the lake replace spontaneous flights to the Riviera for midnight swims, and bobbing for baubles becomes a game best left to the grandkids. If you are concerned your Dragon is getting too sedentary—perhaps a little paunchy around the tail—connect with other Dragon keepers, arrange get-togethers

---

6. With what we know today, people were obviously confusing various species of pseudo-dragon and morphing them into a True Dragon at various stages of development.

7. This also explains why so few of these fabled beasties were ever as large as their purported years should have made them.

for your charges, and just let them play. It will prove invigorating for them and alleviate any guilt lingering round the edges of your mind.

Death is one of the last human taboos, especially in the West. Whether young and indestructible or old and afraid of the dark, with hushed tones and euphemisms, we delude ourselves into believing mortality is only for the other guy. A Dragon keeper does not have the luxury of such self-deception. The covenant between you and your Dragon does not end simply because you are no longer around. The guard will change, not once but many times during her lifetime, and provisions—both legal and financial—must be made for her care and protection.

Estate planning is essential, not to mention an iron-clad will. You don't want to be worrying that your dracophobic great-grandnephew Ernie can swoop in after you're gone and parcel out your land to the local urban sprawl czar. Of course, your Dragon may have something to say about that, but if it gets that far you can be sure it'll to be a bloody mess all around. A few hours with a first-rate, sympathetic attorney can make all the difference. Anything less is as irresponsible as letting a pet crocodile loose in the Central Park Reservoir.

Dragon loyalties are passionate and their attachments profound. They will not be handed off to just anyone. If at all possible, keep their care in the family. It's easier on them and less assailable in the courts. If this is not an option, you might consider the people in your Dragon keepers' network or even a like-minded friend for guardian-ship.[8] Once you've worked out the bare bones of an agreement, set up a series of regular get-togethers between your Dragon and the blessed beneficiary. Let them get to know each other: the most meticulous plan will come to naught if the parties don't get along. If all goes well, your Dragon will soon consider this person-in-waiting as part of the family, making the transition as natural as these things can be when the time comes.

Some Dragons refuse to connect with a new person—even a blood relative. Behaviourists, tending to over-anthropomorphize

---

8. If you're still stuck, consult WAFDE.

these things, insist this is a demonstration of the depths of draconic affection and grief, and there is merit to this belief. One has only to look at other companion creatures to know that many animals—cats, dogs, degus, alpacas—can feel the loss of a house or stable mate intensely. While a period of mourning is to be expected, our friends can go to draconic extremes. There are reports of bereft Dragons turning their backs on food, becoming withdrawn, depressed, even getting aggressively snappish with others.[9]

Of course, no one can anticipate the course of another's grief; chances are your Dragon won't even know how she'll feel until after you're gone. This means: Legatees, listen up!

If you have recently "inherited" a Dragon and, after a month, she still refuses to eat or bathe or stretch her wings and the family Alsatian is cowering under the bed and your Maine Coon's tail is singed beyond recognition, it is time to call in a professional. They will likely recommend you get her around other Dragons—wild, woolly, rip-snorting Dragons—as soon as possible. Kindred company—especially if it includes frisky Dragonlets—can seduce her into shedding her heartsick mien and immersing herself in the joys of being a Dragon. This fix can be either temporary or permanent. Some beings thus renewed choose to stay in the wild, while others, try though they might to adjust to weyr life, find they miss rubbing scales with elbows and wend their way back to the peopled world. It may take a while, so be patient. In the end, there is no explaining the whys and wherefores of such decisions. Simply accept them as a Dragon's right and support your friend.

When the essential documents are signed, sealed, and filed with the court and county, it's time for a gala of majestic proportions. After all, honoring a lifetime shared when one of the parties can't attend is inanely anemic to Dragon eyes. Celebrate while you are both very much of this world lest you regret the lost chance when it's too late.

---

9. Behaviourists suspect this last is from dread not sorrow, though why it must be one or the other is a puzzlement. As C. S. Lewis pointed out, "No one ever told me grief felt so much like fear" (*A Grief Observed*).

And do it in empyreal style: invite family and friends both Dragon and human, serve rare viands, play divine music, tell tales, sing songs, and dance.

And when all is said and done and the last of your guests has departed, quietly welcome the new day with laughter in your soul and your Dragon by your side.

Intimations of Mortality: Letting Go

Despite faërie-tale rumors and mystical hypotheses to the contrary, a Dragon's days are not beyond number. Eventually someone, somewhere, will be a Dragon's last keeper.

Cryptogerontology is the last frontier when it comes to Dragon science, and with good reason. Dragons do not slip into old age like most creatures. Inherently farsighted, their eyes stay bright and sharp to the end, allowing them to continue hunting with precision; they don't get all wizened or rheumy in their joints—not that scientists have noticed—though Dragons are stoic at the worst of times and so unlikely to make a fuss about a few aches and pains; and if their diet and dental care are good, they should have no problems with their teeth. What can be said is that, like people, all Dragons age at different rates with different "symptoms," making a Dragon's history—if known—the most reliable way to gauge her journey into senescence. Naturally, species and bloodlines have to be taken into consideration, too: two hundred may be ancient for a Feathered Green from Belize but barely late-middle age to a Tibetan Namtso Snow. Certainly any Dragon over three hundred can be thought of as a senior, and you should be alert to subtle changes in behaviour and aspect: flat, lackluster hue, brittle horns, talons, even scales, diminished appetite and body mass, more time spent in the sun than on the wing, etc. Taken together, these are reasonably accurate indicators of advancing age.

At this point, the best a Dragon keeper can do is continue being attentive to their Dragon's needs. In particular, keep her warm. Elderly Dragons feel the cold more than most and welcome extra UV lamps or radiant heating to make their dens comfortable. You will want to charm any ragged horns or talons and rasp down any chipped scales. This is primarily a safety issue for Dragon and person, yet also boosts a Dragon's spirits.[10] Monitor your Dragon's diet; provide her favorite foods generously supplemented with vitamins, minerals, and antioxidants and laced with a liberal dose of single malt.[11] This won't stop time but can make its passage more pleasant. If your charge is turning churlish, give her some space. While music is usually appreciated, loud noises can be particularly troublesome, so follow her lead when it comes to visitors—especially kids, dogs, and other Dragons—and keep fireworks to a minimum. Basically, try to put yourself in her scales and remember that—as with people—quality of life is as important as quantity.

Now, the great question: How do ancient Dragons die? What actually happens when these noble beings depart this world, not at the unseemly tip of a sword but by simply running out of time? It is a mystery to test the minds of Laozi, Paracelsus, and Einstein together.

The truth is, no one knows. There are no records, no eye-witness accounts of Dragons dying from natural causes. They are simply here one day and then…gone. Perhaps they fade into the mists like Merlin, or turn to dust like Dracula. Perhaps they ascend to the heavens: life being but star stuff, to the stars it shall return.

Fortunately, the lack of verifiable information never stopped us from spinning skeins of draconic yarns, and the annals of Dragon lore are tapestried with *fabulae draconis mori*. One such tale speaks of an island in the middle of the Sacred Sea. On this island grows a Great Rowan Tree, its branches aching upwards, lost in the clouds. Around the tree, tails entwined, sleep six Dragon Guardians, one from each corner of the Dragon World. When a Dragon has reached her end of days, she makes her way to the Island of the Great Tree. With fire and fang and the roar of a thousand-thousand wings, the Guardians

---

10. There's nothing like having a fuss made over you when you're just too weary to do it yourself.

11. Or kava, mead, shaojiu, vodka—whatever your Dragon prefers. Strictly medicinal, of course.

honour her centuries of passions lived and send her on her way, up through silvered boughs to the Kingdom of the Eternal Dragon.

Non-Dragon types insist this is just a pretty fiction, of course. And yet...

...Set in the crystal waters of Lake Baikal in Siberia is the island of Olkhon. On the island grows an ancient rowan tree. Around the tree dwell the six Enchantments of the Weyr of the Eternal Dragon. There is always some truth in Dragon lore.

When the day comes—as it will—that the well-worn nest long filled with a Mountain of Wonder lies empty, you will feel the world sigh and know it is the poorer for her passing. Hold tight to the memories of shared years and blazing passions, to her spirit filled with the thunder of a million stars.

Imagine her soaring strong across the Sacred Sea.

Hear in your heart the roar of a thousand-thousand Dragons.

Then...let her go.

And though you fade from earthly sight,
declare to the silent earth: I flow.
To the rushing water say: I am.

—Rainer Maria Rilke, "Sonnets to Orpheus 29"

epilogue

Standing Alone Together

From the scrappy, ooze-covered creatures emerging from Earth's primal seas to the majestic beauties dancing across modern skylines, There Be Dragons.

Dangerous, terrible, wise, and sublime, Dragons are the universe in miniature, a blinding link in the chain of being. They gouge out rivers and cast up mountains, roil the oceans and swallow stars whole. Beyond good or evil, they see what was, what is, and what will be. Dragons are the burden of dreams; the mystery of the invisible made visible, of raw chaos and eternal power.

Dragons are here, now.

And they were there then—when we humans, barely upright, turned our eyes to the heavens and went positively chartreuse with Dragon envy. These were beings beyond understanding, wild and fearless with power, flight, and freedom. Oh, to be a Dragon! we humans thought, shuddering from brutish head to callused toe. For in the shadow of such overwhelming existence, we suddenly knew we were small and insignificant—a mere fleck on a mote in the eye of the universe. To survive, humans turned wonders to monsters, envy to fear,

fear to loathing. For what we could not understand, we felt compelled to destroy.

Through millennia we fought Dragons, setting blade and myth against tooth, talon, and blazing breath. Once puny interlopers, we were now swarming Earth like locusts through Egypt. Brandishing our claim to dominion like a sword, we soured the waters, felled the forests, and butchered the creatures of air, sea, and wood. We persecuted Dragons, victimized them in the name of progress and prejudice. In the name of our fear, we drove them to the very edge of existence. This was our world. It held no room for their magic.

Still, There Be Dragons.

We humans have not always been the brightest of beings. In our nearsighted greed and arrogance, we have all but removed wildness from our planet. But, try though we might, Dragons held on. In the ephemeral mists of imagination they lingered, generous with the world, patient with our all-too-human failings—far more patient than we had any right to expect. For all our slander, for all our theft of life and land, Dragons knew, on inked page and skin, that we honored them still. Deep down, in childish tales and mystic fancies, they knew we kept them close.

How could we not?

For all our flaws, somewhere in the metaphysical recesses of our souls, we know that to lose Dragons is to lose a part of ourselves. Without their majesty, how mean and narrow become our lives! Without their wisdom, their wonder, how diminished becomes the world! Dragons waited centuries for us to wake up, to embrace their wildness, not only for their sake but for our own. They waited for us to *get it*.

Perhaps we were waiting, too.

Back in 1845, Henry David Thoreau left the tameness of Concord, Massachusetts, to wrap himself in the solitude of meadow mouse and striped squirrel, goshawk and lynx, and "suck out all the marrow of life." One likes to believe that, one evening, as Thoreau walked his woods, he looked out over Walden Pond and beheld a pair of Dragons soaring through the gentle gloaming. One likes to believe that, in that moment, he discovered with certainty what Dragons have known since the dawn of time:

"In Wildness is the preservation of the world."

Fierce and elegant, dark and lustrous—all fire and grace and wonder, Dragons are Wildness. Pure, dangerous, divine Wildness.

It is now the twenty-first century. By the grace of the Great Dragon, we have made it past the Dark Times and further than many thought possible.

Out of the darkness, Dragons roar, reminding us we need them. Reminding us of their right to be. With horns charmed and scales ashimmer, they walk amongst us. They share our lives and lend mystery to the mundane. They fill the skies and sing in thunderous tones for all to hear: "We are Everywhere!" Magic is again in the world. The future rolls out, a grass carpet beneath our feet.

But as we look forward, we must never forget the past. There will always be people who cling to what is safe and familiar, who look at Dragons and see only monsters to fear and slay. The fault, dear reader, is not in our Dragons but in ourselves.

It's up to us to change. We did it before; we can do it again. It is up to us—Dragons and Dragon lovers alike—to keep the flames of magic, the songs of Dragons, alive.

Here, There Be Dragons, standing with us, alone in one place together. And when we are gone, a Dragon will be here still, shouting to the Universe: I am!

glossary

Adopt-a-Dragon Initiative (AAD): Project started by the Dragon Conservancy Program modeled after the U.S. Bureau of Land Management's National Wild Horse and Burro Program and the American Bear Association's Friend of the Cubs. It is a way Dragon lovers around the globe can, for a modest fee, stay connected to these marvelous creatures and feel like they are contributing to the continuance of Dragon welfare the world over. http://mackenziesdragonsnest.com/adoptadragon.html

agathos daimones: "Good Spirits" to the Hellenes. They were winged draconic guardians of the ancient Aegean, often considered the hovering incarnation of one's ancestors.

Aido Hwedo: The Great Rainbow Serpent of the Fon people of Africa who was both aide and friend to the Creator, Mawu. After the world was made, Aido Hwedo wrapped her coils tightly round it to hold it together until the end of time.

Alkha: Cosmic Dragon from the tales of Siberia's Buriat people, so massive his wings covered the heavens. Occasionally he would nibble on the sun and the moon but would throw them up again when their heat became too much for him to stomach. Lunar craters are said to be Alkha's tooth marks.

Altjeringa: The Dreamtime of the Australian Aborigines through which the Rainbow Serpent travelled.

amphiptere: A winged, legless pseudo-dragon similar in appearance to the *Agothos daimones* and the French guivre. Ill-tempered and much feared, the creature's image was often used on warriors' shields to frighten the enemy.

Ananta: Cosmic Dragon from the Hindu Vedas. Ananta served as bed and shade for the god Vishnu, who, in turn, is referred to as Ananta-Shayana, or He Who Sleeps on Ananta.

Anomodontia: Group of extinct herbivores from the Permian Period (approx. 250 MYA). These mammal-like reptiles were stocky and beaked and highly successful in their zoological niche. Some people who subscribe to the Dragon Drift Theory of draconic evolution consider them a distant ancestor of today's Dragons.

antienne eclorsion: Birthing anthem. The song a Queen Dragon and her attendant family sing to spur her eggs into hatching. This is an essential and spectacular part of the birthing ritual.

ANWR: Arctic National Wildlife Refuge, one of the last great wild expanses. It is located in Alaska's North Slope and is home to things rare and wonderful, including numerous Polar Dragons. This is a region we must protect.

après les Chute: "After the Fall." A turning point in the course of Dragon history, and not for the better.

archaeopteryx: A crow-sized creature from the late Jurassic Period (150 MYA) which is the earliest known bird. Archaeopteryx fossils from Germany display distinct flight feathers, tail feathers, and teeth—something modern birds gave up but Dragons sport with glee.

Archosaurs: Literally, "ruling lizards." As their name implies, Archosaurs were the head honchos during the Cretaceous Period. They are of the same subclass as dinosaurs and pterosaurs. Their modern descendents travelled distinct branches up the evolutionary tree, one leading to birds, the other to crocodilians. The Rise of the Feathered Serpent Theory of Dragon evolution has small proto-Dragons struggling for survival in the shadow of the fierce Archosaurs of time.

Ardeshir: Legendary third-century CE founder of the Sassanid dynasty, ruler of Istakhr (later to be Persia), and dragon slayer. His dragon-slaying prowess is generally considered more political hyperbole than truth, but one never knows.

Asdeev: The rare and wondrous white Dragon slain by Rustam as part of his seven heroic trials.

aspis: Very dangerous European pseudo-dragon, whose bite and touch are said to be fatal. It is susceptible to the entrancing force of music, so much so that aspises are known to stick their tail in one ear and place the other to the ground. This contorted posture allows their victims to escape with relative ease. If you find a dead aspis, do not touch. They can be lethal even in death.

Azhi Dahaka: Zoroastrian cosmic Dragon purported to have had a ravenous appetite, first for livestock, then for people. Azi Dahaka was captured and imprisoned under Mount Demavand, though legend states that he will break free at the end of time, wipe out one-third of mankind, and be stopped only through the valiant efforts of the dragon slayer Keresaspa.

Cadmus: Greek dragon slayer, Dragon's-teeth sower, and founder of Thebes. The Dragon Cadmus slew was sacred to Ares, which ticked off the god of war to no end. After years of servitude and torment, in an act of truly karmic proportions, Cadmus, believing the gods favored Dragons over people, chose to live out his days as a Dragon.

Campacti: Cosmic Dragon of Mexico from whose body the Earth was made.

carmina draconium: Latin for "Dragon song." See *antienne eclorsion.*

caveat spector: "Watcher beware." Good advice for anyone out Dragon watching in the wild.

cenotes: Water-filled sinkholes found in the Yucatan and environs. They were often sacred to the indigenous peoples of the area and treasured as bathing/watering spots for local Feathered Dragons.

charming: The act of burnishing horns. A common grooming ritual for Dragons and Unicorns.

chronobiology: Scientific field that examines how living organisms—including Dragons—are affected by and adapt to the rhythms of time, including but not exclusive to solar and lunar rhythms.

Clovis peoples: Prehistoric Western Hemisphere peoples who ranged across the New World circa 11,000 BCE. They are considered the ancestors of indigenous cultures from Oregon to Chile and most places in between.

cornicles: Small horns found on a Dragon's blaze. Unlike a Dragon's large horns, cornicles are believed to be largely ornamental. Not that they can't inflict injury—any Dragon horn can—but that's not their primary function. (To the best of our knowledge.)

crepuscular: Active at dawn and dusk, like most Dragons.

crypto sciences: Crypto = hidden or secret. The crypto sciences are studies of all things not readily apparent to the casual observer. Some people believe the subject creatures are complete fabrications; a crypto scientist believes they are simply hidden. When it comes to Dragons, pertinent branches of the crypto sciences include:

Cryptoanthropology: The study of the impact fabulous creatures have on human culture. Some cryptoanthropologists are tipping the field on its head and looking at the social structure within a particular clan of creature. This is particularly germane to Dragons given the tight-knit nature of their society.

Cryptoherpetology: aka Secret Serpent Science, Remarkable Reptile Research, and Dragon Studies. *The* field for serious dracophiles. Cryptoherpetology also covers such non-dragons as the cockatrice, chimera, and a wide variety of water beings who fall in that grey area between fish and reptile.

Cryptomythology: The study of sifting through what is real and what is myth in human lore, oral history, and ancient epic.

Cryptopaleontology: Fossil science as it relates to the exploration of the world of hidden beings. When it comes to Dragons, the lack of fossil record has frustrated cryptopaleontologists greatly.

Cryptotheriogenesis: Secret creature reproductive science, specifically as it relates to Dragons.

Cryptoveterinary: The medical branch of the crypto sciences. Crypto vets look at diseases and treatments for mundane ailments which may cross over to the mystical as well as those specific to our friends in the crypto kingdom. Dragons, being by and large hale and hardy, tend to have little use for cryptoveterinary aid.

Cryptozoology: The umbrella field of study for all creatures strange and unusual, from abadas to zlatorogs. And, naturally, Dragons.

Dark Times: A particularly rough period in Western Dragon history when our friends were under attack on all sides. It lasted roughly from the rise of Western monotheism until the Late Middle Ages (c. 1500 CE). The Dark Times did not feature humanity at its best.

Degei: The Cosmic Dragon atop the animalistic hierarchy of Fiji.

Divine Darwinism: Theory that the ancient gods and demigods—both human and not, including some Dragons—mixed their blood with humans to give them an evolutionary edge. A familiar example is Zeus's proclivity to bed humans, producing a slew of heroes and heroines, who in turn mated with more humans, strengthening the species' bloodlines. Many heroic and powerful figures from the East trace their divine lineage back to Cosmic Dragons.

dracophile: A Dragon lover. Like you.

Dragon Conservancy Program: Modern movement dedicated to preserving Dragons and Dragon habitat for the present and future. The Dragon Conservancy is behind the Adopt-a-Dragon initiative, among other efforts. http://mackenziesdragonsnest.com/dragonconservancy.html

Dragon Drift Theory (DDT): The oldest of the theories of draconic evolution which believes proto-Dragons first emerged from the primordial seas during the Permian Period over 250 MYA.

Dragon lay-by: A Dragon-friendly patch of land established for the rest and recreation of itinerant Dragons.

Dragon sanctuaries: Internationally recognized safe havens surrounding every known wild weyr in the world. Dragon sanctuaries are essential for keeping wild Dragons safe and sound.

dragon slayers: Their numbers are, woefully, legion. Some were canonized: George, Margaret, Michael, etc. Some were given hero's laurels and royal crowns: Gilgamesh, Rustam, Teoma, Hercules. For our purposes, the less said about them, the better.

Dragon studies: See *cryptoherpetology*.

drakes/draks: Heavy set, wingless pseudo-dragons. In the past, drakes were frequently beset by dragon slayers and their deaths counted in the anti-Dragon tally.

Druids of the Keltoi: Ancient sages and mystics of Europe. The Druids were instrumental in keeping Dragons in the world.

Echidna: According to myth, Echidna was the mother of all Greek monsters, including the Lernaean Hydra and the wise Dragon Ladon.

***Edda (Poetic)*:** Icelandic masterpiece from the thirteenth century and attributed to Snorri Sturluson. It speaks at length of the Twilight of the Gods and the role the Miðgard Dragon plays therein.

enchantment: The basic draconic family unit or clan. A modern enchantment includes from 10–15 individuals.

endo-, ecto-, and kleptothermic: Terms referring to how organisms regulate their temperature. Endotherms are warm-blooded, ectotherms are cold-blooded, and kleptotherms borrow (steal?) heat from others. Dragons are all of these things and more. See *gigantotherm*.

Epirotes: The maternal Dragon Apollo placed in charge of rearing Python's children at what was, essentially, the first Dragon Sanctuary of record.

Eurynome: Primal Mother of ancient Pelasgian cosmology. She created—then married—the great Dragon, Ophion, and from their union created all things in the Universe.

***fabulae draconis mori*:** Latin for "tales of Dragon deaths."

Fibonacci sequence: A numerical sequence in which each number after the second is the sum of the two preceding numbers: 0, 1, 1, 2, 3, 5, 8, 13, 21, 34, 55, 89, 144, 233, 377, 610, 987, 1597, 2584, 4181, 6765 … The spiral based on this sequence is the divinely geometric form Eastern Dragons take when growing in their shell. Once hatched, True Dragon scales multiply in precise Fibonacci progression. See *sacred geometry*.

Fire Dragon: Genial Cosmic Dragon of the Huron and Iroquois people. Fire Dragon spent time with Chief-of-All-the-Earth's young bride, Aataentsic, which roused the old green-eyed monster. Rumors circulated through the heavens that Fire Dragon impregnated Aataentsic which led to a very messy situation for all involved. Not even Fire Dragon was immune to the god's wrath.

flying ointment: A medicinal concoction for Dragons who are having a little trouble getting aloft. It can be very unstable and must be handled with the greatest of care.

Four Dragon Kings: A quartet of Chinese Dragons—Ao Chin, Ao Kuang, Ao Ping, and Ao Shun—who ruled the rains, seas, and depths below.

Fu-Ts'ang: Dragon of Hidden Treasures. The epitome of the hoarding Dragon, Fu Ts'ang protects and rules all ores and precious stones under the ground.

Gandareva: Cosmic Dragon from Sumer who stretched from the ocean floor to the starry firmament. For all his ferocious ways, Gandareva kept an even more dangerous Dragon in check. Unfortunately, he was slain by Keresaspa and the second Dragon—possibly Azhi Dahaka—was free to destroy the universe.

Giant's Causeway: Formation of basalt columns rising up out of the sea on the northern coast of Ireland. A once-familiar recreation spot for Gaelic Dragons.

gigantotherm: Any creature, like the largest dinosaurs and, of course, Dragons, massive enough to maintain a constant, active body temperature even though they are not, strictly speaking, warm-blooded.

Gilgamesh: Babylonian hero-king and dragon slayer who merited an epic of his own: the eponymous *Epic of Gilgamesh*. Among his string of "heroic" deeds, he killed a Dragon guarding a tree sacred to the goddess Inanna.

Glacial Egg Theory (GET): The youngest of the theories of Dragon Evolution. It suggests that Dragons arose from the survivors of the Cretaceous/Triassic Extinction c. 65 MYA.

Golden Lung: The First Celestial Dragon of China.

Golden/Divine Ratio: a+b/a = a/b = φ [φ ≈ 1.618]. This mathematical equation is a foundation of sacred geometry. As perfect beings, True Dragon proportions follow the Golden Ratio to a T.

gowrow: Legendary New World pseudo-dragon found in the Ozarks and surrounding wilderness. Their habitat has been seriously threatened by recent human sprawl in Arkansas and Missouri.

Great American Interchange: A paleozoological event during which prehistoric fauna from North America migrated south and those from South America went north. It figures prominently in the Glacial Egg Theory of draconic evolution, explaining how primitive New World Dragons and pseudo-dragons wandered across the continents.

guivre: Lake dragon from France. Seldom seen today, though quite numerous during the Middle Ages, guivres are frequently confused with the amphiptere.

hemorrhagic hemotoxin: Venom which virulently attacks the blood system, causing massive internal bleeding and, if left untreated, death. Feathered Dragon fangs are loaded with the stuff. Fortunately, they use it defensively only as a last resort.

henge: Not to be confused with Neolithic stone circles dotting the British landscape, *henge* are a group of shape-shifting beings from Japan. Playful, at times malicious, they include the Kitsune (Fox), Tengu (Bird Man), Tanuki (Racoon Dog) and, of course, the Dragon.

Himalayan quad: A Dragon-rich region in the high Himalayas, home to four known weyrs, possibly more.

hornfels: Fine-grained metamorphic rock excellent for charming Dragon horns.

household dragons: Pisuhänds, puuks, aitvaras, et al. A class of small pseudo-dragons who, if treated well, will protect your home, guard your valuables—especially your children—and even increase your wealth. The latter can be at your neighbors' expense, which can lead to unanticipated incivility and local feuds.

hydra: A multi-headed water pseudo-dragon indigenous to Mediterranean lands. The most famous hydra is the Lernaean Hydra, offspring of Echidna and victim of Hercules's labors.

iaculus: Winged pseudo-dragon from Africa. They are protectors of tombs and mediators between the living and dead. Known as the javelin snake, they will hurl themselves at anyone trespassing on their territory.

Iguazu and Canaima Uplands: Upland rainforests of South America, still wild enough for Dragons—especially Feathered Dragons—to enjoy.

jagua fruit: Rainforest harvest and New World Feathered Dragon staple. The indigenous peoples use the juice of the unripe jagua for body ink.

Keresaspa: Quasi-divine dragon-slaying hero from Sumer. See *Gandareva*.

kiaus: Pseudo-dragons who watch over rivers and lakes of eastern Asia and keep them ecologically sound. Not to be confused with the mythical monster Kiau from China who spent his life giving the fisher folk in his bailiwick grief.

Kurgan civilizations: Ancient peoples who moved from Central Asia into Europe, bringing their Dragons with them.

Ladon: Wise Dragon of ancient Greece. The son of Echidna, Ladon lived in the garden of the Hesperides where he guarded Hera's golden apples. He spoke fluent Greek and was very content until, fulfilling his eleventh labor, Hercules killed him and stole the apples.

lake dragons: A vast class of pseudo-dragons who are literally found across the globe. They come in all shapes, temperaments, and sizes. Champs in Vermont, Ogopogo in British Columbia, and the Misiganabic of Quebec are examples of notorious lake dragons.

ley lines: Aka Dragon Currents or energy lines. The electromagnetic grid which crisscrosses the planet. Dragons are very sensitive to ley lines and will take up residence on or near a ley line nexus whenever possible.

***Lung Tik Chuan Ren*:** "Children of the Dragon." The people of China.

Marduk: God of Ancient Babylon and slayer of the Cosmic Dragon Tiamat.

marsh draks: Pseudo-dragons known for their oversized appetites. Unrestrained marsh draks have driven numerous wetland species to the brink of extinction.

Mawu: Androgynous Creator of the Fon universe. A very Dragon-friendly individual. See *Aido Hwedo*.

megafauna: The huge land creatures of post-dinosaur Earth, including mammoths, indricotheres, giant sloths, cave bears, and Dragons. Today megafauna are few and far between and include elephants, rhinoceros, and, of course, Dragons.

microraptors: Small flying dinosaurs with feathers on all four limbs and tail. Seen as an ancient relative of modern birds, microraptors shared the world with simple Dragons at the start of the Rise of the Feathered Serpents.

Miðgard: The middle realm—the Earth—of the Norse cosmos.

Miðgarðsormr: Cosmic Dragon of the Norse people. The unruly son of Loki. As a Dragonlet, Miðgarðsormr was hurled into the ocean that surrounds Earth. With the Twilight of the Gods, he hauls himself up onto Earth and partakes in its destruction until slain by Thor.

Minia: Cosmic Dragon of the ancient Sahara from whose sacrifice the world was created.

molting balm: Palliative treatment for Dragons having a hard time shedding their skin. It's good for sunburn, too.

Mongolian death worm: A vicious crypto-creature from the depths of the Gobi Desert.

monitors: Family of large lizards including Komodo dragons and the fast, whippy-tailed Perenties of the Australian outback.

Mucalinda: Benevolent naga who sheltered Siddhārtha beneath his hood as a torrential storm rage about them.

MYA: Million years ago.

Nazca lines: Mysterious geoglyphs in Peru's Nazca Desert. Local Dragons are known to use them as guides for their flying workouts.

***nemet*:** A sacred grove, particularly one used by the Dragon-friendly peoples of Europe.

Niðhögger: Cosmic Dragon of the Norse who is wrapped round Yggdrasil, the World Tree, constantly nibbling away at its roots, working towards the destruction of the world.

Olkhon: Island in Siberia's Lake Baikal, known in the *fabulae draconis mori* as the place of departure for passing Dragons.

ophidian: Serpentine. See *Ophion*.

Ophion: Cosmic Dragon created by Eurynome. A bit of a braggart, a trait which, ultimately, led to his downfall.

Otherworld: Celtic realm of the dead, the faërie (*sidhe*), and other deities and spirits. It is believed the *sidhe* welcomed beleaguered Dragons into the Otherworld to weather the worst of the Dark Times.

ouroboros: Pseudo-dragon frequently depicted holding his tail in his mouth. The ouroboros is symbolic of the eternal circle of life.

paleontology: Study of fossils and Earth's fossil record.

Pan Gu: Chinese Creator deity who, with the aid of the Divine Quartet—one of whom was a Dragon—made the Universe.

Pangaea: Pre–continental drift landmass that extended virtually from pole to pole on one side of Earth. According to Dragon Drift Theory, during the Permian migration, primitive Dragons roamed across Pangaea, thus explaining their global presence.

passion ball: Aka ardor orb. A draconic aphrodisiac that a mating Queen shares with her mate to help ensure a fecund bonding.

pax loci: "Peace of the Place." The rule that governs all Dragon lay-bys and guarantees a civil stay for all who drop by.

Pelasgians: Neolithic Greeks. Eurynome and Ophion are central to Pelasgian cosmology.

perchloric acid ($HClO_4$): Highly corrosive—and flammable—compound believed by some cryptoherpetologists to be a byproduct of a violent Dragon death, eating through flesh and bone and assuring no fossil record is left behind.

Permian Extinction: The most devastating extinction-level event the planet has experienced. Occuring 250 MYA, the Permian Extinction wiped out 90 percent of all marine life and 70 percent of all land vertebrates. According to Dragon Drift Theory, Dragon ancestors retreated to the seas and managed to survive.

Permian Migration: In Dragon Drift Theory, the Permian Migration is cited to explain the ubiquitous presence of Dragons in the world.

Pliny the Elder: Roman naturalist and philosopher who travelled extensively and wrote about the strange and wondrous creatures he saw, including numerous pseudo-dragons. He died from exposure to toxic fumes spewing out of Vesuvius in 79 CE.

Popol Vuh: The sacred book of Maya cosmology. It speaks extensively of the various Feathered Dragons—Sovereign Plumed Serpent, Vision Serpent, et al.—central to the Maya faith.

pre-Raphaelites: Nineteenth-century school of artists, writers, and aesthetes. Their dedication to Renaissance ideals and their interest in ancient Celtic and Arthurian legends helped revive the interest in the Druids and, consequently, in Dragons. The Pre-Raphaelite Brotherhood included Dante Gabriel Rossetti, John Millais, Edward Burne-Jones, and William Morris.

proto-Dragons: The very first hardly-recognizable-as-Dragons Dragons who walked the earth, swam the seas, and filled the skies at the start of draconic evolution.

pseudo-dragons: A broad class of creatures who, in the popular imagination, are frequently lumped together with True Dragons but who are distant relatives at best. The ranks of pseudo-dragons include wyverns, nagas, household dragons, wyrms, and drakes, to name but a very few.

pterosaur: "Winged lizards." Flying reptiles who filled the skies from the late Triassic to the late Cretaceous periods (220–65 MYA). Due to their leathery wings, it was erroneously believed for many years that pterosaurs were the direct ancestors of Dragons. Though they were contemporaneous with early Dragons, they are most definitely not related.

pyrometric cones: Idiot-proof temperature gauges commonly used by potters and extremely useful when monitoring the temperature in a hatching kiln.

pyronic sacs: Anatomical structure essential to the production of Dragonfire. Pyronic sacs are vestigial at birth and only develop fully as a Dragon enters her second year.

Python: The prophetic Dragon of Delphi. Apollo slew her and buried her beneath the Delphic temple so that her oracular powers might transfer to the women who served in her stead. In her honor, the Delphic oracles were called the Pythia.

Quaternary Dragons: The first modern Dragons. Though larger than their twenty-first-century cousins, the Quaternary Dragons of the late Cenozoic were, in other aspects, indistinguishable from the Dragons of today.

Queen: A breeding female Dragon.

Quetzalcoatl: The Cosmic Feathered Serpent (Dragon) of Mesoamerica.

Ragnarök: The End of Days in Norse mythology. It is the time when the destroyer Dragons Miðgarðsormr and Niðhögger break their bonds and wreak havoc upon the worlds of men and gods.

Rainbow Serpents: Cosmic Dragons who travel the Dreamtime and serve as right hands to the Creators. Aido Hwedo, Minia, and Degei are but a few Rainbow Serpents who have helped shape the world. In Australia, the Rainbow Serpent is one of the most powerful totemic figures of the Aboriginal peoples.

Ratatöskr: The chatty squirrel who spends his days running up and down Yggdrasil, the World Tree, carrying messages to and from the Dragon Niðhögger.

Remembrance of Names: Solemn event in the life of every True Dragon when they, quite literally, remember their name. This usually happens in a Dragon's third year, though some youngsters are more precocious than others. For Dragon keepers and their Dragons, it is a time of great celebration.

Rise of the Feathered Serpent Theory (RFST): Middle theory of draconic evolution which places primitive Dragons 100 MYA during the Cretaceous period. It sees Dragons as offshoots of the more upright thecodonts, surviving on their wings and their brains. RFST believes that the proto-Dragons of the time flourished thanks to strong family units, forming what are considered the world's first enchantments and weyrs.

ropen: Small, bipedal pseudo-dragon from the rainforests of Papua New Guinea. The ropen can be easily mistaken for a large fruit bat but is actually one of the last descendents of ancient ptero-saur/proto-Dragon hybrids from the Triassic Period.

Rustam: Hero and dragon slayer from ancient Zabulistan. See *Asdeev*.

ryu-jin: Generic water dragon spirits in Japan. They're very important to the island nation which depends so extensively on water for health and livelihood.

Ryu-jin: The Dragon King who lives in the sea off the coast of Japan. His daughter fell for a human and their descendents became the imperial line of Japan. See *Divine Darwinism*.

sacred geometry: Geometric study of specific, perfect proportions in the natural world which led the ancients to believe there was a divine mathematician at work in the creation of the Universe. The tenets of sacred geometry have been used in the planning of temples, and churches and the planting of holy labyrinths, etc. One of the basic proportions is the Golden Ratio, which can be applied to the structure/dimensions of all True Dragons. This leads cryptoherpetologists to say, with conviction, that Dragons are perfect beings.

Saints Petroc and Carantoc: A pair of medieval Welsh saints who, when challenged to remove pesky Dragons, were wise enough to approach the tasks with words and faith rather than swords. Their approach may be indicative of the long-standing Welsh affinity for Dragons.

saurian paleontology: Study of dinosaur fossils.

Seleucid Empire: Dragon-rich realm created out of the eastern portions of Alexander the Great's conquests. It was assimilated by the Roman Empire around 188 BCE.

Shen Lung: The spiritual Dragon who rules the rains of China. The Emperor alone could display his likeness.

Sire: A breeding male Dragon.

Smok Wawelski: Legendary Polish Dragon who lived on the banks of the Vistula and was brought low by a cobbler. Smok's lands were appropriated by the civil and religious authorities of what was to become the thriving metropolis of Krakow.

snallygaster: A pseudo-dragon from the mid-Atlantic wilds of New Jersey. Once a not-uncommon sight, the urban sprawl in the area has pushed the snallygaster into legendary territory.

Sovereign Plumed Serpent: Aka Gucumatz. The Cosmic Feathered Dragon of Maya cosmology (see *Popol Vuh*). Gucumatz joined with Heart of Sky and brought the world into being. It took them several tries, but eventually they got it right. With creative duties behind him, Gucumatz transformed. See *Vision Serpent*.

Sparti: The Sown Men. The surviving warriors sprouted from the Dragon teeth sown by Cadmus. They worked with Cadmus to found the city of Thebes.

Ssu-Ling: The Divine Quartet or four sacred creatures of Chinese cosmology: Lung Wang the Dragon, Qi-Lin the Unicorn, Gui Xian the Turtle, and Feng Huang the Phoenix. They represented the four cardinal directions, the seasons, and the elements and were instrumental in the making of the world.

taiga: The boreal ecosystem of the Northern Hemisphere just south of the Arctic tundra. The taiga is marked by coniferous forests and is home to wolverines, martens, bears, various deer, and hardy Dragons.

TANSTAAFL: "There ain't no such thing as a free lunch." Wise words well remembered by Dragons and humans alike.

thecodonts: A group of Archosaurs who made a big impression during the Triassic Period. Thecodonts are believed by some to be distant cousins of drakes and other wingless, terrestrial pseudo-dragons.

Tiamat: Cosmic Dragon of the ancient Near East. Tiamat was Chaos personified. Her downfall led to the creation of the world and the dawn of civilization.

Trans-Atlantic Transmigration: An exodus of a passel of adventurous European Dragons who were fed up with the rampant anti-Dragon sentiments coursing through Britain and the Continent in the Dark Ages. Shortly after the Saxon invasion of the British Isles, they heeded the call to "Go west, young Dragons!" and crossed the Atlantic. In the New World they made their way amongst the enchantments of North America.

True Dragons: The three species of Big D Dragons: Western or European Dragons, Eastern or Asian Dragons, and Feathered or Southern Dragons. All others are pseudo-dragons. Accept no substitutes.

Turukawa: Divine hawk of Fiji and friend of the Dragon Degei.

Typhon: Draconic son of Gaia, mate of Echidna, and father of Ladon and the Hydra. Typhon was considered the most dangerous of all Greek monsters. Zeus imprisoned him beneath Mount Ætna.

Unity Theory (UT): The theory of draconic evolution which is increasingly *en vogue* among modern cryptoherpetologists. According to UT, Dragon genesis is a continuum following highly resilient threads of draconic DNA which, no matter how primitive, managed to survive, informing each subsequent generation, until we have the beings we know and recognize as Dragons today. In short, UT takes the best of all other theories of draconic evolution and connects—or unifies—them.

Vasuki: Great naga who, according to the Hindu Vedas, helped the gods recover the elixir of eternal life. Also known as Basuki.

Vision Serpent: Aka Kukulcan. A transformation of Sovereign Plumed Serpent, Kukulcan is the Cosmic Feathered Dragon who perches atop the Mesoamerican foliate World Tree. He brought civilization to the people and was invoked as a war god when necessary.

Vritra: Three-headed Vedic Chaos Dragon. Vritra drank the waters of the world dry, only disgorging them when he was defeated by Indra and his thunderbolt.

water horses and kelpies: Cryptozoological creatures frequently mistaken for lake dragons.

weyr: A Dragon community. In the old days, a weyr could easily accommodate five to seven enchantments. Unfortunately, everything is downsized today: modern weyrs are two or three enchantments large at most.

Weyrsickness: Aka Dragon Despondency. An ailment of the spirit which can afflict Dragonlets just out of the egg, especially those who are orphaned or abandoned. The best course of treatment is time, affection, and liberal doses of Weyrsickness Remedy.

World Association for Dragons Everywhere (WAFDE): A global organization whose sole purpose is to preserve and protect the world's Dragons. WAFDE serves as a resource center for Dragon keepers and dracophiles, is charged with inspecting and licensing Dragon lay-bys, and works with various mundane conservation organizations to put an end to poaching of Dragons and the more familiar creatures integral to their ecosystems. http://mackenzies-dragonsnest.com/WAFDE.html

wyrms: Massive, legless pseudo-dragons frequently found in underground caverns, wells, and old mines.

wyverns: One of the most recognizable of the pseudo-dragons, the wyvern has wings but only hind legs. Much smaller than True Dragons, wyverns frequently bore the brunt of Dragon hunting zeal and were mistaken by artists no less than Leonardo da Vinci, Raphael, and Paolo Uccello for True Dragons.

Y Ddraig Goch: The Red Dragon, draconic guardian of Wales.

Yggdrasil: The World Tree in Norse cosmology. The Dragon Niðhögger is coiled around its roots, noshing away as the spirit moves him, until such time as he gnaws them through, heralding the Twilight of the Gods and the end of the world.

žaltys: Benevolent and mild guardian pseudo-dragon from the Baltic. Sacred to the goddess of the sun, if treated with respect, a žaltys will loyally protect you and yours.

zapovednik: A wilderness research station in Russia.

zeitgeben: The external clues which help a creature adjust their internal clock. Common zeitgeben for Dragons are sunlit hours, temperature, and the daily habits of enchantment life—hunting and foraging, bathing, playing, etc.

bibliography & suggested reading

Allan, Tony. *The Mythic Bestiary: The Illustrated Guide to the World's Most Fantastic Creatures.* London: Duncan Baird, 2008.

Bently, Peter, ed. *The Dictionary of World Myth.* New York: Facts On File, Inc., 1995.

The Bhagavad Gita. Juan Mascaro. New York: Penguin Classics, 1962.

Blanpied, Pamela Wharton. *Dragons: The Modern Infestation - Reprint.* Woodbridge, Suffolk, UK: Boydell Press, 1997.

Bronowski, J. *The Ascent of Man.* Boston: Little, Brown & Company, 1973.

Buchman, Dian Dincin. *Herbal Medicine.* New York: Wing Books/ Random House, 1996.

Calasso, Roberto. *The Marriage of Cadmus and Harmony.* New York: Alfred A. Knopf, Inc., 1993.

Campbell, Joseph. *Transformations of Myth Through Time.* New York: Harper & Row, 1990.

Campbell, Joseph, and Bill Moyers. *The Power of Myth.* New York: Doubleday, 1988.

Conway, D. J. *Magical Mystical Creatures.* St. Paul: Llewellyn Publications, 2001.

Cunningham, Scott. *Encyclopedia of Magical Herbs*. St. Paul: Llewellyn Publications, 1996.

Dickinson, Peter. *The Flight of Dragons*. New York: Harper & Row, 1979.

Durrell, Gerard, and Lee Durrell. *The State of the Ark*. New York: Doubleday, 1986.

Ellis, Peter Berresford. *The Druids*. Grand Rapids, MI: Wm. B. Eerdmans Publishing Co., 1994.

The Enchanted World: Dragons. Alexandria, VA: Time-Life Books, 1984.

Epic of Gilgamesh. George Andrew, trans. New York: Penguin Classics, 2003.

Frazer, Sir James G. *The Golden Bough, Abridged: Vol 1*. New York: Macmillan Co., 1922.

Graves, Robert. *The Greek Myths*. London: Penguin Books, 1992.

———. *The White Goddess*. New York: Noonday Press; Farrar, Straus & Giroux, 1975.

Greer, John Michael. *Monsters*. St. Paul: Llewellyn Publications, 2001.

Johnsgard, Paul, and Karin Johnsgard. *A Natural History of Dragons and Unicorns*. New York: St. Martin's Press, 1982.

Kynes, Sandra. *Whispers from the Woods: The Lore & Magic of Trees*. Woodbury, MN: Llewellyn Publications, 2006.

Lorenz, Konrad. *The Year of the Greyleg Goose*. New York: Harcourt Brace, 1979.

The Mabinogion. Jeffrey Gantz, trans. New York: Dorset Press, 1976.

Mack, Carol K., and Dinah Mack. *A Field Guide to Demons, Fairies, Fallen Angels and Other Subversive Spirits*. New York: Henry Holt & Co., 1998.

The Mahabharata. John D. Smith, trans. New York: Penguin Classics, 2009.

Matthews, John, and Caitlin Matthews. *The Element Encyclopedia of Magical Creatures.* London: Harper Element, 2005.

Maybury-Lewis, David. *Millennium: Tribal Wisdom and the Modern World.* New York: Viking, 1992.

McGinn, Bernard. *Anti-Christ: Two Thousand Years of the Human Fascination with Evil.* San Francisco: Harper, 1994.

Popol Vuh. Dennis Tedlock, trans. New York: Touchstone Books, 1996.

Radcliffe-Brown, Alfred. "The Rainbow-Serpent Myth of Australia." *The Journal of the Royal Anthropological Institute of Great Britain and Ireland*, 1926: 19–25.

Randolph, Vance. "Fabulous Monsters of the Ozarks." *The Arkansas Historical Quarterly, Vol. 9, No. 2*, Summer 1950: 65–75.

Robinson, James M., ed. *The Nag Hammadi Library in English.* New York: Harper & Row, 1988.

Rose, Carol. *Giants, Monsters & Dragons: An Encyclopedia of Folklore, Legend, and Myth.* New York: W.W. Norton & Co., 2000.

Santayana, George. *The Life of Reason.* New York: Charles Scribner's Sons, 1917.

Schele, Linda, and David Freidel. *A Forest of Kings: The Untold Story of the Ancient Maya.* New York: William Morrow & Co., 1990.

Schele, Linda, David Freidel, and Joy Parker. *Maya Cosmos: Three Thousand Years on the Shaman's Path.* New York: William Morrow & Co., 1993.

Simpson, Jacqueline. *British Dragons.* Ware, Hertfordshire, UK: Wordsworth Editions Limited, 2001.

Thoreau, Henry. *The Journals of Henry David Thoreau.* New York: Dover Publications, Inc., 1962.

Whitmore, Timothy L. Cannon, and Nancy F. *Ghosts and Legends of Frederick County.* Frederock, MD: T. Cannon & N. Whitmore, 1979.

Wood, Matthew. *The Book of Herbal Wisdom: Using Plants as Medicines.* Berkeley, CA: North Atlantic Books, 1997.

Yeats, William Butler. *Mythologies.* New York: Macmillan, 1969.

Young, Dudley. *Origins of the Sacred.* New York: St. Martin's Press, 1991.

Internet References, accessed June 2011

Crystal, Ellie. "Chinese Dragons." *crystallinks.* 1995. http://www.crystalinks.com/chinadragons.html.

DESA, UN. "UN DESA: The World at Six Billion." *UN DESA.* 2010. http://www.un.org/esa/population/publications/sixbillion/sixbillion.htm.

"Enuma Elish: The Epic of Creation. First Tablet." L. W. King, trans. *Internet Sacred Texts Archive.* 2010. http://www.sacred-texts.com/ane/enuma.htm.

Jule, Kristen R. "Revisiting the Effects of Captive Experience on Reintroduction Survival in Carnivores." *Current Conservation Issue 3.4.* 2009. http://www.currentconservation.org/cc_3-4-7.php.

Lai, Prof. David Chuenyan. "The Dragon in China." *Chinese Canadian Heritage Fund.* http://www.cic.sfu.ca/cchf/.

Lindemans, Micha F. , ed. *Encyclopedia Mythica.* MCMXCV-MMVII. http://www.pantheon.org/.

Parkinson, Danny J. "British Dragon Gazetteer." *Mysterious Britain & Ireland.* http://www.mysteriousbritain.co.uk/england/legends/british-dragon-gazetteer.html.

Poetic Edda. Vol. I. "Voluspo." Bellows, H.A., trans. *Internet Sacred Texts Archive.* 2010. http://www.sacred-texts.com/neu/poe/poe03.htm.

Rig Veda. Ralph T. H. Griffith, trans. *Internet Sacred Texts Archive.* http://www.sacred-texts.com/hin/rigveda/.

Spalding, Tom. *Dragons in Art and on the Web.* 2000–2005. www.isidore-of-seville.com/dragons/.

University of Aberdeen. *The Aberdeen Bestiary.* 2010. www.abdn.ac.uk/bestiary.

Suggested for Fun

Ashman, Malcolm. *Fabulous Beasts.* Woodstock, NY: Overlook Press, 1997.

Bissell-Thomas, J. *The Dragon Green.* London: Robert Hale Ltd., 1936.

Calasso, Roberto. *Ka: Stories of the Mind and Gods of India.* New York: Alfred A. Knopf, 1999.

Campbell, Joseph. *The Masks of God Vol. I–IV.* New York: Viking Penguin, 1977.

Conway, D. J. *Mystical Dragon Magic.* Woodbury, MN: Llewellyn Publications, 2009.

Drake, Ernest. *Dragonology.* Somerville, MA: Candlewick, 2003.

Grant, John, and Bob Eggleton. *Dragonhenge.* London: Paper Tiger, 2002.

Lewis, C. S. *The Chronicles of Narnia.* New York: Collier Books, Macmillan, 1972.

————. *A Grief Observed.* New York: HarperCollins, 1996.

————. *Out of the Silent Planet/Perelandra/That Hideous Strength.* New York: QPBC/Simon & Schuster, Inc., 1997.

McCaffrey, Anne. *A Diversity of Dragons.* New York: HarperCollins, 1997.

————. Dragonriders of Pern series, consisting of more than twenty novels/novellas and short stories. All first published by Del Rey in New York.

Nesbit, E. *The Book of Dragons.* San Francisco: Chronicle Books, 2001.

Scamander, Newt. *Fantastic Beasts & Where to Find Them.* New York: Scholastic, 2001.

Schele, Linda, and Peter Mathews. *The Code of Kings: Language of the Seven Sacred Maya Temples & Tombs.* New York: Scribner, 1998.

Trumbauer, Lisa. *A Practical Guide to Dragons.* Renton, WA: Mirrorstone, 2006.

da Vinci, Leonardo. *The Notebooks of Leonardo da Vinci.* Edward MacCurdy, ed. New York: Reynal & Hitchcock, 1939.

Wrede, Patricia. *The Enchanted Forest Chronicles: Dealing with Dragons/Searching for Dragons ...* New York: Scholastic, Inc., 1993.

DANCING WITH DRAGONS
Invoke Their Ageless Wisdom & Power
D. J. CONWAY

As magickal allies or guardians, dragons can help you solve everyday problems, protect your home, and grow spiritually. Exploring the fascinating history of dragons
in legend and mythology, this unique book will help you understand these ancient,
powerful creatures that thrive on the astral plane. Conway describes many different kinds of dragons and explains how they are magickally linked to the elements
and the planets. Through spells and rituals, you'll discover how to contact dragons,
befriend them, draw on their power, and channel dragon energy.

978-1-5671-8165-4
264 pp., 7 x 10, illus., charts, index, $18.95

Mystical Dragon Magick
Teachings of the Five Inner Rings
D. J. Conway

Dragons have been sharing their power with humanity throughout history and across cultures. These magickal creatures can strengthen your spellwork and guide you to new realms of consciousness.

D. J. Conway's sequel to *Dancing with Dragons* takes dragon magick to the highest level. Discover how to attract dragons, draw on their legendary energy and wisdom, and partner with them as co-magicians. Each of the five "Inner Rings"—apprentice, enchanter, shaman, warrior, and mystic—introduces new methods for working dragon magick and guides you to a higher path of spiritual consciousness. From shape shifting to herbal spells, this guide to dragon magick also offers plenty of practical methods for working with these otherworldly creatures.

978–0-7387-1099-0
312 pp., 7 x 10, illustrations, $18.95

To order, call 1-877-NEW-WRLD
Prices subject to change without notice
Order at Llewellyn.com 24 hours a day, 7 days a week!

MONSTERS
An Investigator's Guide to Magical Beings
JOHN MICHAEL GREER

Most of us don't believe that entities such as vampires, shapeshifters, and faeries really exist. Even those who study UFOs or psychic powers dismiss them as unreal.

The problem is, people still keep running into them.

What do you do when the world you think you inhabit tears open, and something terrifying comes through the gap? Join ceremonial magician John Michael Greer as he takes you on a harrowing journey into the reality of the impossible. In *Monsters* he examines the most common types of beings still encountered in the modern world—vampires, ghosts, werewolves (and other shapeshifters), faeries, mermaids, dragons, spirits, angels, and demons—surveying what is known about them and how you can deal with their antics.

978-0-7387-0050-2

312 pp., 7 ½ x 9 ⅛, illus. $19.95

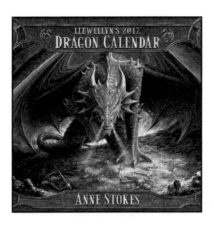

LLEWELLYN'S 2012 DRAGON CALENDAR
Anne Stokes

Back by popular demand—another breathtaking showcase of dragons from internationally acclaimed illustrator Anne Stokes! Once again, she brings these mythological beasts to life in all their glory—as fierce warriors, noble protectors, and sacred creatures. Inspired by popular legends, these vivid images recreate an entire world ruled by striking, majestic, and fearsome dragons—and tell a fascinating story of their history, magic, and power..

978-0-7387-2565-9

24 pp., 12 x 12 $13.99

To order, call 1-877-NEW-WRLD
Prices subject to change without notice
Order at Llewellyn.com 24 hours a day, 7 days a week!

AUTUMNQUEST
The DragonSpawn Cycle: Book One
TERIE GARRISON

It is unlawful for anyone but cruel King Erno to have dragons. So when Donavah finds one, newly hatched, in her brother Breyard's room, she begs him to let it go. The Royal Guard discovers the crime and takes Breyard away to be executed. Heartbroken and guilt ridden, Donavah runs away from school to save him. Pursued by the king's savage soldiers, her treacherous journey turns into one of self-discovery as Donavah learns to use her "maejic" gift for animal communication. She forms a special bond with Xyla, who turns out to be no ordinary dragon. When Xyla is captured, everyone is depending on Donavah—whose destiny is somehow linked with this mystical beast—to rescue her. As her brother's execution looms near, Donavah wonders how she can possibly save both of them...

978-0-7387-0926-0
192 pp., 5 ³⁄₁₆ x 8   **$8.95**

To order, call 1-877-NEW-WRLD
Prices subject to change without notice
Order at Llewellyn.com 24 hours a day, 7 days a week!

WinterMaejic

The DragonSpawn Cycle: Book Two

Terie Garrison

In this captivating sequel to AutumnQuest, Donavah is learning to control her vast maejic powers under the tutelage of Yallick, a revered mage. Maejic is outlawed in Alloway, and dreadful news of the Royal Guard drives the majes—along with Xyla the red dragon—from their hidden forest sanctuary. No one realizes the traitor in their midst until it's too late and Donavah is brutally attacked. Stripped of her voice, the use of her hands, and her maejic, she is utterly helpless until rescued by a handsome and mysterious young man.

Evil forces are scheming to dispose of the mages and overthrow the king. Their fate rests on Donavah—perhaps their only hope for restoring the rightful rule of the dragons. Crippled physically and spiritually, can the young mage break free from the terrible spell before all is lost?

978-0-7387-1028-0

192 pp., 5 ³⁄₁₆ x 8 $8.95

To order, call 1-877-NEW-WRLD

Prices subject to change without notice

Order at Llewellyn.com 24 hours a day, 7 days a week!

THE CELTIC DRAGON TAROT
D. J. Conway and Lisa Hunt

Are dragons real? Since they do not live on the physical plane, scientists cannot trap and dissect them. Yet magicians and psychics who have explored the astral realms know firsthand that dragons do indeed exist, and that they make very powerful co-magicians. Dragons tap into deeper currents of elemental energies than humans. Because of their ancient wisdom, dragons are valuable contacts to call upon when performing any type of divination, such as the laying out of tarot cards. Tarot decks and other divination tools seem to fascinate them. The Celtic Dragon Tarot is the first deck to use the potent energies of dragons for divination, magickal spell working, and meditation.

Ancient mapmakers noted every unknown territory with the phrase "Here be dragons." Both tarot and magick have many uncharted areas. Not only will you discover dragons waiting there, but you will also find them to be extremely helpful when you give them the chance.

978-1-5671-8182-1
Boxed set includes 78 full-color cards, and book: 216 pp., 6 x 9 $34.95

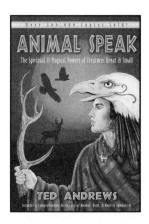

ANIMAL SPEAK
The Spiritual & Magical Powers of Creatures Great & Small
TED ANDREWS

The animal world has much to teach us. Some animals are experts at survival and adaptation, some never get cancer, and some embody strength and courage, while others exude playfulness. Animals remind us of the potential we can unfold, but before we can learn from them, we must first be able to speak with them.

In this book, myth and fact are combined in a manner that will teach you how to speak and understand the language of the animals in your life. Animal-Speak helps you meet and work with animals as totems and spirits—by learning the language of their behaviors within the physical world. It provides techniques for reading signs and omens in nature so you can open yourself to higher perceptions and even prophecy. It reveals the hidden, mythical, and realistic roles of 45 animals, 60 birds, 8 insects, and 6 reptiles.

Animals will become a part of you, revealing to you the majesty and divine in all life. They will restore your childlike wonder of the world and strengthen your belief in magic, dreams, and possibilities.

978-0-87542-028-8
400 pp., 7 x 10 $21.95

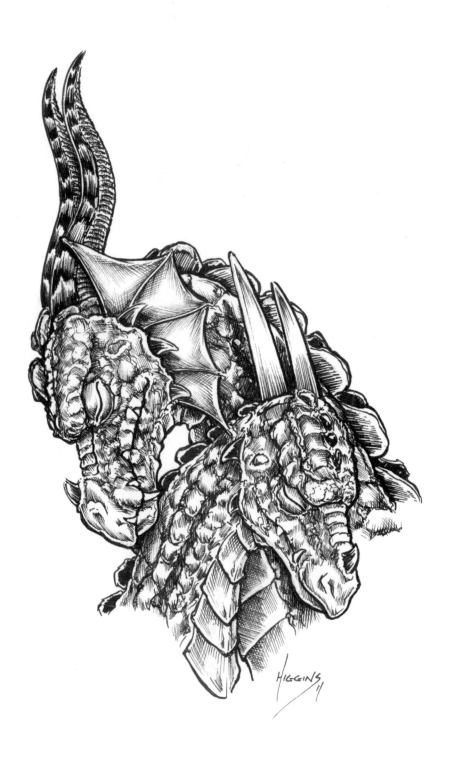